Translated Texts for Historians

This series is designed to meet the needs of students of ancient and medieval history and others who wish to broaden their study by reading source material, but whose knowledge of Latin or Greek is not sufficient to allow them to do so in the original languages. Many important Late Imperial and Dark Age texts are currently unavailable in translation and it is hoped that TTH will help to fill this gap and to complement the secondary literature in English which already exists. The series relates principally to the period 300-800 AD and includes Late Imperial, Greek, Byzantine and Syriac texts as well as source books illustrating a particular period or theme. Each volume is a self-contained scholarly translation with an introductory essay on the text and its author and notes on the text indicating major problems of interpretation, including textual difficulties.

Front cover drawing: Representation of a fourth-century Alamannic soldier.

For a full list of published titles in the Translated Texts for Historians series, please see pages at the end of this book.

Translated Texts for Historians
Volume 17

LIBER DE CAESARIBUS

OF

SEXTUS AURELIUS VICTOR

TRANSLATED WITH AN INTRODUCTION
AND COMMENTARY
BY

H. W. BIRD

Liverpool University Press

First published 1994 by
Liverpool University Press
PO Box 147, Liverpool, L69 3BX

British Library Cataloguing-in-Publication Data
A British Library CIP Record is available
ISBN 0 85323 218 0

Printed in the European Community by
Bell & Bain Limited, Glasgow

CONIUGI
MEAE

CONTENTS

Preface   v

Special Abbreviations   vi

Translation: The *De Caesaribus*   vii

Introduction   1

Commentary   55

Maps   208

Select Bibliography   212

Index   223

PREFACE

This book is intended as a companion volume to my *Sextus Aurelius Victor: A Historiographical Study* (Liverpool, Francis Cairns, 1984), and *Eutropius: Breviarium* (Liverpool University Press, 1993). In general I have attempted to avoid replicating material found in them. The text followed, with a few exceptions noted in the commentary, is the Teubner edition of F.R. Pichlmayr and R. Gruendel, Leipzig, 1966. For purposes of comparison I have consulted the English translation of C.E.V. Nixon (Ann Arbor, 1971), the French translation of P. Dufraigne (Paris, 1975), and, very occasionally, the Russian translation of V.S. Sokolov (Moscow, 1963). In order to accommodate students the Loeb editions of classical sources were used when available.

I should again like to thank Gillian Clark for some kind and useful suggestions, also Mrs. Margie Prytulak, our secretary, for her indefatigable efforts, my university for granting me a Research Professorship when it was most needed, and my wife for her patience.

H. W. Bird
Windsor, Ontario
Christmas, 1993

SPECIAL ABBREVIATIONS

Alföldi, *Conflict* = A. Alföldi, *A Conflict of Ideas in the Late Roman Empire* (trans. H. Mattingly, Oxford, 1952).

Barnes, *Constantine* = T.D. Barnes, *Constantine and Eusebius* (Cambridge, Mass., 1981).

Barnes, *New Empire* = T.D. Barnes, *The New Empire of Diocletian and Constantine* (Cambridge, Mass., 1982).

Bird, *S.A.V.* = H.W. Bird, *Sextus Aurelius Victor: A Historiographical Study* (Liverpool, 1984).

Bird, *Eutropius* = H.W. Bird, *Eutropius: Breviarium* (Liverpool, 1993).

den Boer, *S.M.R.H.* = W. den Boer, *Some Minor Roman Historians* (Leiden, 1972).

Dufraigne, *A.V.* = P. Dufraigne, *Aurelius Victor: Livre des Césars* (Paris, 1975).

Howe, *P.P.* = L.L. Howe, *The Praetorian Prefect from Commodus to Diocletian* (Chicago, 1942).

Jones, *L.R.E.* = A.H.M. Jones, *The Later Roman Empire 284-602* (Oxford, 1964).

Matthews, *R.E.A.* = J. Matthews, *The Roman Empire of Ammianus* (London, 1989).

Nixon, *Caesares* = C.E.V. Nixon, *An Historiographical Study of the Caesares of Sextus Aurelius Victor* (diss. University of Michigan, Ann Arbor, 1971).

Syme, *Ammianus* = R. Syme, *Ammianus and the Historia Augusta* (Oxford, 1968).

Syme, *Emperors* = R. Syme, *Emperors and Biography* (Oxford, 1971).

Williams, *Diocletian* = S. Williams, *Diocletian and the Roman Recovery* (London, 1985).

INTRODUCTION

SEXTUS AURELIUS VICTOR: HIS LIFE AND CAREER

We know little for certain about Sextus Aurelius Victor. He was born probably on a small but flourishing farm in North Africa (perhaps near Cirta/Constantina) a little after A.D. 320, and he appears to have been at Rome in 337 to witness the anger of the populace when Constantine was buried at Constantinople. Furthermore he must have been reasonably mature for Julian to appoint him consular governor of Pannonia Secunda in 361[1]. His father was of humble means and not educated, but clearly he was wealthy enough to have his son educated, locally at first, possibly at Cirta or Carthage, and subsequently at Rome, for otherwise Victor would not have obtained a fairly high post in the imperial bureaucracy at Sirmium, from which he rose to the positions of consular governor and urban prefect. Africa's relative prosperity under Constantine probably helped Victor's father provide the necessary financial support for his son's education, which, in turn, as Victor admits, enabled him to climb the bureaucratic and social ladder.[2]

Between c. 337 and c. 357 Victor may have resided at Rome, and, in his early years, have studied law,[3] like Alypius, Augustine's friend, and many others from all over the empire. While there he seems to have observed the lack of celebrations for Rome's eleven hundredth anniversary in 348 (41.17; 28.2), the civil turmoil caused by Magnentius' seizure of power, and Nepotianus' disastrous revolt and savage suppression by Magnentius' forces in 350 (41.25; 42.6), for his brief but graphic descriptions give the appearance of autopsy.

Victor's student days were over by about 345 and he must have made an impression by his diligent application for he evidently obtained a position in the imperial bureaucracy. But in which branch? Two posts appear likely. Victor's education and background would have equipped him well to serve in the corps of notaries which underwent rapid expansion under Constantius II. Senior notaries performed important, confidential missions, became personally acquainted with the emperor and obtained rapid promotions. In this period a number, like

Felix, Domitian, Taurus, Philippus and Dulcitius, came from humble backgrounds and rose to such positions as *magister officiorum*, *quaestor*, consul, praetorian prefect or proconsul of Asia. Two others, Jovianus and Procopius, nearly became emperors in 363 and 365. Victor's career would fit neatly into this picture. On the other hand his special knowledge (or peculiar choice of material) of the imposition of taxation on *Italia annonaria* by Diocletian, the building schemes at Carthage, Nicomedia and Milan, the origins, nature and abolition of the special oil and grain taxes on Tripolis and Nicaea, the establishment of a Flavian priesthood in Africa and the reconstruction and renaming of Cirta (Constantina) could indicate service in the *scrinium epistolarum*, which drafted rescripts to judges and responses to delegations of provincial councils and cities. In this small but important secretariat, which served the *magister scriniorum* and the *quaestor* and employed barristers and rhetoricians, promotion depended upon education and seniority. Victor might have served for a time in this branch, since judicial expertise was expected in the two known posts which he subsequently filled, consular governor and urban prefect.

On April 30th, 357 Constantius came to Rome and held a triumphant procession through the city which Victor had grown to love. He left there on May 29th for Sirmium via Tridentum.[4] For almost two years the emperor was either at Sirmium or campaigning against the Quadi and Sarmatians (c. 10, note 16) in the general area between Sirmium (Mitrovica) and Brigetio (Szóny). It appears feasible that Victor had by now been seconded to the staff of Anatolius, the praetorian prefect of Illyricum based at Sirmium from 357, for Victor inserts into his account of Trajan's reign a surprising but surely not gratuitous comment praising Anatolius.[5] That Victor knew of Anatolius' sound and beneficial administration in Illyricum and chose to mention it, while diplomatically lodging it in Trajan's reign, leads me to conjecture that Victor was by now a senior member of Anatolius' fiscal staff, perhaps even a department head (*numerarius*).[6] Certainly his subsequent promotions indicate an important post, granting access to the prefect and perhaps even to emperor, who may have taken him to Sirmium and encouraged him to write the *De Caesaribus*. That would account for his almost unstinting praise of Constantius and his omission of anything that might detract from his eulogistic portrait.

Even in the final postscript he carefully distinguishes between the outstanding emperor and his frightful subordinates, a lesson not wasted on the Epitomator (45.6).

Our first reasonably firm date for Victor's career comes from Ammianus.[7] Probably in the summer of 361[8] Julian met Victor at Sirmium and was clearly impressed by him. Julian spent barely two days there, to win over the populace with games, organize his commissariat, and establish an orderly and loyal administration. Victor may well have been instrumental in this. Julian then moved on to Naissus (Nish), seized the pass of Succi three days later, fortified it and returned to Naissus. There he may have read the De Caesaribus, for it is doubtful that he would have had the leisure to do so earlier. At any rate he summoned Victor to Naissus, interviewed him, and not only sent him back to Sirmium as consular governor of Pannonia Secunda, but also honoured him with a bronze statue.[9] Julian did not put Victor in charge at Sirmium (a vital post) and grant him the statue without good reason. Despite the very laudatory description of Constantius and the implicit criticism of Julian at the end of the De Caesaribus,[10] Julian must have shared Ammianus' assessment of Victor with respect to his integrity and have been impressed with the general sentiments of his book. Victor's job performance and experience at Sirmium and Julian's need to replace unshakable supporters of Constantius would also have been factors considered by Julian in making the appointment.

Victor's new office, recently upgraded,[11] carried with it the clarissimate, i.e. entry into the senate, and the chance to obtain the ordinary consulship, quite a promotion for a country-boy from North Africa. How long he served there is not known for certain: Fortunatus held the post on May 28th, 365.[12] It is likely, then, that Victor was governor until replaced probably by Valentinian, in spring 364 or perhaps in spring 365.[13] The latter had been cashiered by Julian in 357 while serving as a tribune in Gaul[14] and had retired to Sirmium. He clearly knew what had happened in the city in 361 and would hardly have favoured Julian's appointee. Victor's career, unexpectedly accelerated by the events of 361, may have suffered a reversal of fortune through the sudden deaths of Julian (363) and Jovian (364) and the acclamation of Valentinian.[15] Julian and his appointees did not lack enemies.[16] On the other hand Victor had probably served three or four years as governor, which would be an above-average tenure, and could expect to be replaced. What seems likely, however, is that he did not receive another appointment for some time if at all from an emperor who was suspicious of Julian's ministers, detested educated men, among others,[17] and restricted the careers of senatorials between 368 and his death in 375.[18]

Victor's next known office, that of urban prefect of Rome, came nearly a quarter of a century later, in 388/389.[19] It is highly unlikely that a commoner such as Victor would have obtained this very prestigious and much sought-after post without holding intermediate ones. Senatorials normally held at least a proconsulship between consular governorships and the city prefecture. What other positions, then, might Victor have held? Possibly none until 375 when Valentinian died and Gratian, much more sympathetic to scholars and literary men, came to the throne. Thereafter he might have held a further provincial governorship or lesser prefecture at Rome and then have gone on to the vicariate of Rome, or the proconsulship of Africa, which seems to have been a common stepping-stone to the urban prefecture during these years. Victor's immediate predecessor, Julianus Rusticus, was proconsul of Africa from 371 to 373 and he, too, was not of senatorial origin. Three other urban prefects between 381 and 385 had also previously been proconsuls of Africa.[20] Finally, Victor was an African, though this probably had little significance.

Julianus Rusticus, Rome's urban prefect and *iudex sacrarum cognitionum*, died in or just before August, 388.[21] The emperor Theodosius, who had a penchant for history and a high regard both for men of learning and integrity and for tried and honest officials,[22] needed a successor. Aurelius Victor was admirably suited; certainly the emperor and his advisers thought so. Thus probably that same August the self-made man from Africa joined the ranks of the exalted, like Q. Aurelius Symmachus, Ceionius Rufius Albinus, Faltonius Probus Alypius and Nicomachus Flavianus, who held this post during these years. Though not exceptional,[23] Victor's prefecture was hardly commonplace. Ammianus clearly thought that the man and his achievement deserved mention, though this may well have been an office of friendship. Victor, too, was not without gratitude, hence the dedicatory inscription to Theodosius, which he set up in the Forum of

Trajan presumably during his prefecture. Victor was in office about nine months, which is only slightly shorter than the average term of a year. It does not indicate that he died in office or displeased the emperor. Theodosius was in Rome in 389 and the appointment of Rufius Albinus in June of that year was probably one of the steps he took to conciliate the pagan aristocracy. Accordingly the date of Victor's death, like that of his birth, remains a matter for conjecture.[24]

THE DATE AND TRADITION OF THE *DE CAESARIBUS*

Internal evidence seems to indicate that Victor commenced work on the *De Caesaribus* after the earthquake of Nicomedia, which took place on August 24th, 358, during the consulship of Naeratius Cerealis.[25] Furthermore, in 42.20-21 Victor states that Constantius had been ruling for twenty-three years as Augustus, i.e. from September 9th, 337[26] (which I interpret to indicate that Victor was writing this section after September 9th, 360), and that he had given a king to the Sarmatians, which occurred in 358.[27] The subscript to the book's title referring to the tenth consulship of Constantius and third consulship of Julian, probably added by the editor of the *corpus*, also refers to 360.

Nevertheless, in 42.17 Victor notes the capture of famous kings, which, as Nixon argues, surely includes the capture of Vadomarius in the spring of 361,[28] otherwise Julian had only captured one famous king, Chonodomarius. Thus it seems likely that Victor began his book in late 359 or 360 and completed it in the spring of 361, when it was first published, possibly in a limited edition. It ended, so I believe, at 42.23 with the eulogy of Constantius. Later that summer, however, when Victor no longer had reason to fear repercussions, he added the postscript (42.24-25) which bitterly denounced Constantius' ministers and commanders but reinforced Victor's praise of the emperor himself.[29] It was in this completed form that the *De Caesaribus* subsequently appeared. Only two manuscripts of it are extant, both of the fifteenth century, in a corpus containing the *Origo gentis Romanae*, the *De Viris Illustribus*, and other works.

The earlier, *codex Bruxellensis* or *codex Pulmani* (*p*) is in the Royal Library at Brussels (nos. 9755-9763). Its text contains fewer errors than the other but does have some adventurous emendations.

xii

The *codex Oxoniensis* (*o*), residing in the Bodleian Library at Oxford (*Canon. Lat.* 131), dates from the mid-fifteenth century and contains more *lacunae*. Nevertheless both share common *lacunae*, in particular the one at 34.7, and clearly derive from a common exemplar. A.Schott, the first editor of the corpus, for his Antwerp edition of 1579, in which he divided the work into the chapters which appear in all modern editions with the exception of c. 43, used only *p*, despite Dufraigne's contentions (LIV-LVI). F. Pichlmayr, however, in his first edition of 1892, (*Programma gymnasii Ludoviciani Monacensis*) was able to use both *p* and *o*. He afterwards produced a Teubner edition at Leipzig in 1911 which was reissued with *addenda* and *corrigenda* by R. Gruendel at Leipzig in 1961. This was reproduced in 1966 with the addition of an *index verborum* of the *De Viris Illustribus* to form the basis for the current translation and commentary.[30]

THE SOURCES AND INFLUENCE OF THE *DE CAESARIBUS*

Despite the serious reservations of den Boer and Dufraigne[31] most scholars nowadays accept that Aurelius Victor, like his contemporary Eutropius for the imperial section of his *Breviarium*, made first-hand use of only one basic source, the so-called *Kaisergeschichte*.[32] In 1883 A. Enmann attempted to explain the numerous verbal similarities, shared errors and idiosyncrasies found in Victor's *De Caesaribus*, Eutropius' *Breviarium* and parts of the *Historia Augusta* by postulating a common source which has since come to be known as the *Kaisergeschichte* (*KG*), which he considered to be the main if not the only source they used.[33] Quite independently A. Cohn examined the first eleven chapters of the *De Caesaribus* and concluded that from Augustus' sole reign to Domitian's death Victor, Eutropius and the Epitomator followed a common source which he entitled *Suetonius auctus*, an abbreviation of Suetonius with some new material added[34] in the fashion of Livy's *Epitome*. Since Enmann had already described the early chapters of the KG in this manner the two were readily identified.[35] Syme regarded the KG as a work of no great compass, otherwise it would hardly have so many elementary mistakes and Victor and Eutropius would have exhibited more variants in their selection.[36] Barnes noted that the only hypothesis which could explain the nature and extent of the similarities between Victor and Eutropius was that Victor grafted his reflections onto the KG whereas Eutropius reproduced it largely unchanged.[37]

A close comparison of the accounts of Victor, Eutropius, the *Epitome* and parts of the *H.A.* lead me to infer that it was little more than thirty-five to forty Teubner pages long and covered the years 30 BC to 357 A.D.[38] Victor's account, including personal comments, is fifty-three pages long, that of the *Epitome* to the death of Constantius is thirty-eight, while Eutropius' economical account of the imperial period covers twenty-nine pages. The KG, which culminated with the Battle of Strasbourg and probably ended with a eulogistic description of Constantius similar to Victor's, was perhaps written in Gaul[39] and published in late 357 or in 358. It appears to have been a rather simple account, quite meagre on most of the third century emperors between Caracalla and Diocletian, and particularly concerned with usurpers. Enmann (p. 432 ff.) was able to demonstrate the general outline of each biography as follows:

(1) the emperor's name and origin, remarks on his previous life, the place of his proclamation if he gained power by rebellion; (2) wars against barbarians and pretenders; (3) public works, legislation and character of the reign; (4) the place and manner of the emperor's death, place of burial, posthumous honours, length of reign. Victor presumably acquired a copy of this work in 358 and felt that he could do better.

Of course not all of the material in the *De Caesaribus* and in Eutropius' *Breviarium* derives from the KG. As Nixon correctly noted, all of the extant historical writers of the fourth century have points in common stemming from a common pool of information, which each used according to his needs and objectives.[40] Victor had read quite widely and had discussed Roman history with a variety of people, as he states.[41] It was, therefore, from this general pool of information, from his (occasionally faulty) recollections of earlier authors, read during his schooldays or subsequently, and from his discussions with friends, colleagues and acquaintances that he added to the basic account he had before him. Differing in background, tastes, attitudes and experience from Eutropius, he stamped the *De Caesaribus* with his own personality and predilections and set it apart from the *Breviarium*, the KG and other fourth century epitomes.[42]

This, however, did not make Victor a popular author, which Eutropius soon became.[43] His tortuous, pretentious style and frequent moralizing were passed up by the majority who preferred the chronologically broader scope and lucid simplicity of Eutropius. Jerome does cite and use Victor,[44] but makes more use of Eutropius. The *H.A.*, however, borrows much from the *De Caesaribus*, which is the strongest single argument for the post-Constantinian dating of that work,[45] and far less from Eutropius. In addition, in the middle of the sixth century at Constantinople, John Lydus both names and cites Victor,[46] and in the eighth century Paul the Deacon cites the authority of our author, though it appears that he is really referring to the *Epitome* and not to the *De Caesaribus*.[47] Otherwise it seems that by the fifth century Victor's work was generally gathering dust, eclipsed by the more pliable survey of his contemporary. That may well account for the paucity of manuscripts of the *De Caesaribus* in comparison with the abundance of manuscripts of the *Breviarium*.[48] In a literary sense Victor was out of step. On the other hand we have no manuscripts of the KG, in spite of its significant influence on the writers of the second half of the fourth century. It, too, covered only the imperial period, probably emphasized the west, and was soon overshadowed by Eutropius' more comprehensive and accessible work.

METHOD OF PROCEDURE

Victor's *modus operandi* appears to have been quite simple. He chose a recent and relatively short factual account of the lives of the emperors which conveniently covered the whole period he intended to describe, the KG. This work he used as the basis for his historical narrative, even to the extent that he copied lines and passages from it practically verbatim, as a comparison with Eutropius demonstrates. The KG, however, was probably devoid of any real attempt to explain the historical events which it depicted. Victor considered it his task to interpret the course of Imperial history as he recounted the events and to pass judgement on the individuals and classes involved, hence the frequent moralizing reflections and interjections often introduced by such devices at *uti solet, uti mos est* or *compertum est*.

The author also supplemented his basic source from his own knowledge, especially in his discussions of Septimius Severus' reign and the period following Diocletian's accession, and added *exempla* taken mainly from Republican history to emphasize the points he wished to make and to exhibit his erudition.[49] Indeed the author seems to have been more interested in painting a moral picture than in verifying the accuracy of his statements, which may partially account for his decision to follow only one basic and relatively brief source. This would give him ample opportunity to elaborate upon the simple narrative and infuse the results of his wider reading and historical deliberations. Momigliano states that the pagan historians were not concerned with ultimate values,[50] which is generally correct. Certainly Eutropius, Festus, the Epitomator and presumably the author of the KG were content simply to present the bare facts of Roman history and Eutropius concludes his account with the words "nam reliqua stylo maiore dicenda sunt: quae nunc non tam praetermittimus quam ad maiorem scribendi diligentiam reservamus."[51] Victor, on the other hand, was concerned with ultimate values, hence his stress on the absolute need for education, culture, honesty and respect for tradition. It is in this regard that Victor stands out from the other pagan historians of his era.

STYLE AND LANGUAGE

Victor's style[52] differs markedly from that of Eutropius or Festus and his personality permeates his work. He uses terms like *ego, mihi, nos, nobis* and *meus* and verbs in the first person[53] and expresses his personal views vigorously in his many moralizing passages.[54] To each reign he attempts to give a certain tone by his choice of material, his interpretation of events and his assessment of character. Moreover he frequently inserts scurrilous anecdotes into his factual narrative, quite unlike his contemporary, Eutropius. Consequently the *De Caesaribus* is often uneven and at times incongruous, for Victor was not only a moralist, he also attempted to be a stylist. In his personal interventions, which Victor often used as a transitional device, his language becomes tortuous, tantalizing, even perplexing to the translator. Sokolov, who translated Victor's work into Russian, justifiably described Victor's style as frequently bombastic and difficult.[56]

There appears little doubt that Sallust was the chief influence on Victor's style and the earlier historian's views on the importance of morality in the writing of history and the capricious nature of Fortune in human affairs are clearly discernible in the *De Caesaribus*. Sallust had become the classic model historian by the first century A.D. and his reputation and place in the school curriculum lasted beyond the fourth century.[57] Not only must Victor have read the republican writer during his school days, he almost certainly re-read him in his maturer years for there are a great number of Sallustian expressions and reminiscences in the *De Caesaribus*.[58]

To a lesser extent Victor was also influenced by Tacitus, whose works were anything but popular in antiquity.[59] The opening remarks in the *De Caesaribus* (1.1) echo those of the *Annals* (I.2),and there are many other examples of Tacitean usage or attitudes.[60] Nonetheless, Victor manifests numerous stylistic idiosyncrasies of his own. He begins sentences with a double ablative absolute construction and sometimes has four such constructions in the same sentence.[61] This is probably caused by Victor's need to condense material; it ends up being clumsy and confusing. In addition, Victor sometimes completes his sentences weakly with participles or ablative expressions,[62] or uses present participles instead of causal or relative clauses, with unfortunate consequences.[63] The need to prune might have led to short, truncated sentences so Victor tried to combine diverse and sometimes incongruous notices, as in 5.14, when he confusingly inserts the Parthian envoy in two examples of Nero's treachery and tyranny, or in 10.5 where he inappropriately connects chronological statistics with architectural mentions.[64] The style then became so wayward that it even confused the scribes.

Like most authors Victor exhibits a significant number of personal preferences in his choice of vocabulary and expressions.[65]

abhinc	13.12; 24.9; 37.5; 41.15
adhuc	3.2; 4.3; 9.8; 13.5; 24.6; 35.14; 39.23; 39.45; 40.20; 40.26; 41.23; 42.24

aegre/aegerrime	9.9; 11.10; 13.2; 33.25; 39.48; 40.23; 41.17; 42.20
arduus/ardua	16.9; 20.20; 33.13; 38.5; 41.6; 42.4
confestim[66]	11.2; 16.3; 17.10; 20.32; 24.2; 24.9;41.23
gratia + genitive	4.11; 5.2; 20.20; 29.1; 39.16; 40.10; 41.6; 41.14
hincque	1.6; 11.6; 14.8; 16.5; 19.3; 23.1
huiuscemodi	3.5; 3.12; 5.4; 20.3; 20.12; 27.5; 35.7; 35.11; 39.12; 41.24
longe	2.1; 3.5; 5.2; 8.4; 9.2; 11.12; 14.9; 15.5; 16.1; 20.23; 28.8; 33.7; 35.12; 39.18
magis magisque	11.7; 12.4; 23.3; 39.12
mortales = homines[67]	3.20; 12.3; 16.14; 24.11; 28.7; 33.30
plus quam	11.2; 13.5; 20.13; 24.5; 39.3
praecipue /praecipua	8.7; 11.13; 17.1; 20.2; 40.12; 40.15
sanus / sane	3.17; 4.11; 5.6; 5.13; 10.6; 20.33; 27.1; 31.3; 33.29; 36.1; 37.3; 39.26; 39.32; 39.40; 39.46; 40.11; 41.6; 41.17; 41.23
satellites	4.10; 9.2; 17.7; 33.31

usque	13.3; 13.9; 16.13; 17.1; 33.3; 35.6; 40.20
uti solet/uti mos est	5.14; 13.9; 16.7; 20.33; 29.2; 31.3; 32.2; 33.17; 34.8
bonis indocti	9.12
boni malive/ boni malique	13.7; 24.9
malos e bonis	3.5

In the use of *ac* and *atque* Victor is particularly strict: before vowels *atque* is invariably employed, before consonants generally *ac* except before *c* when *et* is normally used.[68] In the choice of coordinating conjunctions, however, the author displays a good deal of variety although he reveals a distinct preference for *tamen*, which occurs thirty-three times, and *namque*, which occurs on twenty-nine occasions. His other favourites are *ita* (21), *nam* (18), *at* (17), *sed* and *igitur* (16 each), *qua causa* (10), *quin etiam* (8), *dein / deinde* (6), *ceterum* (5) and *idcirco / iccirco* (5). Other very common coordinatives such as *autem* (3), *itaque* (2) and *enim* (1) are conspicuous because of their rarity in the *De Caesaribus*.

On occasions Victor was clearly guilty of the monotonous repetition of certain words and constructions but in general he did strive for diversity. For example he admitted such abstract nouns as *honestas, humanitas, felicitas* and *sanitas* which are not to be found in Sallust's extant works.[69] Furthermore, like Tacitus, he sometimes couples nouns governed by *per* with modal ablatives or locatives or recasts phrases in common use (*non modo domi, verum militiae quoque*).[70] Alliteration, which plays a large part in Sallust's style, is employed by Victor too, mostly with moderation[71] but not always. In the final eighteen lines of his book commencing with *cum externis motibus modo civilibus exercetur, aegre ab armis abest. quis tyrannide tantorum...,* he intemperately overworks the technique.

The *De Caesaribus* also includes a number of metaphors and

bon mots to animate the narrative. Some were perhaps borrowed from previous writers like Suetonius, probably via the KG[72] or were commonplace[73] but one or two may have been original, such as the one traducing Julia Domna *quippe quae pudorem velamento exuerat* or the anecdote about the pretender Marius.[74] Finally, in this regard, on several occasions Victor seems to have modified the plain wording of his source in order to introduce more impressive words and phrases or to give the narrative polish and elegance. Thus, whereas Eutropius in describing the death of Pertinax writes quite simply: *octogesimo imperii die praetorianorum militum seditione et Iuliani scelere occisus est,*[75] Victor moralizes and elaborates: *eum milites, quis exhausto iam perditoque orbe satis videtur nihil, impulsore Didio foede iugulavere octogesimo imperii die.*[76] Immediately afterwards he eschews what was probably the KG's unadorned statement of Julianus' background, *vir nobilis ac iure peritissimus*, and concocts instead: *genus ei pernobile iurisque urbani praestans scientia.*[77] Further examples of Victor's embellishment of his source are probably to be seen in his descriptions of Valerian's capture, Aurelian's death, the reign of Tacitus, Diocletian's execution of Aper *et al.*[78]

    Victor wrote in a style which he considered fitting for an educated man of his day and suitable for a moralistic interpretation of imperial history. In the fourth century that meant modelling oneself on one of the great republican writers, in particular Sallust, whose reputation flourished in the fourth century A.D. and apparently never waned. Unfortunately Victor lacked the ability to assimilate the style of his chosen model and make it his own. Furthermore he was incapable of animating his prose with a mordant phrase here and there or a striking figure of speech. He quite lacked the incisive brevity of Sallust or the majestic dignity of Tacitus and deliberately avoided the easy simplicity of Eutropius. As a consequence Victor's Latin was heavily affected, its word order often tortuous, full of unnecessarily involved sentences and artificial conceits. Probably it was his style more than any other aspect of his work which made the *De Caesaribus* unpopular in later years, when readers turned with apparent relief to the direct and unembellished account of Eutropius.

XX

CONCLUSIONS

When Constantine became sole emperor in 324 that segment of his ambition had been achieved, others supervened. A new capital to rival Rome and overshadow Trier, Milan, Nicomedia or Sirmium was immediately commenced at Byzantium, equipped with libraries, and museums. A new, unifying religion, cleansed of internal conflict, was envisaged, and to that effect the Council of Nicaea was convened in 325, under the aegis of the emperor. Teachers and professors were encouraged by the imperial edicts of 321, 326, and 333,[79] which granted them privileges and exemptions, "in order that they may more readily instruct many in the liberal studies." A new literary and cultural renaissance began under this superpatron who was interested in reviving Roman cultural traditions. His example was followed by Constantius and Julian[80] (and subsequent emperors) who issued an edict in 358 concerning the acquisition and copying of the manuscripts of earlier authors.[81] New authors like Victor were encouraged. A liberal education, if possible with demonstrable literary skills, had become the surest passport to a place in the imperial service and advancement within it. The most striking example of this was Decius Magnus Ausonius, a professor from Bordeaux, who became prefect of the Gauls and, in 379, consul. Victor, of course, had preceded him; so it appears, had the author of the KG, possibly like Ausonius another product of the Gallic schools and burgeoning literary environment in the province.

There were, I believe, four factors which caused Victor to turn his mind to writing: the conducive literary ambience of the day, the personal encouragement of a patron such as Anatolius or even Constantius himself, personal ambition and the desire to be recognized,[82] and, finally, the appearance in 358 of the KG. That work, a series of brief imperial biographies seemingly written in the manner of Suetonius, formed the basis for the De Caesaribus. But Victor did not wish to be merely an epitomator or a breviarist.[83] His work differs markedly from those of his contemporaries, Eutropius and Festus, and of his successor, the anonymous Epitomator.

The latter writers were content merely to chronicle events in a concise, straightforward manner and write in a simple, unaffected style. They had neither literary nor historical pretensions. Indeed, one discerns in the compositions of Eutropius and Festus no distinct personal imprint and no attempt at historical explanation. The Epitomator, however, does demonstrate one idiosyncrasy, a pronounced interest in the personalities of his subjects, and he evidently took great pains to discover their qualities and foibles.[84] His work is therefore characterized by its emphasis on biographical details.

Victor, on the other hand, was intent upon writing history rather than biography. Consequently he was prepared to use facts for theorizing, to pass judgement upon rulers and regimes, to evaluate the different phases of the empire and to suggest remedies for the afflictions of the state as he saw them. The *De Caesaribus*, then, is not intended to be a mere factual record of the history of the empire or a catalogue of emperors and their exploits but is an attempt to interpret and account for the historical events which are described. Victor was evidently following the precedent of his moralizing model, Sallust. Like Sallust he connected the decline of the state with the deterioration of moral standards.[85] Yet he clearly realized that the situation of the state in the third and fourth centuries A.D. was different from that of Sallust's time and he adduced other causes for Rome's degeneracy, the diminishing importance of education and culture, the increase in the power of the army and, in the final phase, the pernicious influence of the *agentes in rebus*. Unfortunately Victor was not a profound historical thinker and he failed to distinguish between cause and effect. Thus, in the same way as Sallust (and Ammianus), he construed moral decadence as the cause rather than the symptom of political degeneration and considered that only a moral (and cultural) regeneration was required to restore its pristine vigour to the state. Nevertheless he was quite correct in assuming that the growing power of the military, its preoccupation with emperor-making[86] and the greed and depredations of officials and soldiers[87] were major contributory factors in the disintegration of the empire.

Victor appears to have done no extensive research with the result that he was at the mercy of his one fundamental source, the KG. Accordingly he seems to have accepted uncritically the numerous factual errors and historical misconceptions of that source and, at the same time, he also committed further blunders of his own.[88] Moreover he occasionally omitted facts which would tend to disprove his own contentions.[89] It would, therefore, be hazardous to accept Victor's testimony as reliable unless that testimony is corroborated by additional evidence.[90]

The style and form of the *De Caesaribus* were mainly influenced by the works of Sallust and by the KG. Following the biographical format of the latter Victor sought to infuse a Sallustian spirit into his composition and transform it into an historical treatise. He thus became the victim, so to speak, of both of these authors, for he could neither escape the generalized *schema* of the KG nor the magnetism of Sallust's style and moralistic interpretation of history. Hence he attempted to write in a dignified, majestic style, embellishing the sentences he borrowed from the KG with Sallustian expressions and inserting moralizing disquisitions in a mock Sallustian manner. Unfortunately the resultant prose became tortuous, involved and artificial: it lacks vitality and vividness. Similarly the form of the *De Caesaribus* is a peculiar new hybrid of history and biography,[91] since Victor was attempting to write a history set in a biographical framework. In the process his character depictions suffered and often appear flat or stereotyped.[92] Occasionally Victor compensates with brief flashes of insight; for example he realized that Claudius' accession in 41 signified the continuation of monarchical rule at Rome.[93] In general, however, one must admit that he lacked historical perception. He quite failed to understand the reasons for the concentration of power in the hands of the military, for the long-standing political impotence of the senatorial class. Furthermore, he was blind to the role played by his countryman, Septimius Severus, in the militarization of the empire and to the difficulties encountered by Gallienus whom he impugned with almost hysterical vehemence. In lieu of these considerations Victor presented his readers with what were basically historical clichés and contemporary commonplaces.[94]

Nonetheless, in spite of these strictures, Victor has one claim to originality. Whereas the other extant historical writers of the fourth century (with the notable exception of Ammianus Marcellinus) were content to write biographies or biographical breviaries, Victor attempted to integrate his biographies into a coherent history.[95] His efforts to make the history of the Roman Empire significant and meaningful for his contemporaries should, for this reason alone, merit our respect.

NOTES

[1]Bird, *S.A.V.*, 5. Nixon (*Caesares*, 21) gives c. 325, Dufraigne (*A.V.*, xiv) c. 327.

[2]*De Caes.* 20.5; Bird, *S.A.V.*, 5, 128. For other reconstructions *vid.* Nixon, *Caesares*, 1 ff.; Dufraigne, *A.V.*, ix ff.

[3]For a full discussion, *vid.* Nixon, *Caesares*, 5-6.

[4]Ammianus, 16.10.1 ff.; 16.10.20.

[5]*De Caes.* 13.6 and note 10; Nixon, *Caesares*, 12.

[6]Bird, *S.A.V.* 9-10. *De Caes.* 20.31 could refer to Anatolius or Constantius.

[7]Ammianus, 21.10.6.

[8]C.E.V. Nixon, *C.Ph.* 86, 1991, 113.

[9]According to Ammianus (14.6.8) statues had become fashionable among senatorials so Victor would have been flattered. For further discussion *vid.* Nixon, *Caesares*, 16.

[10]*Ibid.*; cf. B. Baldwin, *Klio* 60, 1978, 457 for the intriguing suggestion that Julian and Victor may have influenced one another through conversation and consultation.

[11]Nixon, *loc. cit.*

[12]*Cod. Theod.* VIII.5.27; Nixon, *Caesares*, 17.

[13]Jovian made few appointments in his 7 1/2 month reign and was cautious with those he did make (Ammianus, 25.10.15). Valentinian made his brother, Valens, co-emperor on March 28th, 364 in a suburb

of Constantinople. New arrangements may have been made then, before they fell ill, or more probably in the following spring at Naessus where Ammianus (26.5.1) informs us that the two emperors organized their separate spheres and shared their commanders.

[14]Ammianus, 16.11.6-7.

[15]Cf. Ammianus, 26.1.3.

[16]Ammianus, 26.4.4.

[17]Ammianus, 30.8.10; cf. *Epit.* 45.6. Zosimus states that Valentinian and Valens replaced governors appointed by Julian (IV.1.2).

[18]C. Schuurmans, *L'Antiquité Classique* 18, 1949, 34-38.

[19]Ammianus, 21.10.6; *I.L.S.* 2945 = *C.I.L.* VI 1186. Nixon, *Caesares*, 20; Bird, *S.A.V.*, 13. Cf. Matthews, R.E.A., 24, giving 389/90, and 457, giving 388/89. Syme (*Ammianus*, 9) accepts the latter.

[20]For fuller description *vid.* Nixon, *Caesares*, 18-19, 39; Bird, *S.A.V.*, 12-13; Jones, *L.R.E.* I.381-382.

[21]Bird, *loc. cit.* The appended title of judge went with the office.

[22]*Epit.* 48.9 ff.

[23]Nixon, *Caesares*, 42; cf. Dufraigne, *A.V.* XIII.

[24]One might speculate that Ammianus' mention reads like a death notice, which would indicate that Victor was dead by the summer of 391. For the dating of Ammianus' mention *vid.* Syme, *Ammianus*, 9; Nixon, *Caesares*, 20.

[25]*De Caes.* 16.12; cf. Ammianus, 17.5.1; 17.7.1 ff.

[26]*Chron. Min.* I.235; Nixon, *C.Ph.* 86, 1991, 120.

[27]Chapter 42, note 16. It was also probably in 358 that Victor learned of Sapor's demand for the return of Mesopotamia: cf. *De Caes.* 39.37; Ammianus, 17.14.1-3.

[28]*Vid.* Nixon, *loc. cit.* for arguments and sources.

[29]Cf. chapter 42, note 19; Nixon, *op. cit.*, 124-125; *Caesares*, 36. On methods of publication *vid.* H.L. Pinner, *The World of Books in Classical Antiquity*, Leiden, 1958, 30-45. Victor, as a new author, would not merit a large number of initial copies. Furthermore, the addendum would be easy to make, both in existing copies and for additional ones.

[30]For fuller discussions *vid.* Dufraigne, *A.V.*, LII-LX; S. D'Elia, *Studi sulla tradizione manoscritta di Aurelio Vittore*, Naples, 1965; *Ricerche sulla tradizione manoscritta e su testo di Aurelio Vittore e duell'Epitome de Caesaribus*, Naples, 1969. *Bolletino di Studi Latini* 3, 1973, 52-75; R.J. Tarrant, *Gnomon* 50, 1978, 355 ff.

[31]*S.M.R.H.*, 20 ff.; *A.V.*, xxv ff. But even Dufraigne is forced to admit the existence of a common source for some notable shared errors (p. xxxvii).

[32]Bird, *S.A.V.*, 16-23; *Eutropius*, xlvii-xlix.

[33]A. Enmann, *Philol.* suppl. 4 (1884), 335-501, published in June, 1883.

[34]A. Cohn, *Quibus e fontibus Sex. Aurelii Victoris et libri de Caesaribus et Epitomes XI capita priora fluxerint*, Berlin, 1884.

[35]Enmann, *op. cit.*, 407 ff.; 431 ff.

[36]*Ammianus*, 106; cf. Alföldi, *Conflict*, 98.

[37]T.D. Barnes, *The Sources of the Historia Augusta*, Brussels, 1978, 92.

[38]Cf. Barnes, *loc. cit.*; *B.H.A.C. 1968/69* (1970); 20, Bird, *C.Q.* 23,

1973, 375-377; *S.A.V.*, 17; *Eutropius*, 157-160. R.W. Burgess' as yet unpublished paper, *On the Date of the Kaisergeschichte*, which he kindly sent to me, comes out strongly in favour of 357.

[39]Enmann, *op. cit.*, 435-436. R.W. Burgess (*C.Q.* 43, 1993) conjectures that it was written by Eusebius Nanneticus.

[40]Nixon, *Caesares*, 330; cf. den Boer, *S.M.R.H.*, 22-24, 54; 67; 110.

[41]*De Caes.* 11.13; *cf.* 5.8-9; 14.8; 20.10; 20.34; 29.5; 39.48.

[42]*E.g.* 24.7-11; 33.13; 33.23-26; 39.7; 39.26-27; 39.45; 40.25.

[43]Bird, *Eutropius*, lv-lvii.

[44]Hieron. *Ep.* 10.3; *Chron.* 213d; 217e; 226b.

[45]A. Momigliano, *Studies in Historiography*, London, 1966, 152; Bird, *S.A.V.*, 122-126 and the commentary to this book, *passim*.

[46]*De Mag.* 3.7.

[47]*Hist. Lang.* 2.18; on which *vid.* D'Elia (*op. cit.*, 1965) 29.

[48]Eighty manuscripts of Eutropius' *Breviarium* survive, eleven written before the fifteenth century (Bird, *Eutropius*, lv). This, in addition to the Greek translations of Eutropius, testify to the greater popularity of the latter.

[49]*De Caes.* 3.14; 4.15; 11.12; 14.2; 18.1; 33.1; 35.12; 37.2-3; 39.6; 42.22.

[50]A. Momigliano, *The Conflict between Paganism and Christianity in the Fourth Century*, Oxford, 1963, 85.

[51]Eutrop. 10.18; For what remains must be told in a more elevated style. Right now we do not really omit these matters but rather reserve them

for a more careful composition." Cf. *H.A. Car.* 21.2-3. *Stylo maiore* seems to indicate the grand, historical style and mode of composition of such authors as Sallust, Livy and Tacitus. The biographers and epitomators, in spite of their popularity, recognized their literary inferiority. Festus, who succeeded Eutropius as *magister memoriae* in 370, completed a twenty-page *Breviarium* of Roman History that year, which he also dedicated to Valens.

[52]For a full discussion *vid.* Bird, *S.A.V.*, 90-99.

[53]*E.g.* 5.9; 8.7; 11.12-13; 20.6; 28.8; 39.48; 40.14; 41.10; 42.5; 42.22; 42.25.

[54]Unlike the Epitomator (E. Wölfflin, *Rh.M.* 29, 1874, 285) or Eutropius. Wölfflin describes the Epitomator as a mechanical contaminator (302).

[55]*E.g.* 5.1 ff.; 14.7 ff.; 16.2.

[56]V.S. Sokolov. *Vestnik Drevnej Istorii* 86, 1963, 216. This echoes the words of M. Schanz, *Geschichte der römischen Literatur bis zum Gesetzgebungswerk des Kaiser Justinian IV* [2], Munich, 1914, 73.

[57]R. Syme, *Sallust*, Berkeley, 1964, 274 ff.; H.I. Marron, *A History of Education in Antiquity*, trans. G. Lamb, London, 1956, 374.

[58]Bird, *S.A.V.*, 91-94.

[59]H.W. Benario, *An Introduction to Tacitus*, Athens, Georgia, 1975, 159. The *H.A.* makes three references to Tacitus, none showing profound knowledge of him (*Aur.* 2.2; *Tac.* 10.3; *Prob.* 2.7), but Ammianus, Victor's acquaintance, was influenced by the earlier historian.

[60]Bird, *S.A.V.*, 95.

[61]*De Caes.* 26.5; 28.10; 29.3; and 28.1; 41.12.

[62]*De Caes.* 5.2; 16.4; 17.7; 18.2; 20.14; 27.8; 32.3; 33.15; 33.28; 35.11; 37.6; 40.23.

[63]*De Caes.* 3.16; 20.6; 20.31; 21.2; 33.13.

[64]Nixon, *Caesares*, 405.

[65]This list does not include those of Sallustian or Tacitean provenance, for which *vid.* Bird, *S.A.V.*, 91-95.

[66] Never used by Tacitus (Syme, *Tacitus*, 734).

[67]A Sallustian usage.

[68]*De Caes.* 2.2; 3.5; 9.8; 10.4; 20.10; 20.25; 39.45; 42.18; but cf. 33.30; 42.7.

[69]Syme, *Sallust*, 309.

[70]*De Caes.* 11.12; 37.5; 42.4.

[71]*De Caes.* 9.3; 9.12; 13.9; 24.9; 33.11; 39.48; 40.13.

[72]*E.g. De Caes.* 11.5-6 (cf. Suet. *Domit.* 3.1; 22); *De Caes.* 20.6 (cf. Sen. *N.Q.* 18.4; *Epit.* 1.28); *De Caes.* 21.3 (cf. Cic. *Pro Quinct.* 30.94).

[73]*De Caes.* 33.3.

[74]*De Caes.* 21.3; 33.11.

[75]*Eutro.* 8.16; cf. *Epit.* 18.1 ff.

[76]*De Caes.* 18.2.

[77]Eutrop. 8.17; *Epit.* 19.1; cf. *De Caes.* 19.2.

[78]*De Caes.* 32.5; cf. Eutrop. 9.7; *Epit.* 32.5; *De Caes.* 35.8; cf. Eutrop.

xxix

9.15; Epit. 35.8; *De Caes*. 36.1-2; cf. Eutrop. 9.16; *Epit*. 36.1; *De Caes*. 39.13; cf. Eutrop. 9.20.

[79]*Cod. Theod*. XIII.3.1, 2, 3.

[80]*Cod. Theod*. XIV.1.1.

[81]Them. *Or*. 4.59; *Cod. Theod*. xiv. 9.2.

[82]P. Petit, *Libanius et la vie municipale à Antioche*, Paris, 1955, 384-385.

[83]Basically an epitome is a summary or abbreviated version of a longer work, often with minor additions from other sources, *e.g.* Florus and the *Periochae* of Livy. A *breviarium* is an abbreviated account of an often substantial historical period from a particular point of view and relying on more than one major source, e.g. Eutropius and Festus. For discussion of E. Wölfflin. *A.L.L.* 12, 1902, 333 ff.; E. Malcovati, *A.F.L.C.* 12, 1942, 23 ff.; *R.L.A.C.* 38, 1961, 447 ff.; J. Eadie, *The Breviarium of Festus*, London, 1967, 10-20; Dufraigne, *A.V.*, xxxix-xli.

[84]*E.g. Epit*. 43; 45; 46; 47; 48: it is more noticeable after the KG had ended, but the author clearly used a number of sources (Wölfflin, *op. cit.*, 584).

[85]Cf. Sall. *Jug*. 1-4; *Cat*. 1-13. Ammianus (14.6.1 ff.) also dwells upon the moral decline of Rome and implicity contrasts it with the moral uprightness of the Romans of Marcus Aurelius' day (31.5.14).

[86]*De Caes*. 24.9 ff.; M. Cary, *A History of Rome*, 2nd ed., London, 1954, 779.

[87]*De Caes. passim*; R. MacMullen, *Soldier and Civilian in the Later Roman Empire*, Cambridge, Mass., 1963, 85 ff.

[88]Syme, *Emperors*, 195; *Ammianus*, 106. For some examples, *vid.* H.W. Bird, *C.B.* 65, 1989, 95-98.

[89]This is most noticeable in Victor's account of the reigns of Constantine and Constantius II. Sokolov (*op. cit.*, 220) observes that Victor wrote with a certain disregard for the accuracy of his statements since he was more interested in moralizing.

[90]E.g. *De Caes.* 37.6; 39.1, with reference to the Edict of Gallienus and the early existence of the *domestici*.

[91]F. Leo, *Die Griechisch-römische Biographie*, Leipzig, 1901, 307.

[92]Not always; cf. *De Caes.* 4.1; 39.26-27.

[93]*De Caes.* 3.18-20; also 39.26.

[94]*E.g.* the decline of morality, education, and culture, the excessive greed and power of the army, and the waning influence of the senatorial class.

[95]C.G. Starr, *A.H.R.* 61, 1955/56, 576.

SEXTUS AURELIUS VICTOR'S
Book on the Emperors

The abbreviated histories of Aurelius
Victor from Augustus Octavian, that
is, from the end of Titus Livy to the
tenth consulship of Constantius
Augustus and the third of Julian
Caesar.

1.   In about the 722nd year of the city the custom commenced at
Rome of obeying one man alone.[1]   For Octavian, son of
Octavius, received the *cognomen* Caesar after being adopted by
his great uncle and subsequently, through a decree of the
nobility, that of Augustus[2] because he had exploited his party's
victory leniently,[3] won over the soldiers with bribes and the
common people by his apparent concern for the grain supply
and subdued the rest without difficulty.[4]   When roughly 44
years had passed in that manner he died of an illness at Nola,[5]
having added Raetia and Illyricum[6] to the empire of his fellow
citizens and tamed the fierce spirits of foreign nations except
for Germany, though he was the third after Numa to close the
temple of Janus[7] when he had defeated Antony. This would
occur according to Roman law when all wars had ceased. The
man possessed a charming and gracious disposition but he had
an excessively ardent passion for luxury and the games and an
immoderate desire for sleep.[8]   He was a great supporter of
learned men, who were numerous, and his friends, since he
was remarkably devoted to the study of eloquence[9] and
religious practices, and he was called "Father of his country"[10]
because of his clemency and granted permanent tribunician
power.[11]   Consequently temples, priests and sacral colleges
were dedicated to him as a god at Rome and in the most
famous cities in all provinces both while he was alive and after
his death.[12]   He was so fortunate (except, however, for his
children and also his marriage), that the Indians, Scythians,
Garamantes and Bactrians sent envoys to beg for an alliance.[13]

2.	Thereafter Claudius Tiberius Nero, admitted by adoption from the position of stepson to be among Augustus' children,[1] when he realized that those circumstances which were causing alarm were safe enough, embraced the imperial power while shrewdly refusing its title.[2] Cunning and rather secretive, he often pretended to oppose what he especially desired and insidiously supported what he detested.[3] His mind was far sharper in making sudden decisions.[4] After a good beginning he subsequently became pernicious,[5] given to the most unnatural lusts for persons of practically every age and sex and punishing all too cruelly the innocent and the guilty, his own relatives and strangers alike.[6] Moreover in the period when he detested cities and assemblies he sought out the isle of Capri as a cover for his shameful activities. Therefore, since military affairs were neglected, a great part of the Roman empire was ravaged[7] and no (new) province was formed except for Cappadocia, and that at the beginning of his reign when King Archelaus had been removed.[8] The predatory raids of the Gaetuli, which had broken out everywhere under the leadership of Tacfarinas, were suppressed.[9] At the same time Marobodus, king of the Suebi, was cunningly entrapped.[10] Furthermore he collected from every quarter the praetorian cohorts, which had been kept dispersed and lodged in private homes at Rome or in the nearby municipalities, and concentrated them in a camp near the city, calling the authority by which they were controlled the praetorian prefecture, which was an increase in status, for Augustus had instituted other bodyguards and guards units.[11]

3.	And so Claudius, when he had ruled for 23 years and was 79 years old, was overcome by a fever or a plot[1] and Gaius Caesar, surnamed Caligula, was appointed with universal consent because of his ancestry and his father.[2] For Augustus, through his daughter, was his great-grandfather and his grandfathers were Agrippa on his mother's side and Drusus, father of Germanicus, who was his father. The common people were greatly moved by their modesty and by their untimely deaths, except for Octavian's, as well as by the deaths of his mother and brothers whom Tiberius had eliminated in various ways.[3] For this reason everyone strove to mitigate the misfortune of such a great family with their expectations of the very young man; then again, because he had been born in the army[4] (where he had acquired his surname from a military boot) he was loved and accepted by the legions. Furthermore, all the most sensible people believed that he would be like his relatives, but it turned out quite differently, as if by some law of nature which frequently, as if by design, produces bad men from good, boors from quite learned men and others of this kind or the opposite. In fact from his example many intelligent men have decided that it is more beneficial not to have children.[5] Moreover in Caligula's case they were not very far from the truth inasmuch as for a long time he had so concealed the enormities of his nature by his proper behaviour and pretence of obedience that it was justly said in public that there had never been better servants nor a harsher master than he.[6] Finally, after obtaining power, as is customary with people of such a disposition at the beginning, for several months of that year he granted extraordinary benefits to the people, the senators and the soldiers,[7] and when a conspiracy had been reported, as if he did not believe it, he declared that it could hardly have been undertaken against him whose life was a burden or detriment to no one.[8] But suddenly, after he had first killed a few innocent people through various crimes, he revealed the nature, as it were, of a wild beast that has tasted blood.[9] And so thereafter three years passed while the world was defiled with the widespread murders of senators and nobles. Furthermore he amused himself by debauching his sisters and (mockingly) marrying noblewomen, and would go about dressed like a god since he claimed that he was Jupiter on account of his incest, but also Liber because of his chorus of Bacchants.[10] Similarly he concentrated his legions in one place with the expectation of crossing over into Germany, then ordered them to gather mussels and cockles on the shore of the Ocean while he himself went among them at times in the flowing robe of Venus,[11] at other times, in full armour, he would say that he was taking spoils not from men but from the gods, doubtless because he had heard that according to the Greeks, who love to embellish everything, fish of this kind are (called) Nymphs' eyes. Elated by this he had attempted to have himself addressed as "Lord" and to fasten royal insignia to his head.[12] Consequently, at the instigation of Chaerea, those who possessed Roman courage were impelled to deliver the state from such a terrible scourge by stabbing him to death;[13] and that outstanding exploit of Brutus when he expelled Tarquinius would have been repeated, if only the true Romans[14] had been performing their military service. But when, through apathy, the citizens conceived the desire to draft foreigners and barbarians into the army, morals were corrupted, freedom was suppressed and the craving for possessions increased.[15] In the meantime, while in accordance with a decree of the senate armed men were hunting down the family of the Caesars, even those of the female sex, and all their relatives by marriage, by chance Vimius, a native of Epirus and a centurion from the cohorts which were occupying strategic locations throughout the palace, discovered Titus Claudius concealing himself in a disgraceful hiding-place, dragged him out and exclaimed to his comrades that if they were smart, there was the emperor.[16] And certainly because he was foolish he seemed extremely mild to unsuspecting men. This had helped him against the wicked intentions of his uncle Nero (Tiberius) and prevented him from being envied by his nephew, Caligula.[17] Moreover he had won over the hearts of the soldiers and plebs until he himself could be considered more pitiable than contemptible through the violent tyranny of his family.[18] As most of them were recalling these facts the crowd which was present suddenly surrounded him with no opposition and the rest of the soldiers and a great throng of ordinary people began to flock to him. When the senators had learned this they quickly sent to see if they could suppress the bold coup.[19] But, after the state and people of all ranks were torn by various frightful dissensions, as if on command they all surrendered.[20] Thus at Rome the royal power was confirmed[21] and it was all too plainly revealed that men's efforts are rendered vain and futile by Fortune.[22]

4. Consequently Claudius, although he was a shameful slave to his stomach,[1] foolish as well and forgetful, of timid disposition and rather cowardly,[2] nevertheless, mostly because of his apprehension, made some outstanding decisions, particularly on the advice of the nobility whom he courted through fear. Simple-minded people, you see, do what their advisors tell them. In short, because of his good counsellors, vices were suppressed by him[3] as were the notorious rites of the Druids[4] throughout Gaul, the most beneficial laws possible were established, military matters were dealt with, frontiers for the Roman Empire were retained or furnished, Mesopotamia in the east,[5] the Rhine and Danube to the north,[6] and in the south the Moors were added to the provinces since their kings had been removed after Juba,[7] a band of Musulamii was destroyed,[8] and at the same time, (in) the lands of the extreme west, parts of Britain were subdued, which was the only place he visited, setting out by sea from Ostia, for his generals had taken care of the rest.[9] Furthermore he relieved the grain shortage which Caligula had brought on when he had collected cargo ships from all over the world and attempted at the expense of the people to make the sea a thoroughfare for theatres and chariots.[10] Similarly, after he had carried out a new census and had removed quite a lot from the senate, since he had retained a dissolute young man whose father had asserted that he approved of him, he (Claudius) had justly added that a father should also be a censor for his children.[11] But when he had been dragged into depravity through the enticements of his wife, Messalina, and at the same time of his freedmen, to whom he had subordinated himself,[12] not only were tyrannical acts committed, but also whatever the worst sort of women and slaves are capable of, if their husband or master is a fool. For his wife in the first place committed adultery indiscriminately,

as if it were her right, and to such an extent that very many who refused her, whether because of their character or through fear, were killed along with their families as she, with typical womanly wiles, charged those whom she had solicited with soliciting her. Aroused to greater enormities by this she had forced certain women from the nobility, married and unmarried, to act as prostitutes with herself, like common whores, and men were made to participate. But if anyone recoiled from such depravities she would fabricate a charge and savagely attack him and his whole family. You see his own household used to terrify Claudius, who was, as we have shown above, extremely timid by nature, in particular by instilling in him the fear of a conspiracy, so that by means of this machination even his freedmen would ruin whomsoever they wished. At first they connived at her crimes but when they became as powerful as their patroness they killed her, too, through their agents without their master's knowledge, yet as if he had given the command. And indeed the woman had gone to such extremes that she celebrated a marriage with another man at Rome when her husband had gone to Ostia to enjoy himself with his mistresses, and she became even more notorious through this as it appeared astonishing that at the emperor's palace she had married a man other than the emperor.[13] Thus the freedmen,[14] after acquiring complete power, corrupted everything with their depravity, exiles, murders and proscriptions and so prevailed upon their master's folly that, though he was an old man, he set his heart on marrying his brother's daughter.[15] Although she was considered more irrational than her predecessor and therefore feared a similar fate,[16] she murdered her husband with poison.[17] In his sixth year (as emperor), although he reigned fourteen years, the 800th anniversary of the city was celebrated in magnificent style[18] and in Egypt the Phoenix was seen, a bird which, they say, flies every five hundred years from Arabia to places (which are) on record,[19] and in the Aegean Sea a huge island suddenly emerged one night during which a lunar eclipse had occurred.[20] Furthermore the death (of Claudius) was concealed for a long time, as had once happened in the case of Priscus Tarquinius, while the guards, corrupted by the woman's guile, pretended that he was sick and that the management of the state had been entrusted by him to his stepson whom he had quite recently adopted.[21]

5. In this manner L. Domitius[1] (for that was certainly Nero's name, since his father was Domitius) was made emperor. He, although he had reigned as many years as his stepfather while a very young man,[2] nevertheless was so outstanding for five years especially in enhancing the city, that Trajan quite often justifiably asserted that all emperors fell far short of Nero in his (first) five years[3] during which he even reduced Pontus to provincial jurisdiction, with the consent of Polemon, for whose sake it is called Pontus Polemoniacus, and similarly the Cottian Alps after King Cottius had died.[4] Consequently it is reasonably certain that age is no barrier to virtue, that it is easily transformed if one's nature has been corrupted by unrestricted freedom, and that the law of adolescence, as it were, if it is omitted, recurs more destructively. For Nero, in fact, spent the rest of his life so disgracefully that it is disgusting and shameful to record the existence of anyone of this kind, let alone that he was the ruler of the world.[5] He, while he had begun by singing to the cithara in public in competition for a crown, a Greek innovation,[6] went to such extremes that he spared neither his own nor anyone else's decency and finally, dressed in the fashion of young girls getting married, openly in the presence of the senate, after a dowry had been given and everybody was celebrating in a festive manner, was married to someone chosen from among all his coterie of perverts. Yet this must be considered rather trivial in his case for, in fact, while decked out in the skin of a wild beast he would nuzzle the genitals of people of either sex who had been chained up like criminals and, in an even more disgusting act, he compelled couples to copulate.[7] Furthermore among these activities many consider that he even had intercourse with his mother since she, too, in her passion

for power, was willing to commit any crime whatever to subject her son to her.[8] I personally think this is true although there are writers with different opinions. For, in fact, when vices have entered the mind humans in no way feel the obligations of decency in dealing with strangers and habitual sinning, which leads to novel and therefore sweeter pleasures, finally turns them to their own families.[9] This is demonstrated more forcefully by the following: while she, in a sort of progression went via other men to marriage with her uncle[10] and from the torture of strangers[11] to the murder of her husband, he by degrees proceeded to defile a priestess of Vesta,[12] then himself, and finally each defiled the other. Nevertheless such delights could not unite them,[13] but they were drawn into danger on that account and, while they plotted against each other, the mother was forestalled and killed. Accordingly, when he had violated every law, human and divine, by parricide[14] and was attacking the nobility with greater and greater violence[15] many men plotted, naturally at different times, to liberate the state.[16] After these had been betrayed and executed he decided even more monstrously to destroy the city with fire,[17] the common people with wild beasts let loose everywhere and the senate with a similar fate,[18] and he sought a new capital for his empire principally through the encouragement of the Parthian ambassador[19] who happened to be at a feast. The entertainers were singing, as is the custom, when he demanded a cithara-player for himself. Upon being told in response that the player was a free man Nero had added that he should take whomsoever he wished from his household, indicating to those who were attending the banquet that under imperial rule no one was considered free.[20] And if Galba, who was governor of Spain, upon learning that his execution had been ordered, had not come to the rescue by seizing power,[21] although he was of advanced age, such a great crime would without doubt have been committed. But at his approach Nero was deserted on all sides except by a eunuch, whom he had once tried to make into a woman by surgery, and he stabbed himself since, although for a long time he begged for someone to kill him, he had not deserved anyone's assistance even to die.[22]

This was the end of the family of the Caesars, which many portents foretold, in particular the withering on their estates of a grove of laurel dedicated to them for their triumphs and the death of the chickens which were so numerous and white and so suitable for religious rites that even today a place is kept for them at Rome.[23]

6. But when Galba, who was no less noble (than they) as a descendant of the extremely renowned family of the Sulpicii,[1] had entered Rome, as if he had come to promote excesses or even cruelty, he pillaged, plundered and harassed, and in a disgraceful manner he destroyed and defiled everything. Becoming more detestable through these actions (for those who were expected to govern more mildly offend more grievously), and at the same time, because, in his excessive greed for money, he had reduced the pay of the soldiers,[2] he was killed at the instigation of Otho. The latter, hurt insufferably because Galba had preferred to adopt Piso, had led angry, armed cohorts into the forum. When Galba, wearing a cuirass, hurried there to quell the disturbance he was killed near the Lacus Curtius on the seventh day and in the seventh month of his reign.[3]

7. Consequently Salvius Otho, once, to his shame, a close friend of Nero, seized power[1] though he was hardly more than an adolescent.[2] He ruled in a predictable manner for nearly eighty-five days,[3] but after he had been beaten in battle at Verona by Vitellius, who had come down from Gaul, he took his own life.[4]

8. Thus the power was passed to Aulus Vitellius and from such a beginning it would have become progressively more destructive[1] if Vespasian had been detained any longer by the Jewish War which he had undertaken on the orders of Nero.

He, when he had learned of Galba's actions and of his
suppression and also, because envoys from the Moesian and
Pannonian armies had arrived among those encouraging him,
seized the imperial power. For the soldiers mentioned above,
after they had discovered that Otho had been made emperor by
the praetorians and Vitellius by the German legions, in rivalry,
as is their custom, so that they should not seem different,
urged on Vespasian, upon whom the Syrian cohorts had
already agreed because of his outstanding qualities.[2] In effect
Vespasian, a senator from a new family with ancestors from
Reate, was regarded as a member of the high nobility because
of his hard work and his civil and military achievements.[3]
When his legionary commanders had crossed into Italy and the
Vitellian forces had been routed at Cremona[4] Vitellius had
come to an agreement with Sabinus, the urban prefect and
Vespasian's brother, with the soldiers as mediators, that he
would abdicate his imperial position for a hundred million
sesterces,[5] but subsequently, after he imagined that he had been
deceived by the reports[6] with his fury compounded, so to
speak, he burned Sabinus and the rest of the opposing faction
together with the Capitol, which they had seized as a refuge
for their safety.[7] But when it was revealed that the reports
were true and that his enemies were approaching,[8] he was led
out of a porter's hut where he had hidden himself, a noose was
tied around his neck, as they do with parricides, and he was
dragged to the Gemonian steps and down them. At the same
time his body was stabbed with as many blows as each man
could inflict and it was thrown down into the Tiber[9] in the
eighth month of his tyranny when he was more than fifty-
seven years old.[10]

All these whom I have briefly touched upon, and
particularly the family of the Caesars, were so refined in
literature and eloquence that, had they not been excessive in all
their vices, with the exception of Augustus, their great talents
would surely have cloaked ordinary misdemeanours.[11]
Although through these instances it is generally agreed that

character is of paramount importance, nevertheless all good men and especially a supreme ruler need both qualities equally, if it is possible; otherwise, if the purpose of life should take a giant step backwards, at least let him assume the dignity of refinement and learning.[12]

9. Vespasian likewise was a man of this kind, honourable in all respects and not lacking the eloquence to express what he felt,[1] and he quickly restored a world long debilitated and exhausted.[2] For first he preferred to reform rather than to torture and destroy the accomplices of tyranny,[3] except for those who had perhaps gone too far in committing atrocities, since he very sensibly realized that evil tasks are carried out by most people through fear. Then he allowed many conspirators to escape with their crimes unpunished,[4] demonstrating in a kindly manner, as was his nature, the foolishness of those who did not know how much work and harassment there was in ruling.[5] At the same time, as a devotee of soothsayers (whose veracity he had ascertained from frequent use) he was confident that he would be succeeded by his sons, Titus and Domitian.[6] Furthermore, by the fairest of laws,[7] by counselling and, what is even more compelling, by the example of his own life he eradicated the majority of vices. Nonetheless he was weak when it came to money, so some people wrongly believe, although it is generally agreed that he had sought new revenues from taxes because of the depletion of the treasury and the ruined state of cities and these (taxes) were not kept in place very long afterwards.[8] For at Rome the Capitol, which had burned down as I mentioned above, the Temple of Peace, the monuments of Claudius, the massive structure of the amphitheatre, many other buildings, too, as well as a forum were started or completed.[9] In addition, through all the lands where Roman law prevails cities were restored with exceptional care and roads were constructed at enormous cost in labour and the mountains along the Flaminian Way were excavated to make the crossing level.[10] That so many enormous enterprises were completed in a brief time without

harming the peasant farmers testified more to his good sense than to his avarice.[11]   At the same time when a census had been held according to ancestral practice all the more shameful men were removed from the senate and a thousand families were formed from the best men selected from all over the empire, since he had with the greatest difficulty found only two hundred because the majority had been destroyed by the savagery of the tyrants.[12] Furthermore Vologeses, king of the Parthians, was forced by war to make peace and the Syrian district which is called Palestine became a province together with the Jews,[13] through the efforts of his son Titus, whom he had left behind for the foreign campaign when he travelled across to Italy[14] and whom subsequently, after his victory, he promoted to the praetorian prefecture.[15]   Consequently that office, too, which had been powerful from the beginning, was further inflated and became second to the emperor in authority. But at the present time, when the integrity of public office is despised, the ignorant are confused with the good and the inept with the capable, many have made it a title empty of power, arrogant to the poor, but subservient to all the most wicked men and, under the guise of collecting the annual tax, simply rapacious.[16]

10.   However, after Titus had acquired the imperial power, it is incredible how much he surpassed the man he imitated, particularly in learning, clemency and favours.[1] In short, since it was customary for indulgences granted by previous emperors to be confirmed by their successors, as soon as he took power he voluntarily assured and guaranteed such grants to their possessors by edict.[2] And no less scrupulously he was ready to protect those who had chanced to conspire against him, so much so that when two men of the highest rank were unable to deny the crime that they had planned and the senators had decreed that they should be punished as confessed criminals, he led them to the show, ordered them to sit on either side of him, deliberately asked a gladiator, whose fight they were watching, for his sword and handed it to one and then to the

other as if they should test its sharpness. They were astonished and admired his composure. "Do you see," he said, "that powers are granted by fate and it is futile to attempt a crime in the hope of acquiring it or through fear of losing it." [3] So, after two years and about nine months, when work on the amphitheatre had been completed in a splendid manner, he died of poisoning in his fortieth year (though his father had died in his seventieth after being emperor for ten years).[4] His death was truly such a source of grief for the provinces that they called him the darling of the human race and mourned for a world that had been left fatherless. [5]

11. And so Domitian, becoming more frantic in his criminal acts, both in public and in private, through the murder of his brother, the best of emperors, began simultaneously to commit the robbery, murder and torture (characteristic of) a depraved youth.[1] He became more extravagant in his shameful acts of lust[2] and treated the senate with excessive arrogance inasmuch as he demanded to be addressed as lord and god, which was immediately abandoned by his successors but revived more forcefully much later by one emperor after another. [3] But at first Domitian pretended to be compassionate and since he was not thus far inactive he appeared quite resolute in both domestic and military affairs.[4] For that reason, after he had crushed the Dacians and a band of Chatti, he renamed the months of September and October and called the former Germanicus and the latter by his own name, [5] and he completed many of the building projects begun by his father or through the efforts of his brother, in particular the Capitol.[6] From then on he was frightful for his murders of honourable men[7] and absurdly indolent,[8] for he would send everyone away and chase swarms of flies after finding himself with less energy for sexual pursuits, a disgraceful exercise which he used to call in Greek "bed-wrestling." This produced a lot of jokes, for when someone asked whether there was anyone in the Palace, the reply was: "Not even a fly, unless perhaps in the wrestling-room."[9] Accordingly, as his cruelty grew more and more

excessive and, therefore, he became more mistrusted even by his friends, through a plot of his freedmen, of which his wife was not unaware, for she preferred the love of an actor to her husband's, he paid the (ultimate) penalty[10] in the forty-fifth year of his life after a tyrannical reign of approximately fifteen years.[11] Then the senate decreed that he should be buried in the manner of a gladiator and that his name should be obliterated.[12] The soldiers, angered by this because they had received quite generous private benefits (from him) at public expense, began in their habitually rebellious manner to seek out those responsible for his death to punish them. Although they were barely restrained and only with difficulty by sensible men, eventually they came to an agreement with the nobility. Nevertheless they continued to stir up hostilities by themselves because the change of government made them resentful at losing the perquisites provided by (Domitian's) generous gifts.[13]

Up to this time men born at Rome or in Italy had ruled the empire, afterwards foreigners did, too; perhaps, as was the case with Tarquinius Priscus, they were far better. And to me at least, from the many things I have heard and read, it is perfectly clear that the city of Rome grew great in particular through the qualities of outsiders and imported talents.[14]

12.   For who was wiser or more moderate than the Cretan Nerva?[1] Since he had taken up the supreme power as the choice of the legions in extreme old age while he lived among the Sequani, where he had retired in fear of the tyrant, when he realized that the position could not be handled except by people mentally more able and physically stronger than he, he abdicated in the sixteenth month,[2] after previously dedicating a forum, which is called the Pervium, where the temple of Minerva rises with even more imposing splendour.[3]   Whereas it is always extraordinary to judge what you are capable of, and not to be driven on headlong by ambition, it is particularly so in the case

of supreme power, which mortals desire to such an extent that they avidly seek it even in extreme old age.[4] Furthermore he revealed more and more clearly how sensible he was through the merit of his successor.[5]

13.   For he adopted Ulpius Trajan, a native of Italica, a Spanish city, but of the highest (i.e. senatorial) order and also of consular rank.[1] It would be difficult to find a more distinguished man than he whether in civil or in military affairs.[2] Indeed he was the first or even the only one to extend Roman power across the Danube when he subdued and formed into a province the bonnetted Dacians and Sarmatian tribes under King Decebalus and the Dardanians.[3] At the same time in the east he crushed in war all the nations which live between the famous rivers the Indus and the Euphrates and he demanded hostages from the king of the Persians named Chosroes,[4] and amid those achievements he built a road through barbarous nations by which one might easily travel across into Gaul all the way from the Black Sea.[5] Forts were erected in the more critical and strategic locations, a bridge was constructed over the Danube, and very many colonies were settled.[6] Furthermore at Rome he improved and decorated in a more than magnificent fashion a forum and many other structures begun by Domitian,[7] and showed an admirable concern for the permanent grain supply by reviving and strengthening the guild of bakers.[8] At the same time, in order that he might be informed more rapidly of whatever state business was being transacted anywhere (in the empire) the resources of the public postal system were employed.[9] In fact this quite useful service turned into the bane of the Roman world through the greed and arrogance of later generations, except that in these (recent) years its resources have been adequate in Illyricum because of the reforms of the prefect Anatolius.[10] Indeed, there is nothing good or bad in the state that cannot be changed to the opposite by the character of its rulers.[11] Trajan was fair, merciful, extremely patient and very loyal to his friends,[12] since he dedicated to his friend Sura the

building which is called the Suranae,[13] and was so sure of his integrity that whenever he gave his praetorian prefect, Suburanus by name,[14] the dagger that was the symbol of his power, as was the custom, he would frequently advise him: "I am entrusting you with this for my protection, if I act properly; if not, use it rather on me," for it is less proper for the ruler of all to make any kind of mistake.[15] Furthermore he had prudently moderated his excessive fondness for wine, a fault with which he was afflicted like Nerva, by prohibiting his orders from being carried out after prolonged banquets.[16] After he had governed the empire with these qualities for almost twenty years,[17] since he was utterly devastated by the severe earthquake at Antioch and through the rest of Syria,[18] on his way back to Italy at the request of the senate he died of an illness at an advanced age,[19] but not before he had appointed Hadrian, his fellow-countryman and relative, as emperor, although there are others who think that the imperial power was acquired through the favour of Plotina, Trajan's wife, who had pretended that Hadrian had been designated heir to the throne in her husband's will.[20] Henceforth the titles of Caesar and Augustus were separated and the practice was introduced into the state of having two or more men share the supreme power, but with different titles and unequal power.[21]

14. And so Aelius Hadrian, who was more suited for declamation and civil pursuits,[1] established peace in the east[2] and returned to Rome. There, in the fashion of the Greeks or Pompilius Numa, he began to give attention to religious ceremonies, laws, schools and teachers[3] to such an extent, in fact, that he even established a school of liberal arts, called the Athenaeum,[4] and celebrated at Rome in the Athenian manner the rites of Ceres and Libera which are called the Eleusinian Mysteries.[5] Then, as is normal in peaceful circumstances, he retired somewhat negligently to his country retreat at Tivoli, leaving the city to Lucius Aelius Caesar.[6] He himself, as is the custom with the fortunate rich, built palaces[7] and devoted himself to dinner parties, statuary and paintings, and finally took sufficient pains

to procure every luxury and plaything.[8] From this sprang the malicious rumours that he had debauched young men and that he burned with passion for the scandalous attentions of Antinous and that for no other reason he had founded a city named after him or had erected statues to the youth. Some, to be sure, maintain that these were acts of piety and religious scruple because when Hadrian wanted to prolong his life and magicians had demanded a volunteer in his place, they report that although everyone else refused, Antinous offered himself and for this reason the honours mentioned above were accorded him.[9] We shall leave the matter unresolved, although with someone of a self-indulgent nature we are suspicious of a relationship between men far apart in age.[10] Meanwhile, after the death of Aelius Caesar, since he himself was not mentally strong enough and was for that reason treated with contempt, he convened the senators to appoint a Caesar. As they were hurriedly assembling by chance he caught sight of Antoninus supporting with his hand the faltering steps of an old man, his father-in-law or his father. Singularly delighted by this he gave orders for him (Antoninus) to be formally adopted as Caesar[11] and for a large number of the senators, to whom he had been a laughing-stock, to be immediately executed by him.[12] Not long afterwards he died of consumption at Baiae at a rather ripe old age in the twenty-second year of his reign less a month.[13] On the other hand the senators were not even swayed by the entreaties of the emperor to accord him the honour of deification, so deeply did they mourn the loss of so many men of their order. However, after those whose death they were grieving suddenly appeared and each one embraced his relatives and friends, they sanctioned what they had refused.[14]

15. Meanwhile Helius Antoninus acquired the surname Pius. He was virtually unblemished by the taint of vices.[1] A man of a very old family from the municipality of Lanuvium, he was a senator of Rome.[2] He was so fair and of such upright character[3] that he plainly showed that perfect dispositions are

not corrupted by continuous peace and long-lasting leisure[4] and, in fact, that on that account, cities will be fortunate if wise men rule them.[5] In short, he remained the same for the twenty years during which he managed the affairs of state[6] and celebrated in magnificent manner the nine hundredth anniversary of the city.[7] Yet perhaps his lack of triumphs appears to be a sign of inactivity, which is far from the truth since it is undoubtedly more important that no one dared to disturb the established order[8] nor did he make war on peaceful nations to make a vain display of himself.[9] Furthermore, lacking male heirs he provided for the state through the husband of his daughter.[10]

16.   For he adopted into his family and into the imperial power M. Boionius, who is known as Aurelius Antoninus, and was from the same town and of equal nobility,[1] but far superior in the pursuits of philosophy and eloquence.[2] All his actions and decisions, both civil and military, were divinely inspired:[3] but his inability to restrain his wife spoiled this for she had erupted to such a degree of shamelessness that while staying in Campania she would haunt the beauty spots along the coast to pick out those sailors, because they mostly work in the nude, (who would be) particularly suitable for her disgraceful passions.[4] Accordingly, when his father-in-law had died at Lorium at the age of seventy-five,[5] Aurelius straightway admitted his brother, Lucius Verus, to a share of the power.[6] Under his leadership, the Persians under their king, Vologeses, though at first they had been victorious, finally yielded a triumph.[7] Lucius died within a few days, thus providing material for the invention that he had been destroyed by the treachery of his brother who, they say, was vexed with envy at his exploits and had devised the following deception at dinner. For, with one side of a knife smeared with poison, he cut a piece of a sow's udder with it and deliberately set it aside. He ate one slice and, as is customary among close friends, he offered the other, which the poison had touched, to his brother.[8] Only minds with criminal inclinations can believe

this of such a great man, especially since it is generally acknowledged that Lucius died of illness at Altinum, a city in Venetia,[9] and that Marcus possessed such wisdom, gentleness, integrity and learning[10] that as he was about to march against the Marcomanni[11] with his son Commodus, whom he had substituted as Caesar,[12] he was surrounded by a throng of philosophers begging him not to commit himself to a campaign or to battle before he had explained some difficult and very obscure points of the philosophical systems. So in their eagerness for learning they feared that the uncertainties of war would endanger his safety:[13] and fine arts flourished to such an extent during his reign that I consider precisely this to have been the glory of the times.[14] Ambiguities of the law were admirably clarified and, by eliminating the custom of posting bail, the right of laying a charge and having it disposed of on the determined date was duly established.[15] Roman citizenship was granted without discrimination to all[16] and many cities were founded, settled, restored or embellished and in particular Punic Carthage, which fire had terribly ravaged, and Ephesus in Asia and Nicomedia in Bithynia, which had been levelled by an earthquake,[17] just as Nicomedia was in our time during the consulship of Cerealis.[18] Triumphs were celebrated over nations which, under King Marcomarus, used to extend all the way from the Pannonian city which is called Carnuntum to the centre of Gaul.[19] So in the eighteenth year of his reign he died in the prime of his life at Vienna, to the very great distress of all people.[20] Finally the senators and common folk, who are divided in other matters, voted everything to him alone, temples, columns and priests.[21]

17.   But his son was considered quite detestable for his despotism, which was savage from its beginning,[1] especially when contrasted with the memory of his predecessors. This is such a burden on successive generations that, apart from our common hatred of the undutiful, they are more loathsome for being, as it were, the corruptors of their kind.[2] Clearly energetic in war, because of his success against the Quadi he

had called the month of September Commodus.[3] He constructed a building to serve as a bath that was hardly worthy of Roman might.[4] Indeed he possessed such an utterly harsh and cruel nature that he frequently butchered gladiators in mock battles, since he would use an iron sword, his opponents swords made of lead.[5] When he had finished off very many in that manner, by chance one of them named Scaeva, who was very bold, physically powerful and a skilled fighter, deterred him from this passion. He, spurning his sword, which he saw was useless, said that the one with which Commodus was armed would be sufficient for both of them. Fearing that in the struggle, he might have his weapon torn away from him and be killed, which does happen, he had Scaeva removed[6] and, (now) more fearful of the others, he transferred his ferocity to wild beasts.[7] Since all people were horrified at his insatiable bloodthirstiness through these activities, his closest associates in particular plotted against him. In fact no one was loyal to his regime at all and even his cronies, by whom the power of those men was maintained, while they were wary of a criminal mind that was inclined to cruelty,[8] thought it safer to overthrow him any means whatever, and actually sought to poison Commodus, albeit very secretly at first, in about the thirteenth year of his reign.[9] The poison's strength was rendered ineffective by the food with which he happened to have stuffed himself; since, however, he was complaining of a stomach ache, on the advice of his doctor, a leader of the group, he went to the wrestling hall.[10] There he died at the hands of the masseur (for, by chance, he too was privy to the plot) by having his throat crushed tightly in an arm-lock as if it were part of the exercise.[11] When this was known the senate, which had gathered in full complement at dawn for the January festival, together with the people, declared him an enemy of the gods and men and (ordered) his name to be erased;[12] and straightway the imperial power was conferred upon the prefect of the city, Aulus Helvius Pertinax.[13]

18.   He had matched the Curii and Fabricii with his comprehensive learning, really old-fashioned morality and extreme frugality.[1] The soldiers, to whom nothing seemed sufficient even though the world was already exhausted and ruined, cruelly murdered him at the instigation of Didius on the eightieth day of his reign.[2]

19.   But meanwhile Didius (or Salvius) Julianus,[1] relying on the praetorians whose alliance he had secured with even more extravagant promises, advanced from prefect of the watch to the badge of sovereignty.[2] His family was very noble and he was distinguished for his knowledge of Roman law.[3] In fact he was the first to codify the edict which used to be published by the praetors in varying and confusing ways.[4] Hence it is generally accepted that unless character helps to restrain our passions, learning is a feeble thing[5] since even this really strict professor of more righteous conduct proceeded (to commit) the crime which he had decreed punishable by a new penalty.[6] Not for long, however, did he keep what he had coveted.[7] For, as soon as it was learned what had happened Septimius Severus, who happened to be waging war in distant lands as governor of Syria, was proclaimed emperor and defeated him in battle near the Milvian Bridge.[8] Men sent to pursue him as he fled cut him down in the palace at Rome.[9]

20.   Therefore Septimius Severus, moved by grief and anger at the death of Pertinax and at the same time because of his hatred of their crimes, immediately cashiered the praetorian cohorts[1] and, after executing all of his opponents, enroled Helvius among the gods through a senatorial decree.[2] He ordered the name of Salvius and his writings and achievements erased, but this was the one thing he could not accomplish.[3] So great is the prestige of the learned arts that not even a violent disposition (can) harm the reputation of writers.[4] Moreover a death of this kind glorifies them but makes the agents of the deed detestable, since all men, and especially later generations, consider that those talented individuals could not have been

suppressed except through public villainy and madness. All good men must put their faith in this, and I especially, for I was born in the country of a poor and uneducated father yet I have achieved upper-class status in these times through such important studies.[5] This, in my opinion, is really characteristic of our race which, by some quirk of fate, is sparingly productive of good men, yet those whom it has raised it extols, each according to his own merits. Like Severus himself; no one in the state has been more distinguished than he.[6] Although he died at an advanced age[7] they solemnly decreed that he should be mourned with a public holiday and funeral speech while declaring that it was totally inappropriate for that just man to be born or to die.[8] Clearly this was because they considered him excessive in reforming morality, but after they had attained the level of integrity of their ancestors just as if they had come to their senses, they considered him compassionate.[9] Thus honesty, which at first is deemed troublesome, when it has been achieved, becomes a source of pleasure and extravagance.[10] He defeated Pescennius Niger at Cyzicus,[11] Clodius Albinus at Lyons and had them killed.[12] Of these the former, who held Egypt as military governor,[13] had started a war in the hope of gaining supreme power. The latter, who had brought about the assassination of Pertinax,[14] had seized power in Gaul while he was attempting, through fear of his actions, to cross over to Britain,[15] the province to which he had been appointed by Commodus. Because of the indiscriminate murder of many he was considered too cruel[16] and given the surname Pertinax, although many think that he had rather adopted the name himself on account of their similarly parsimonious lifestyles.[17] I am inclined to believe that it was imposed on him because of his harshness. For when one of his enemies,[18] who had gone over to Albinus because of geographical necessity, as is often the case in civil wars, had nevertheless finally concluded his explanation of the reasons (by saying): "What, I ask, would you have done, if you had been in my place?" he replied, "I would have endured what you will."[19] Nothing is harsher than this saying and action since good and honourable men blame fortune for dissensions of this kind, however eagerly they have been undertaken, and would rather allow the truth to be distorted to protect citizens than to ruin them.[20] But he in particular wanted to destroy opposition groups[21] so that he might then behave in a gentler fashion, and preferred to punish an act of necessity so that the expectation of pardon might not gradually lead to the collapse of the state through conspiracies, to which he realized minds were inclined because of the fault of the times. Nor do I myself deny that those types of crime which have begun to increase excessively must be eradicated in an almost more than severe manner.[22] He was so successful and skilful, especially in military affairs, that he left no battle except as victor[23] and he extended the empire by overcoming the king of the Persians named Abgarus.[24] Similarly he subdued and reduced to provincial status the Arabs, as soon as he attacked them.[25] He would also have consigned Adiabene to tributary status, if he had not despised the barrenness of their territory.[26] On account of these great successes the senators granted him the titles Arabicus, Adiabenicus and Parthicus.[27] He undertook enterprises more serious than these for he defeated the enemy and then protected Britain, up to the point where the country was useful, with a wall which he built across the island right up to the Ocean at both ends.[28] Furthermore he drove the warlike tribes far away from Tripolis where his birthplace, Leptis, was situated.[29] These tasks, difficult to achieve, he would accomplish all the more readily inasmuch as he was implacable with those who failed but would promote and reward all men of action.[30] Finally, not even petty thefts were allowed to go unpunished and he was even more careful with his associates because, as a man of experience, he understood that such things were done through the fault of those in command or through factions.[31] He was devoted to philosophy, to oratory and, in short, to the study of all the liberal arts:[32] similarly he wrote an autobiography which was as impressive as it was honest.[33] He established extremely impartial laws.[34] The scandalous behaviour of his

wife diminished the outstanding reputation of this man, who
was so great at home and abroad, for he was so infamously
attached to her that he retained her even after he had learned
of her wantonness and when she was implicated in a
conspiracy.[35] This is shameful both to a humble man and to
the powerful, but especially to him, since not only were private
citizens, individual soldiers and criminals under his control, but
also magistrates, armies and even vices themselves. For when
he delayed a campaign because of his gout and the soldiers felt
anxious about it and elected as Augustus his son Bassianus,
who was with him as Caesar, he gave orders that he should be
carried to the tribunal and that all who had been responsible
for this affair should attend, both the general, the tribunes, the
centurions and the cohorts, and appear as criminal defendants.
When the army, which had been victorious over such great
foes, was prostrate on the ground in fear at this and begged his
forgiveness, tapping his head with his hand he said; "Don't
you realize that it is the head rather than the feet that rules?"[36]
Not long afterwards he died of illness in the British town
called York in the eighteenth year of his reign.[37] Born of a
fairly humble family he was educated first in literature, then in
the law. Dissatisfied with this, as is common (for people) in
limited circumstances, while he was trying various jobs and
looking for something better he climbed to the imperial
power.[38] After experiencing graver problems in that position,
hard work, cares, fear and, in short, all kinds of uncertainties,
as if he were a witness of the human condition, he said; "I
have been everything; I have achieved nothing."[39] His body,
which his sons Geta and Bassianus had brought to Rome, was
honoured in splendid fashion and buried in the tomb of
Marcus[40] whom he had so admired that for his sake he had
persuaded (the senate) to enrol Commodus among the gods and
called him his brother and added the name Antoninus to
Bassianus,[41] because it was through the former that he, after
many doubtful occurrences, had received the auspicious
beginnings of his career through his appointment as advocate
of the privy purse.[42] Naturally those who work their way up

remember the beginnings of their success and the people responsible.

But his heirs, as if they had received orders to make war on one another, immediately parted company.[43] Accordingly Geta, whose name came from his paternal grandfather, since his brother was affronted by his gentler nature, was attacked and perished.[44] This victory was made more shameful by the murder of Papinian, at least in the opinion of devoted historians, since they state that he was in charge of Bassianus' secretariats at that time and was advised, as is the custom, to compose a report for the Roman people as quickly as possible, but he, in his grief for Geta, had said that parricide was not at all as easy to conceal as it was to commit, and therefore he was put to death.[45] But these statements are outrageously absurd since it is generally accepted that he held the praetorian prefecture, and could not have rudely heaped such great abuse on the very man he loved and served as a minister of state.[46]

21.   On the other hand Antoninus won over the Roman populace with unheard of kinds of gifts since he distributed cloaks which reached the ankles, (for which) he was called Caracalla, although in a similar manner he gave the garments the name Antoninians after his own name.[1] He crushed the Alamanni, a populous nation who fight wonderfully well from horseback, near the River Main.[2] He was patient, accessible and calm and had the same fortune and wife as his father.[3] For, captivated by her beauty, he made every effort to marry his stepmother Julia, whose crimes I have recorded above, since she, in her great eagerness for power, had showed herself unclothed to the gaze of the young man as if unaware of his presence. When he passionately declared; "I should like, if I may, to..."; she replied even more shamelessly, for she had stripped off her modesty with her clothes; "You want to? Certainly you may."[4] The cults of Egypt were brought to Rome by him[5] and the city was endowed with the magnificent addition of a new road and the construction of a public bath with beautiful fittings.[6] After

these had been completed and while he was travelling through Syria he died at Edessa in the sixth year of his reign.[7] His remains were brought back to Rome amid public grief and were buried alongside those of the Antonines.[8]

22.   Afterwards Opilius Macrinus, who held the praetorian prefecture, was declared emperor by the legions and his son, Diadumenus, Caesar.[1] Because of their great grief for the emperor they had lost, the soldiers called the young man Antoninus.[2] However we have discovered nothing about these except that they had cruel and ungracious dispositions.[3] For this reason, when they had with difficulty maintained power for barely fourteen months, they were killed by those who had appointed them.[4]

23.   Then Marcus Antoninus, son of Bassianus, was summoned.[1] After his father's death, fearing treachery, he had fled for asylum, so to speak, into the priesthood of the sun-god, which the Syrians call Heliogabalus, and for this reason he was called Heliogabalus.[2] He transported a statue of the god to Rome and set up an altar in the innermost parts of the palace.[3] Not even shameless and wanton women were more depraved than he; in fact he searched the whole world for the lewdest men so that he might watch them or participate in their practice of filthy obscenities. Since these were multiplying day by day and love for Alexander, whom the nobility had proclaimed Caesar after learning of Opilius' death, was increasing more and more,[4] he (Heliogabalus) was overthrown in the praetorian camp in the thirtieth month of his reign.[5]

24.   Straightway the power of Augustus was conferred upon Aurelius Alexander, who was born in Syria in the town with the double name Caesarea and Arce, with the support also of the soldiers.[1] He, although a young man, nevertheless possessed an intellect beyond his age,[2] and he immediately made large-scale preparations and commenced a war against Xerxes, king of the Persians.[3] After the latter had been

defeated and put to flight Alexander very quickly marched into Gaul, which was being harassed by the plundering raids of the Germans.[4] There he suppressed mutinies in most of the legions with the utmost resolution which brought him renown for the moment but subsequently proved fatal. For the soldiers were horrified at the violence of his great severity (from which he had even earned the surname Severus)[5] and they cut him down in a British village named Sicilia where he happened to be operating with a small retinue.[6] He built for the city a most magnificent monument in his honour,[7] and he was more than dutiful in his reverence for his mother, whose name was Mammaea.[8] Furthermore he showed how devoted he was to the nobility and the pursuit of justice by retaining in the same office Domitius Ulpianus, whom Heliogabalus had put in command of the praetorians, and by recalling Paul to his homeland at the beginning of his reign, both being jurists. [9] Although he ruled for not more than thirteen years[10] he left the state strengthened in all respects. It had grown through its struggles from Romulus to Septimius and by then, because of the policies of Bassianus, it stood at its peak, so to speak. It was due to Alexander that it did not immediately collapse. Henceforth, as long as the emperors were more intent upon dominating their subjects than upon subjugating foreign peoples and preferred to fight among themselves, they threw the Roman state into a steep decline, as it were, and men were put in power indiscriminately, good and bad, noble and base-born, even many of barbarian extraction. In fact when there is universal confusion and nothing is done in its proper manner, all think it right, as is natural amid chaos, to seize the offices of others which they cannot discharge, and they shamefully corrupt any conception of honourable conduct. So the violent power of fortune, once it has acquired unfettered freedom, drives on mortals with destructive desire. For a long time, indeed, it is restrained by virtue as if by a wall, but after almost all were overcome by depravity it entrusted the government even to the lowest in birth and training.[11]

25.   For, in fact, Gaius Julius Maximinus, the governor of Trebellica,[1] though he was practically illiterate, was the first common soldier to seize power as the choice of the legions.[2] However the senators also approved of this since they considered it dangerous for unarmed men to resist one backed by an army.[3] His son, who had the same name, Gaius Julius Maximinus, was made Caesar.[4]

26.   When they had held power for two years and had fought, not without success, against the Germans,[1] suddenly Antonius Gordian, the proconsul of Africa, was made emperor by the army at the town of Thysdrus though he was not present.[2] When he had been summoned and had arrived there, as if he might be made emperor by doing just that, he was greeted with a mutiny. This he easily suppressed and made for Carthage.[3] There, while he was performing the rites according to custom to avert prodigies, for he was not unreasonably troubled by fear of these, suddenly the victim gave birth. The soothsayers and he above all (for he was exceptionally skilled in the practice of this art) interpreted it to mean that he, in fact, was destined to die but he would procure the imperial power for his children. Continuing further with their prophecy they foretold the death of his child, too, predicting that he would be gentle and innocent, like the animal, but he would not live long or be subject to treachery.[4] Meanwhile at Rome, when Gordian's death had been reported, the urban prefect and the rest of the magistrates were murdered in public by the praetorian cohorts at the instigation of Domitius.[5] Indeed Gordian, after he had learned that the imperial power had been conferred upon him, had sent envoys and a letter to Rome promising substantial rewards.[6] When he had been killed the soldiers were angry at being deceived by these promises, being the sort of men who are very greedy for money and loyal and true solely for profit.[7] But the senate, since there was no government and the city looked as if it had been occupied, was afraid that worse things would happen, so first it established a board with shared powers and subsequently conscripted the younger men and

appointed Clodius Pupienus and Caecilius Balbinus as Caesars.[8]

27.   During the same period in Africa the soldiers appointed as Augustus Gordian's son, Gordian, who happened to be on his father's staff though he was a young boy and was subsequently praetorian prefect,[1] and the nobility certainly did not reject this move.[2] Finally, when he had been summoned, the praetorian detachments were destroyed in combat among the hills of the city and its very centre by bands of gladiators and an army of recruits.[3] While this was taking place at Rome the (two) Julii Maximini, who by chance were at that time occupied in Thrace, learned what had happened and hastily made for Italy.[4] At the siege of Aquileia Pupienus killed them after they had been defeated in battle and their remaining troops had gradually deserted.[5] A year was added to their two year reign through delays of this kind.[6] Not long afterwards Clodius and Caecilius were slain in the palace at Rome during a military revolt and Gordian became sole ruler.[7] That very year, when he had extended and consolidated the Quinquennial Games which Nero had introduced to Rome, he set out against the Persians after he had first opened the doors of the Temple of Janus which Marcus had closed according to ancestral custom.[8] There he conducted a brilliant campaign[9] but perished in the sixth year of his reign through the intrigues of his praetorian prefect, Marcus Philippus.[10]

28.   And so Marcus Julius Philippus, an Arab from Thraconitis, took his son Philip as a partner, settled affairs in the east, founded the town of Philippopolis in Arabia, and came to Rome (with his son).[1] They constructed a reservoir on the other side of the Tiber because that region used to be plagued by a shortage of water,[2] and they celebrated the thousandth anniversary of the city with games of all kinds.[3] And since the name has reminded me, in my time, too, the eleven hundredth anniversary passed by in the consulship of a Philip, but it was celebrated with none of the customary festivities, so drastically

has the concern for the city of Rome diminished day by day.[4] In fact they say that this was announced at that time by prodigies and portents, one of which I would like to mention briefly. For when some victims were being sacrificed according to pontifical law, female genitals appeared on a hog's abdomen. This the soothsayers interpreted to predict the decadence of later generations and the aggravation of vices. The emperor Philip, because he thought that this would prove false and then again because he had caught sight of a young boy prostitute resembling his son as he happened to walk past him, took very honourable measures to abolish the practice of male prostitution. Nevertheless it still survives, for if circumstances are altered it is practised even more outrageously as long as men seek more avidly whatever is dangerous and forbidden.[5] Furthermore the Etruscan arts had predicted something quite different, since they asserted that when good men for the most part lie helpless, the most effeminate men would be happy. But I, for one, categorically believe that they were wrong. The fact is that however successfully everything turns out, who can still be happy if he has lost his sense of decency? Yet if that has been retained everything else is bearable.[6] After completing these projects he left his son in the city and set out in person against Decius, even though he was physically weak because of his age. He fell at Verona after the defeat and loss of his army.[7] When news of this had reached Rome his son was killed in the praetorian camp. They had enjoyed five years of power.[8]

29. However Decius, who was born in a village near Sirmium, had conspired to gain the imperial power by virtue of his military position[1] and, overjoyed at the death of his enemies,[2] had appointed his son, named Etruscus, as Caesar.[3] He immediately sent the latter ahead to Illyricum while he remained behind at Rome for a time in order to dedicate the monuments which he had constructed.[4] In the meantime the head of Jotapianus was suddenly brought to him, as is the custom. He, boasting of his descent from Alexander, had been

killed on the authority of the soldiers as he was attempting a rebellion in Syria,[5] and at the same time during those very days the supreme power was offered to Lucius Priscus, who was ruling Macedonia as governor, as a result of an incursion of the Goths, after they had plundered most of Thrace and penetrated that far.[6] When Decius had left Rome as quickly as he could for that reason Julius Valens seized the imperial power at the urgent insistence of the common people.[7] However both were soon killed since the nobility had decreed Priscus an enemy of the state.[8] The Decii, while pursuing the barbarians across the Danube, died through treachery at Abrittus after reigning two years.[9] But very many report that the deaths of the Decii were honourable; that, in fact, the son had fallen in battle while pressing an attack too boldly; that the father, however, while his dejected soldiers were saying many things to console their emperor, had strenuously asserted that the loss of one soldier seemed to him too little to matter. And so he resumed the war and died in a similar manner while fighting vigorously.[10]

30.   When the senators had learned of this they voted the rank of Augustus to Gallus and Hostilianus and appointed Volusianus, the son of Gallus, as Caesar.[1] Thereafter a plague broke out and while it raged ever more violently Hostilianus died but Gallus and Volusianus won popular favour because they meticulously and assiduously arranged the burials of all the poorest folk.[2]

31.   Consequently while they were kept at Rome Aemilius Aemilianus seized the supreme power by suborning the soldiers.[1] They set out to attack him but were cut down at Interamna by their own soldiers who hoped for a greater reward from Aemilius, to whom victory came without labour or losses,[2] and also because they lacked restraint through their self-indulgence and wantonness and had perverted the duties they owed for the benefits they received.[3] While all of these were in power, however, two years elapsed.[4] For Aemilianus,

too, ruled moderately for three months before being carried off by sickness and although at first the senators had declared him an enemy, afterwards, when his predecessor had died, in the face of circumstances, as is usual, they acclaimed him Augustus.[5]

32. On the other hand the soldiers, who had been gathered from all sectors and were detained in Raetia because of the impending war, bestowed the empire on Licinius Valerianus.[1] He, although he was of a reasonably distinguished family, was nevertheless pursuing a military career, as was still the custom at that time.[2] The senate made his son, Gallienus, Caesar, and straightway, though it was high summer, the Tiber overflowed as if it were in spate.[3] Wise men predicted disaster for the state on account of the changeable nature of the young man, because he had been summoned and had come from Etruria, from where the aforementioned river flows.[4] This, in fact, immediately occurred.[5] For when his father was engaged in an indecisive and prolonged war in Mesopotamia, he was captured through the treachery of the Persian king, whose name was Sapor, cruelly mutilated and died in the sixth year of his reign while still a robust old man.[6]

33. At the same time, although he was strenuously attempting to drive the Germans out of Gaul, Licinius Gallienus hurriedly descended on Illyricum.[1] There at Mursa he defeated Ingebus, the governor of Pannonia, who had conceived a desire to be emperor after learning of Valerian's disaster,[2] and subsequently Regalianus, who had renewed the war after rallying the soldiers who had survived the disaster at Mursa.[3] Since his suppression of these was fortunate and beyond what he had prayed for, like men who are lucky he became excessively careless and together with his son, Saloninus, on whom he had conferred the rank of Caesar, he shipwrecked the Roman state, so to speak, to such a degree[4] that the Goths freely penetrated Thrace and occupied Macedonia, Achaea and the border regions of Asia, the Parthians seized Mesopotamia and bandits,

or more accurately a woman, controlled the east. At that time, too, a force of Alamanni took possession of Italy while tribes of Franks pillaged Gaul and occupied Spain, where they ravaged and almost destroyed the town of Tarraconensis, and some, after conveniently acquiring ships, penetrated as far as Africa. Even the territories across the Danube, which Trajan had secured, were lost.[5] Thus throughout the whole world the mightiest things were mixed with the small, the lowest with the highest, as if by winds violently gusting from all directions.[6] And at the same time the plague was ravaging Rome, which often occurs in times of unbearable anxieties and spiritual despair.[7] During these events Gallienus himself frequented taverns and eating-houses, kept up his friendships with pimps and drunkards and abandoned himself to his wife, Salonina, and to his shameful love-affair with the daughter of Attalus, a king of the Germans, whose name was Pipa.[8] For this reason civil wars also broke out which were far more frightful.[9] For first of all Postumus, who happened to be in charge of the barbarians in Gaul, seized the imperial power.[10] After he had driven off a horde of Germans he was involved in a war with Laelianus, whom he routed just as successfully, but he then perished in a revolt of his own men supposedly since he had refused to allow them, despite their insistence, to plunder the inhabitants of Mainz because they had supported Laelianus.[11] At his death, therefore, Marius, a former blacksmith who was not even then particularly well-known to the military, seized power.[12] Accordingly everything had degenerated so far that imperial powers were bestowed on such individuals and the dignity of all noble qualities was an object of derision. Indeed it was because of this that the joke was told that it was hardly surprising if a Marius was attempting to restore the Roman state, since a Marius of the same trade and the founder of the family and name had consolidated it.[13] When he had been murdered after two days Victorinus was chosen, who equalled Postumus in military expertise but was a compulsive lecher. Although he restrained himself at the beginning, he forcibly violated very many women and after a reign of two years, when he forced his attentions on the wife of Attitianus and she informed her husband of the outrage, the soldiers were secretly incited and he was killed at Cologne in a mutiny.[14] So powerful were the companies of quartermasters, in whose ranks Attitianus was serving, that their criminal action was accomplished even though they were attempting a difficult task. They are a kind of people, especially in these times, who are worthless, venal, underhand, rebellious, greedy and, so to speak, fashioned by nature for committing and concealing frauds. They control supplies and therefore they are the enemies of those collecting the produce and of the well-being of the farmers since they are proficient in the opportune bribery of those through whose folly and ruin they have amassed their wealth.[15] Meanwhile Victoria, after the loss of her son Victorinus, bought the approval of the legions with a large sum of money and made Tetricus emperor. He was of a noble family and was serving as governor of Aquitaine, and the title and trappings of Caesar were bestowed upon his son, Tetricus.[16] But at Rome Gallienus was busy dishonestly persuading the people who were unaware of the state's misfortunes that all regions had been pacified, and frequently he even held games and triumphal processions, as is normal when events turn out as one wishes, so that he might more readily substantiate his sham successes.[17] But after danger began to approach he finally left the city. For Aureolus, since he was in command of the legions in Raetia, had seized the imperial power because of the negligence of such an indolent leader, as is customary, and was marching on Rome.[18] Gallienus routed him in battle at the bridge which is named Aureolus after him and drove him to Milan.[19] While he was attacking that city with machines of every kind he was killed by his own men.[20] Aureolus, you see, when he saw that his hopes of raising the siege were futile, cunningly composed a list of the names of Gallienus' generals and tribunes as if they had been assigned by him for execution and threw the document down from the wall as secretly as possible. It happened to be found by those mentioned in it and instilled the fear and suspicion that their deaths had been ordered, but they thought that it had been divulged because of the negligence of his staff.[21] Consequently, in accordance with the plan of Aurelian, whose popularity and prestige in the army were exceptional, they faked an enemy attack and since he was protected by none of his bodyguards, as is normal in a sudden crisis, they led him out of his tent at the dead of night and he was run through with a spear by an assailant who was not identified because of the darkness. Thus his assassination went unavenged because the actual murderer was not known or because what had happened was for the common good.[22] Admittedly moral standards have fallen to such a degree that most men act in their own interests rather than in the interests of the state and in their eagerness for power rather than for reputation.[23] Hence, too, the essence of things and of titles has been corrupted,[24] while for the most part one who has become more powerful through a crime, when he has won the day by arms, calls it the removal of tyranny if he suppresses people to the detriment of the state. Moreover some men who are (Gallienus') equals in lust are enrolled in the ranks of the gods, though they are scarcely worthy of the last rites. If the credibility of history had not prevented this, for it neither permits honourable men to be deprived of the rewards of being remembered, nor allows the wicked to acquire an eternal, illustrious reputation, virtue would be sought in vain,[25] since that true and unique distinction would be granted through favour to all the worst men and impiously denied the good. Eventually the senators were compelled by Claudius to declare Gallienus a god because he had obtained the imperial power through Gallienus' decision.[26] For when the latter realized by the flow of blood from such a serious wound that death was close, he assigned the imperial insignia to Claudius who was commanding the garrison force at Ticinum with the rank of tribune.[27] This was obviously extorted, since the crimes of Gallienus cannot be concealed as long as there are cities, and all the worst (emperors) will always be considered like him and his equal. Actually, as far as one may conjecture, emperors and the best persons reach heaven or, through their reputation among men, are celebrated like gods because of the glory of their lives rather than because of the titles they have sought and amassed.[28]   But the senate, upon learning of his death, decreed that his followers and friends should be thrown headlong over the Gemonian steps and it is generally accepted that a treasury lawyer was led into the senate and was punished by having his eyes torn out, while a mob burst in and with equal clamour begged Mother Earth and even the gods of the underworld to give Gallienus a place among the damned.[29] And if Claudius had not given orders immediately after the capture of Milan that those who had chanced to survive should be spared, ostensibly because the army had demanded it, the nobility and common people would have run riot even more savagely.[30]   And indeed, in addition to the general malaise of the Roman world, the abuse of their own order provoked the senators because he, fearing that the imperial power would be transferred to the best of the nobility through his sloth, was the first to prohibit the senators from undertaking a military career or entering the army.[31]   His reign lasted nine years.[32]

34.   But the soldiers, whom the desperate state of affairs compelled, quite contrary to their natural inclination, to make the right decisions, when they realized that everything was in shambles, eagerly approved and praised the accession of Claudius, a man who could endure hard work, was just and totally dedicated to the state,[1] so much so that after a long interval he revived the tradition of the Decii.[2]   For when he wanted to drive out the Goths, whom the lapse of time had made excessively strong and virtual inhabitants, it was revealed by the Sibylline Books that the foremost man of the most elevated order had to be consecrated to victory. And when the man who seemed to be meant had offered himself, Claudius showed that the responsibility belonged rather to him who was, in fact, the leader of the senate and of all men. Thus the barbarians were routed and driven out with no loss to the army after the emperor had made a gift of his life to the state.[3]   In fact good

emperors consider the safety of their fellow citizens and their own enduring reputation more valuable[4] for these contribute not only to their glory but also, in some way, to the good fortune of their successors.[5]   If indeed Constantius and Constantine and our own emperors[6] . . . and of her body she was more acceptable to the soldiers because of their expectations of rewards or licence.[7] Consequently the victory was sad and rather troublesome, since subjects, as is their custom, more readily defend lax regimes than useful ones through their desire to commit crimes with impunity.[8]

35. Furthermore Aurelian, made more impetuous by his great success, immediately marched against the Persians as if the war were in its final stages. He defeated them[1] and returned to Italy where the cities were being harassed by the incursions of the Alamanni.[2] At the same time, when the Germans had been driven out of Gaul,[3] the legions of Tetricus, whom we have mentioned above, were cut down after being betrayed by their own general. For Tetricus, because he was frequently being assailed by his soldiers who had been corrupted by the intrigue of the governor Faustinus, had begged for the protection of Aurelian by letter and, since the battle line had been led forward for appearances' sake, during the fighting he surrendered to Aurelian as he approached. So, as is usual when there is no commander, the ranks were thrown into confusion and crushed.[4] Tetricus himself, after two years of exalted power, was led in the triumph but then obtained the governorship of Lucania and for his son pardon and senatorial rank.[5] In the same manner the mint workers in the city were destroyed.   Since, at the instigation of the treasurer, Felicissimus, they had been filing off the coin marks, in fear of punishment they had fought so serious a war that after gathering on the Caelian Hill they killed about seven thousand troops.[6]   After so many great successes he constructed a magnificent temple to the Sun at Rome, decorating it with opulent offerings,[7] and to prevent what had occurred under Gallienus from ever happening (again) he enclosed the city

with the strongest walls possible and enlarged their perimeter.[8] And at the same time he carefully supervised generous supplies of pork so that he might allocate sufficient quantities to the Roman populace.[9] False charges laid by Treasury officials or informers, which had distressed the city, were suppressed, registers and documents of dealings of this kind were burned and an amnesty was decreed in the Greek manner. In the meantime he rigorously prosecuted acts of greed, embezzlement and those committing extortion in the provinces, contrary to the customary behaviour of the military from whose ranks he came.[10] For this reason he was entrapped and killed at Coenofrurium through the villainy of an assistant to whom he had entrusted the office of confidential secretary, since that man, conscious of his graft and criminal activity, had handed over to the tribunes, as if doing them a favour, cunningly composed letters containing orders for their execution. Alarmed by fear of that they committed the crime.[11] Meanwhile the soldiers, once they had lost their emperor, immediately sent envoys to Rome to ask the senators to select an emperor of their own choice. When they replied that this was the particular responsibility of the soldiers, the legions again referred it to them. Thus the matter was debated with propriety and moderation on both sides, virtues rare among people, especially in matters of this kind, and almost unheard of with soldiers.[12] So much did that man achieve by his severity and incorruptibility that the announcement of his murder brought destruction to the perpetrators, was a source of fear to the wicked and also to those wavering, a cause of regret to all the best men and a source of arrogance or ostentation to none. And furthermore a sort of interregnum occurred, as it had for Romulus alone, but far more glorious.[13] This action in particular demonstrated that everything revolves in the manner of a circle and nothing happens which the power of nature cannot reproduce in the course of time,[14] and, in addition, that even desperate situations are easily relieved by the virtues of emperors and more stable ones abruptly ruined by their vices.[15]

36.   Finally, therefore, in about the sixth month after the death of
        Aurelian, the senate made Tacitus, one of the former consuls,
        emperor.   He was certainly a kind man and practically
        everyone was happier because the senators had recovered the
        right to choose the emperor from the arrogant military.[1] This
        joy, however, was brief and it did not have a tolerable
        outcome.   For Tacitus soon died at Tyana on the two
        hundredth day of his reign, but not until after he had first
        tortured to death the murderers of Aurelian and in particular
        their ringleader, Mucapor, because he had struck the actual
        blow,[2] and Florianus, Tacitus' brother, seized power without
        any decision being made by the senate or the soldiers.[3]

37.   He, when he had held the absolute power tenuously for one or
        two months, was killed at Tarsus by his own men[1] after they
        had accepted Probus, who had been proclaimed in Illyricum[2]
        and was almost a second Hannibal because of his great
        knowledge of warfare and his versatile training of the soldiers
        and his toughening of the young recruits.[3]   For just as
        Hannibal considered the inactivity of his troops dangerous to
        the state and its leaders and filled many parts of Africa with
        olive trees through their labour,[4] in the same manner he
        (Probus) filled Gaul, the Pannonias and the hills of Moesia
        with vineyards,[5] naturally after he had crushed the barbarian
        tribes which had invaded when our emperors had been killed
        by the treachery of their own men.[6]   At the same time
        Saturninus was cut down in the east and Bonosus with his
        army at Cologne; for both had attempted to seize supreme
        power with the bands of troops they had commanded as
        generals.[7]   For this reason, when all those regions had been
        recovered and pacified, it is reported that he stated that in a
        short time soldiers would be unnecessary.[8]   Eventually,
        therefore, they became even more incensed and they cut him
        down at Sirmium after a little less than six years as he was
        compelling them to drain the city, his birthplace, with
        reservoirs and a ditch since it was damaged by winter rains on
        account of its marshy soil.[9]

From this point on the power of the military increased
and the right of appointing the emperor was snatched from the
senate up to our own times, though it is uncertain whether the
senate desired this through apathy or fear, or because of its
hatred of civil conflicts. In fact it could have regained its right
to military service, which had been lost through the edict of
Gallienus, during the reign of Tacitus when the legions were
duly compliant, and Florianus would not have rashly seized
power nor would it have been granted to any man, however
good, by the decision of the common soldiers if (members of)
that most distinguished and honourable order had been serving
in the army. But as long as they find their gratification in
leisure and simultaneously fear for their wealth, the enjoyment
and abundance of which they consider more important than
what is eternal, they paved the way for the soldiers and
virtually for the barbarians to have absolute power over
themselves and their descendants.[10]

38.   Consequently Carus, who was powerful because he held the
praetorian prefecture, was clothed in the imperial robe and his
sons, Carinus and Numerian, became Caesars.[1] And since all
the barbarians had seized the opportunity to invade once they
had learned of the death of Probus, he sent his elder son to
defend Gaul and, accompanied by Numerian, he straightway
proceeded to Mesopotamia because that land is, so to speak, a
customary cause of war with the Persians.[2] There, after
routing the enemy, while he was advancing beyond Ctesiphon,
Parthia's famous city, with an ill-advised and excessive desire
for glory, he was burnt to death by a bolt of lightning.[3]
Certain men state that he deserved this for although the oracles
had informed him that through his victory he was permitted to
reach the city just mentioned, he advanced further and paid the
penalty. So, you see, it is hard to divert the Fates and for that
reason knowledge of the future is pointless.[4] However
Numerian, after losing his father, at the same time decided that
the war was over, but while he was leading his army back he
was murdered through the treachery of Aper, the praetorian

prefect and his father-in-law. An infection of the young man's eyes provided the opportunity for this. In short the deed was concealed for a long time, while the body was being carried in a closed litter on the pretext that he was ill, so that his eyesight might not be troubled by the wind.[5]

39.   But after the crime had been betrayed by the odour of his decomposing limbs, at a council of generals and tribunes Valerius Diocletian, commander of the household troops, was selected because of his good sense.[1] He was a great man, yet he had the following characteristics: he was, in fact, the first who really desired a supply of silk, purple and gems for his sandals, together with a gold-brocaded robe. Although these things went beyond good taste and betrayed a vain and haughty disposition, they were nevertheless trivial in comparison with the rest. For he was the first of all after Caligula and Domitian to permit himself to be called "Lord" in public and to be worshipped and addressed as a god.[2] From these indications, as far as I can understand, I have concluded that all men from the humblest backgrounds, especially when they have attained exalted positions, are excessive in their pride and ambition. For this reason Marius, in our ancestors' times, and he in ours went beyond the common limits[3] since a mind that has never experienced power is insatiable like a man saved from starvation. Consequently it seems strange to me that most people accuse the nobility of arrogance whereas, in preserving the memory of its patrician origins, it has some right to assert its eminence as compensation for the annoyances by which it is afflicted.[4] But these faults in Valerius were effaced by the other good qualities, and especially by the fact that although he allowed himself to be called "Lord" he acted like a parent; and it is fairly certain that this shrewd man wanted to demonstrate that it was the harshness of circumstances rather than of titles that created obstacles.[5] Meanwhile Carinus, informed of what had happened and in the hope that he might more easily put down the revolts that were breaking out, hastily made for Illyricum by skirting Italy.

There he scattered Julianus' battle line and cut him down. For the latter, while he was governing the Veneti as *corrector*, had learned of Carus' death and in his eagerness to seize the imperial power he had advanced to meet the approaching enemy.[6] Moreover when Carinus reached Moesia he straightway joined battle with Diocletian near the Margus, but while he was in hot pursuit of his defeated foes he died under the blows of his own men because he could not control his lust and used to seduce many of his soldiers' wives. Their husbands had grown increasingly hostile but they had nevertheless put aside their anger and resentment to see how the war turned out. Since it was going quite successfully for him, in fear that a man of such character would become more and more overbearing in victory, they avenged themselves.[7] That was the end of Carus and his children. Narbonne was their native city; they ruled for two years.[8] Consequently Valerius, in his first speech to the army, drew his sword, gazed up at the sun and while attesting that he had no knowledge of Numerian's murder and had not wanted the imperial power, with one blow he transfixed Aper who was standing right beside him. It was through his treachery, as we have shown above, that the good and eloquent young man, his son-in-law, had perished.[9] Pardon was granted to the rest and practically all the enemy were retained, especially one outstanding man named Aristobulus, the praetorian prefect, on account of his services.[10] This was a novel and unexpected occurrence in the history of mankind, that in a civil war no one was stripped of his possessions, reputation or rank, for we are delighted if such a war is waged with all due observances and with mercy and if a limit is set on exiles, proscriptions and also on punishments and murders. Why should I recount that many men, foreigners too, have been admitted into partnership in order to protect and extend Roman authority?[11] For when Diocletian had learned, after Carinus' death, that in Gaul Helianus and Amandus had stirred up a band of peasants and robbers, whom the inhabitants call Bagaudae, and had ravaged the regions far and wide and were making attempts on very many of the cities,[12] he immediately appointed as emperor Maximian, a loyal friend who, although he was rather uncivilized, was nevertheless a good soldier of sound character.[13] He subsequently received the surname Herculius from his worship of that deity, just as Valerius received that of Jovius. This was also the origin of the names given to those auxiliary units which were particularly outstanding in the army.[14] Well, Herculius marched into Gaul and in a short time he had pacified the whole country by routing the enemy forces or accepting their surrender.[15] In this war Carausius, a citizen of Menapia, distinguished himself by his clearly remarkable exploits. For this reason and in addition because he was considered an expert pilot (he had earned his living at this job as a young man), he was put in charge of fitting out a fleet and driving out the Germans who were infesting the seas. Because of this appointment he became quite arrogant and when he had overcome many of the barbarians but had not turned over all of the booty to the public treasury, in fear of Herculius, who, he learned, had ordered his execution, he seized the imperial power and made for Britain.[16] At the same time the Persians were causing serious disturbances in the east, and Julianus and the Quinquegentian peoples in Africa.[17] Furthermore at Alexandria in Egypt someone named Achilleus had donned the insignia of supreme power.[18] For these reasons they (sc. Diocletian and Maximian) appointed as Caesars and made marriage alliances with Julius Constantius and Galerius Maximianus, whose surname was Armentarius. After annulling their previous marriages the former received the stepdaughter of Herculius, the latter Diocletian's daughter, which is what Augustus had once done in the case of Nero Tiberius and his daughter Julia.[19] Illyricum was actually the native land of all of them: so although they were deficient in culture, they had nevertheless been sufficiently schooled by the hardships of the countryside and of military service to be the best men for the state. Consequently it is evident that men are more readily made honourable and sensible by enduring adversity whereas, on the other hand, those who have not experienced misfortunes, as long as they judge everyone according to their own situations, are less considerate. But the harmony of these (rulers) has definitely demonstrated that natural ability and the experience of a successful military career, such as they received through the precedent of Aurelian and Probus, are practically sufficient to ensure merit.[20] Finally, they used to look up to Valerius as a father or like a mighty god. The nature and importance of this attitude have been made conspicuous by the crimes committed by relatives from the founding of the city to our own times.[21] And since the burden of wars, which we have mentioned above, was pressing more insistently, the empire was divided into four parts and all those regions of Gaul which lie across the Alps were entrusted to Constantius, Africa and Italy to Herculius, the coast of Illyricum right across to the Strait of Pontus to Galerius: Valerius retained the rest.[22] As a consequence, then, the immense evil of taxation was imposed upon part of Italy.[23] For although all Italy paid the same moderate levy to support the army and the emperor, who were always or mostly there, a new law for making payments was introduced. It was no doubt bearable in that period of moderation but it has grown into a ruinous monster in these tempestuous times.[24] Meanwhile Jovius set out for Alexandria and his area of command was entrusted to Maximian Caesar so that the latter might leave his territories and advance into Mesopotamia to repel the attacks of the Persians. At first he was seriously troubled by them but he quickly gathered an army of veterans and recruits and marched against the enemy through Armenia which is almost the only or at least the easier route to defeat them. There he eventually captured King Narses, together with his children, his wives and his royal household. He was so successful that if Valerius, at whose command all state affairs were conducted, had not for some unknown reason forbidden it, the Roman *fasces* would now be carried in a new province. But some of the territories which were nevertheless quite useful to us were acquired: the recent very serious and destructive war which has broken out is because they are now

being demanded back with greater insistence.[25] But in Egypt
Achilleus was easily put down by negotiations and paid the
penalty. In Africa the situation was dealt with in a similar
manner[26] and only Carausius was allowed to retain his
sovereignty over the island, after he had been judged quite
competent to command and defend its inhabitants against
warlike tribes. He, in fact, was treacherously overthrown six
years later by a man names Allectus who, after he had been
entrusted by the former to manage the treasury, fearing
execution because of his misdeeds, had seized power through
a criminal act. When he had exercised power for a short
while, Constantius destroyed him through Asclepiodotus, who
was his praetorian prefect and was sent ahead with a
detachment of the fleet and of the legions.[27] In the meantime,
too, the Marcomanni were slaughtered and the whole nation of
the Carpi was transferred to our soil, where some of them had
already been settled from the time of Aurelian.[28] And with no
less regard for the concerns of peace the bureaucracy was
regulated by the most impartial laws[29] and by the abolition of
that malignant clan of *frumentarii*, to whom our current
agentes in rebus (intelligence agents) are very similar.
Although they appeared to have been established to investigate
and report whatever disturbances might crop up in the
provinces, by outrageously fabricating charges and inspiring
fear everywhere, especially in all the most remote areas, they
would shamefully plunder everything.[30] At the same time the
city grain supply and the welfare of the tax-payers were
carefully and responsibly safeguarded[31] and by the promotion
of a better class of men and, on the other hand, by the
punishment of all villains enthusiasm for virtues began to
increase.[32] The most ancient religious cults were looked after
with the utmost respect,[33] and in a marvellous manner the hills
of Rome and other cities, especially Carthage, Milan and
Nicomedia, were embellished with hitherto novel and
beautifully elaborate buildings.[34] Nevertheless, in spite of
these achievements they were not without faults. In fact
Herculius was so driven by lust that not even the bodies of his

hostages were safe from his sick desires. Valerius had too little genuine faith in his friends, doubtless through his fear of conflicts, since he thought that the harmony of the partnership might be disturbed by disclosures.[35] For this reason, too, the forces of the city were, so to speak, pruned down when he reduced the number of praetorian cohorts and common citizens under arms, and very many believe that it was indeed on this account that he laid down the imperial power.[36] For, in fact, he was a close examiner of imminent events and when he discovered that on account of fate intestinal disasters and, as it were, a sort of disintegration of the Roman state were threatening, he celebrated the twentieth year of his reign, and while still in quite good health he gave up the administration of the state after he had with very great difficulty converted Herculius, who had been in power one year fewer, to his point of view.[37] And although regard for the truth has been corrupted because people have different opinions, nevertheless it seems to me that he spurned ambition and stepped down to ordinary life because of the excellence of his character.[38]

40.   Consequently, since Constantius and Armentarius succeeded them, Severus and Maximinus, natives of Illyricum, were appointed Caesars, the former for Italy, the latter for the regions which Jovius had held.[1] Unable to tolerate this Constantine, whose proud and capable spirit had been stirred ever since boyhood by the passion to rule,[2] reached Britain in a planned escape, since he killed all the post horses along the route he had travelled in order to frustrate his pursuers, for he was being detained by Galerius as a hostage on the pretext of obligation.[3] And by chance at the same time and in the same place his father Constantius was approaching the last days of his life.[4] At his death, with the support of all who were present, Constantine assumed the imperial power.[5] Meanwhile at Rome the common people and the praetorian units confirmed Maxentius as emperor, although for a long time his father Herculius restrained him.[6] When Armentarius learned this he hastily ordered Severus Caesar, who happened to be

near the city, to engage the enemy. The latter, while he was operating around the walls, was deserted by his men, whom Maxentius had suborned with the inducement of rewards, and fled to Ravenna where he was besieged and died.[7] Galerius was further enraged by this and, after consulting Jovius, he installed Licinius, a long-standing friend, as Augustus and, leaving him to guard Illyricum and Thrace he marched on Rome. While he was being held up there by the siege, since his soldiers were being tampered with in the same way as their predecessors, he abandoned Italy in fear that he might be deserted.[8] Shortly afterwards, when he had made an area in Pannonia quite useful to the state by cutting down vast forests and draining Lake Pelso into the Danube, he died from an infected wound. Because of this he called the province Valeria after his wife's name.[9] He ruled for five years, Constantius for one, although of course both had held the rank of Caesar for thirteen years.[10] They were so remarkable for their natural abilities that if those abilities emanated from cultivated minds and did not give offence because of their boorishness, without doubt they would be considered exceptional. Consequently it is indisputable that learning, refinement and courtesy are essential, particularly in emperors, since without these qualities natural talents are despised as if they are unfinished or even crude, yet on the other hand those very qualities assured Cyrus, king of the Persians, of everlasting glory.[11] Moreover within my own memory they carried Constantine up to the stars with the prayers of all, even though he demonstrated other such virtues. Certainly if he had set a limit to his lavishness and ambition and to those practices in particular to which mature men of genius progress in their quest for glory and through which they fall too far in the opposite direction, he would have been practically a god.[12] When he learned that the city and Italy were being devastated and that two armies and two emperors had been driven off or bought off he made peace throughout Gaul and marched against Maxentius.[13] At that critical time on Punic territory Alexander, who was acting as deputy-prefect, had foolishly usurped the supreme power although he himself was enfeebled by age, was more dull-witted than his parents who were Pannonian peasants, and his soldiers had been recruited in a hurry and had hardly half of their weapons. To sum up, Rufius Volusianus, the praetorian prefect, and some generals were despatched with a mere handful of cohorts by the pretender (Maxentius) and they polished him off in a minor skirmish.[14] After his defeat Maxentius, the inhuman beast, made more abominable by his excessive lust, had ordered Carthage, the glory of the world, along with the loveliest parts of Africa, to be ravaged, pillaged and burned.[15] In addition he was an unwarlike coward, and shamefully inclined to indolence to such a degree that, while war was raging throughout Italy and his troops had been routed at Verona, he went about his customary business with no less apathy and was unmoved by the destruction of his father.[16] For, you see, Herculius, who was more intractable by nature and at the same time dismayed by his son's apathy, had rashly sought to regain the imperial power.[17] And as he was plotting to make a vicious attack on his son-in-law Constantine, on the pretext of doing him a service, he had eventually met a deserved death.[18] But Maxentius, growing more ruthless by the day, finally advanced with great difficulty from the city to Saxa Rubra, about nine miles away. His battle line was cut to pieces and as he was retreating in flight back to Rome he was trapped in the very ambush he had laid for his enemy at the Milvian Bridge while crossing the Tiber in the sixth year of his tyranny.[19] It is incredible how joyfully and delightedly the senate and people exulted at his death for he had oppressed them so much that on one occasion he permitted the praetorians to massacre the common people[20] and was the first, through a most reprehensible edict issued under the pretext of obligatory state taxation, to compel the senators and farmers to contribute money for him to squander.[21] Because of their aversion the praetorian legions and the support units, which were more useful to factions than to the city of Rome, were entirely eliminated together with the bearing of arms and the wearing of military uniforms.[22] In addition, all the monuments which Maxentius had constructed in magnificent manner, the temple of the city and the basilica, were dedicated by the senate to the meritorious services of Flavius. He also afterwards completed the decorations on the Circus Maximus in a marvellous fashion and built a bathing establishment which was not very different from the others.[23] Statues were erected in the busiest places and most of them are of gold or silver.[24] Then in Africa a college of priests was decreed to the Flavian *gens* and the town of Cirta, which had been demolished during the siege of Alexander, was rebuilt, fully redecorated and given the name Constantina.[25] Indeed nothing is more welcome and more distinguished than those who expel tyrants, and respect for them will actually be so much greater if they are moderate and self-restrained. Naturally people's spirits once they are disappointed in their expectations of something good, are hurt more grievously when the abundance of their hardships remains in spite of the removal of a shameful ruler.[26]

41.   While these events were taking place in Italy, in the east Maximinus, after ruling two years as Augustus, was routed and put to flight by Licinius and perished at Tarsus.[1] Thus the control of the Roman world was acquired by two men who, although they were connected to each other by the marriage of Flavius' sister to Licinius, nevertheless because of their diverse characters only managed to co-exist with difficulty for three years.[2] For, you see, the former possessed other great qualities beyond measure, the latter only frugality, and that, to be sure, of merely a rustic nature.[3] Finally, Constantine received all his enemies with honour and protected them by allowing them to retain their properties, and was so conscious of his obligations that he was also the first to abolish the long-established and utterly frightful punishment of the forked gibbet and the breaking of legs.[4] Consequently he was regarded as a founder or as a god.[5] Licinius carried out tortures reserved for slaves in unlimited numbers even on innocent philosophers of noble rank.[6] He was, indeed, defeated in various battles but, since it

seemed difficult to suppress him completely and at the same
time because of their marriage ties, the partnership was
renewed and their respective children, Crispus and Constantine,
the sons of Flavius, and Licinianus, the son of Licinius, were
admitted to the rank of Caesar.[7] It was, in fact, made clear
that this would hardly be a long-lasting agreement, or
propitious for those who were added, since daylight was
obliterated by a solar eclipse during those same months.[8]
Accordingly six years later peace was broken, Licinius was
defeated in Thrace and withdrew to Chalcedon. There, after he
had admitted Martinianus to the imperial power to assist him,
the two were suppressed together.[9] In that way the state began
to be ruled by the will of one man, while his children retained
their distinct titles of Caesar; in fact it was at that critical time
that the rank of Caesar was given to our Emperor
Constantius.[10] When the eldest of these had died on the orders
of his father, the reason is uncertain,[11] suddenly Calocerus,
commander of the imperial camel herd, insanely seized the
island of Cyprus and pretended to rule. He was tortured to
death like a slave or robber, as was right and proper,[12] and the
emperor turned his remarkable mind to founding a city,
regulating religious practices and, simultaneously, reorganizing
the military.[13] In the meantime, too, the tribes of the Goths
and Sarmatians were subdued and the youngest of all his sons,
Constans by name, was made Caesar.[14] Astonishing omens
announced that because of him there would be turmoil in the
state: in fact on the very night which followed the day of his
imperial appointment the face of heaven blazed with
continuous fire.[15] About two years after this he (Constantine)
designated as Caesar his brother's son, who was named
Dalmatius after his father, even though the soldiers vigorously
objected.[16] Thus, in the thirty-second year of his reign, after
he had controlled the whole world for thirteen years and was
more than sixty-two years old, as he was marching against the
Persians who had just caused a war to break out, he died in a
country villa very close to Nicomedia - they call it Anchyrona,
as that star, so fatal to rulers, which they call a comet, had

portended.[17] His body was carried back to the city bearing his name. This certainly upset the Roman people very seriously since they thought that it was through his arms, his laws and merciful rule that the city of Rome had been practically renewed.[18] A bridge was built across the Danube: camps and forts were strategically placed in many locations.[19] The extraordinary requisitions of grain and oil which used to distress Tripoli and Nicaea quite seriously were removed. The inhabitants of the former of these cities, delighted that Severus was emperor, had given these as an offering to their fellow citizen but duplicity had turned the gratitude owed for these services into the ruin of later generations. Marcus Boionius had punished the others with a fine because they had been unaware that Hipparchus, a man of outstanding genius, had been a native (of their city).[20] Fiscal abuses were severely repressed[21] and everything would have appeared to have been in accord with divine principles if he had not admitted unworthy men to public office.[22] Although this happens all too often, nevertheless in a ruler of the highest character and in a state which enjoys exemplary moral conduct faults however small are more conspicuous and consequently are easily noticed. In addition they often do more serious harm, since, because of the esteem of their author, they are most readily accepted as virtues and encourage imitation.[23] Therefore Dalmatius was promptly killed, though it is uncertain at whose instigation, and just three years later, more or less, Constantine (II) fell in a fateful war.[24] Because of this victory Constans became more arrogant, and at the same time he was wilful and insufficiently cautious on account of his age. Furthermore he was detestable because of the depravity of his subordinates and passionate in his greed and in his contempt for the soldiers, and in the tenth year after his triumph he was overthrown by Magnentius' criminal act, although he had certainly suppressed the uprisings of foreign tribes.[25] Because he had treated too attentively the hostages taken from them, rather attractive boys whom he had sought out and paid for, it was justifiably believed that he burned with a passion of this kind.[26] Yet would that these vices had continued! For everything was so devastated by the awful, savage character of Magnentius, as is natural with a barbarian, and simultaneously by what happened afterwards, that people not without reason longed for the previous reign.[27] It was also because Vetranio, an utter illiterate and quite dull-witted and consequently the worst choice because of his rustic stupidity, while he was commanding the soldiers throughout Illyricum as *Master of the Infantry* had shamelessly seized supreme power although he hailed from the more barren regions of Upper Moesia.[28]

42. Constantius toppled him from the imperial power within ten months by the force of his eloquence and relegated him to private life. He alone, since the birth of the empire, achieved glory through his powers of speech and his clemency. For when a large segment of both armies had gathered together, an assembly was held in the manner of a court and he achieved by his eloquence what could scarcely be obtained by force or much bloodshed.[1] This event adequately demonstrated that the ability to express oneself well is vitally important not only in civil affairs but also in military matters;[2] in short, with this ability even arduous enterprises are all the more effortlessly accomplished if the speaker excels in moderation and integrity. This is particularly evident from the case of our own emperor.[3] Nonetheless a severe winter and the closing of the Alpine passes hindered him from immediately marching on Italy against his other enemies.[4] Meanwhile at Rome, because the common people had been corrupted and Magnentius was hated as well, Nepotianus, a relative of Flavius through his mother's family, was made emperor by a band of armed gladiators after the urban prefect had been murdered.[5] His brutish nature was so destructive to the Roman people and the senators that everywhere the houses, squares, streets and temples were filled with gore and corpses like tombs. Nor was this done by him alone, but also by the advancing troops of Magnentius who had struck down their enemy on the twenty-seventh day.[6] But already prior to this, since they suspected uprisings abroad,

Magnentius had entrusted the Gallic provinces to his brother Decentius as Caesar, and Constantius the East to Gallus, whose name he had changed to his own, also as Caesar. They themselves met in quite bitter battles over a three-year period. Finally Constantius pursued Magnentius as he fled into Gaul and drove both (adversaries) to commit suicide by different means.[7] And in the meantime a revolt of the Jews, who had criminally elevated Patricius to a sort of kingship, was suppressed.[8] Not long afterwards, because of his cruelty and violent disposition, Gallus perished on the orders of the Augustus.[9] Thus after a long interval of almost seventy years the care of the state was returned to one man.[10] Its newly-acquired respite from civil turmoil again began to be disturbed when Silvanus was forced to assume the imperial power. This man Silvanus, you see, had been born in Gaul of barbarian parents and came from the military class. Furthermore, by his desertion from Magnentius to Constantius, he had earned his promotion to *Master of the Infantry* though he was a relatively young man. When he had climbed still higher from that rank through fear or madness, he was slaughtered on about the twenty-eighth day during a mutiny of the legions from which he had hoped for protection.[11] For this reason, so that there might be no rebellion among the Gauls, who are headstrong by nature, especially because the Germans were ravaging most of those districts, Constantius appointed Julian as Caesar in command of the Transalpine regions since he was acceptable to him by virtue of their family relationship, and the latter quickly subdued (those) fierce nations and captured their famous kings.[12] Although these exploits were accomplished by his vigour, they nevertheless came about through the good fortune and planning of the emperor.[13] This is so important that Tiberius and Galerius achieved very much that was outstanding when serving others, but under their own authority and auspices their accomplishments were by no means equal.[14] Moreover Julius Constantius, who has been ruling as Augustus for twenty-three years,[15] has hardly had a break from campaigning since he has been engaged in disturbances abroad and just recently in civil ones. Through these campaigns he removed many a powerful pretender and in the meantime he withstood an attack by the Persians and he appointed a king to the Sarmatian people while he was with great honour seated as a judge among them.[16] We have ascertained that Gnaeus Pompey did this when he restored Tigranes, but very few of our ancestors.[17] Constantius is calm and reasonable in his duties, versed in literature to the point of elegance and has a gentle and agreeable manner of speaking. He is tolerant of hard work and wonderfully quick at shooting arrows, and master of his eating habits, of every passion and all his desires. He is reasonably dutiful regarding the respect owed to his father but excessively concerned with that owed to himself: he is aware that the tranquillity of the state is governed by the lives of good emperors.[18] These qualities, so great and so renowned, have been tarnished by his inadequate attention in approving provincial governors and military commanders and at the same time by the incongruous character of most of his officials and, furthermore, by his neglect of all the best sort of men. And to end on a brief note of truth, just as no one is more outstanding than the emperor himself, so nothing is more frightful than the majority of his subordinates.[19]

COMMENTARY

All dates are A.D. unless otherwise designated.

1

1.   I.e. 31 B.C.. On September 2nd of that year Octavian defeated
      Antony and Cleopatra at the Battle of Actium.   The dating,
      from April 21, 753 B.C., which was when Varro placed the
      founding of Rome, is traditional and in that respect accurate
      (Bird, *Eutropius*, liv). The theme is Tacitean (Tac. *Ann.* I.1.1.)
      but cf. Suet. *Aug.* 27.2l; Flor. 2.14.6; Dio, 53.19.1.

2.   He was granted the title (*cognomen* here) Augustus by the
      senate on January 16, 27 B.C., when the month Sextilis was
      renamed Augustus in his honour (Suet. *Caes.* 83.3; *Aug.* 7.4;
      Epit. 1.2; P.A. Brunt & M. Moore, *Res Gestae* [1967], 77 ff.).

3.   Cf. Vell. Pat. 2.86.2; Dio, 53.16.4.

4.   A Tacitean reflection (Tac. *Ann.* I.1.2).

5.   Augustus died at Nola on August 19, 14, after reigning 13
      days under 44 years, counting from Actium (Dio, 56.31.1;
      Suet. *Aug.* 98.10; Eutrop. 7.8).

6.   Cf. Suet. *Aug.* 21.1; Eutrop. 7.9; *Epit.* 1.4-7, where full lists
      are given. Raetia became a province in 15 B.C. and it was
      probably in 9 that Illyricum was finally pacified and made into
      two imperial provinces.   In his severely restricted account of
      Augustus' reign (cf. *Epit.* 1) Victor chose not to provide a

complete list of the emperor's additions, which he certainly found in his source (cf. Eutrop. 7.9). Instead he mentioned only two Danubian provinces which he knew of personally. It is possible that he had not yet decided how much space to allot each emperor.

7. According to tradition the temple of Janus was closed first by Numa, again by T. Manlius in 235 B.C., and on three occasions by Augustus (Suet. *Aug.* 22; Flor. 2.33.64).

8. Cf. Dufraigne (*A.V.* 67).I retain the text of *o* and *p* which read *intemperantis* (=*tes*). For Augustus' character cf. Suet. *Aug.* 45; 52; 53; 69-71; 78; Eutrop. 7.8; *Epit.* 1.20.

9. For Augustus' dedication to philosophers, writers and religion cf. Suet. *Aug.* 84; 89-93; Dio, 51.16.4; 56.43.2; Julian, *Caes.* 326 ab.

10. On the title *pater patriae*, granted to Augustus in 2 B.C. *vid.* Suet. *Aug.* 83.1; Dio, 53.18.3; Sen. *Clem.* 1.10.3; 1.14.2; *Res Gestae,* 35.1. Cicero received the title in 63 B.C., after the execution of Lentulus and Cethegus, and Caesar in 45 B.C. after the Battle of Munda.

11. Octavian received the sacrosanctity of the tribunes in 36 B.C. and as Augustus the full Tribunician power in 23 B.C., although Dio seems to think that he also received it in 30 B.C. Cf. Dio, 51.19.6; 53.32.5; Suet. *Aug.* 27.10; Tac. *Ann.* I.9.

12. Victor simplifies and exaggerates. Augustus allowed temples and colleges of priests to be dedicated to himself *and Rome* only in the provinces, at least during his lifetime (Suet. *Aug.* 52; Dio, 51.20.7; cf. Eutrop. 7.8.4; Nic. Dam. *Vit. Caes.* 1.1).

13. Cf. *Epit.* 1.9; Eutrop. 7.9; *Res Gestae,* 31; Suet. *Aug.* 21.6; Flor. 2.33.62. The nomadic Garamantes of Tripolitania were defeated in 19 B.C. and are mentioned with the Indians by

Virgil (*Aen.* VI, 794). Tacitus notes a rare appearance of their envoys at Rome in 24 (*Ann.* IV.26). Victor alone includes the Bactrians here. They inhabited the middle Oxus Valley in northern Afghanistan and beyond, and were conquered by Alexander. A Bactrian Greek kingdom was formed by Diodotus which rapidly expanded and for a time governed most of Afghanistan and much of central Asia. The Bactrians are mentioned by Virgil (*Aen.* VIII, 688; *Georg.* II, 138) and Horace (*Od.* III, 29.28), are discussed by Ammianus (23.6.55-58). The Epitomator substitutes Ethiopians for Bactrians, which makes his list more geographically balanced.

2

1. Augustus adopted Tiberius, his stepson through Livia, in 4 after the deaths of his two grandsons, Gaius and Lucius. Victor carefully uses the term *redactus arrogatione* (instead of *adoptione*) because the 44 year old Tiberius had been under his own authority (*sui iuris*) and through adoption fell under the paternal authority of Augustus (Suet. *Tib.* 15.3). He was proclaimed emperor on Sept. 17, 14 (although Augustus had died on August 19) after an embarrassing debate in the senate (Tac. *Ann.* I, 10-13).

2. For his fears and eventual acceptance *vid.* Tac. *Ann.* I.7; Suet. *Tib.* 24-26; Dio, 57.7.1.

3. Cf. Tac. *Ann.* VI.51; Dio, 57.1.1; *Epit.* 2.4.

4. Cf. Suet. *Tib.* 70.2; *Epit.* 2.5. Suetonius makes it clear that this refers to Tiberius' manner of speaking and writing. Victor and the Epitomator generalize, possibly taking their cue from the *Kaisergeschichte* (Nixon, *Caesares*, 112).

5. The expression is Sallustian (Sall. *Cat.* 11.4), the theme a rhetorical commonplace: cf. Tac. *Ann.* IV.6; Dio, 57.19.1;

Dufraigne, *A.V.* 70.

6.   For Tiberius' alleged debauchery cf. Suet. *Tib.* 63-65; Dio, 58.22.1; Eutrop. 7.11; for his cruelty cf. Suet. *Tib.* 50.1; 59.1; Dio, 58. frag. 1; 58.16.5.

7.   Tiberius retired to Capri in 26 and for over ten years governed by means of postal communications with the senate and provincial commanders. Despite Suetonius' claims (followed by Victor) the empire did not suffer unduly through Tiberius' neglect (cf. Suet. *Tib.* 41; Tac. *Ann.* IV.67).

8.   Tiberius detested Archelaus, summoned him to Rome in 17, where he died either by natural causes (he was very old) or by suicide, and annexed Cappadocia (Tac. *Ann.* II.42; Dio, 57.17.3-7; Suet. *Tib.* 37.9).

9.   Tacfarinas, a Numidian who had deserted from the Roman auxiliaries, stirred up a rebellion among the Musulamii and Mauri in the south of Numidia in 17. A master of guerrilla warfare he was able to hold out until 24 when he was crushed and killed by P. Cornelius Dolabella (Tac.*Ann.* II.52; III.20-21; III.73-74; IV.23-25; Vell. 2.129.4). This incident is not mentioned by Suetonius or Dio and only Victor and the Epitomator call Tacfarinas' followers the Gaetuli (*Epit.* 2.8).

10.   Maroboduus, king of the Marcomanni (Suebi), caused his people to move into Bohemia sometime after 9 B.C. where he beat off Roman incursions. The rebellion in Illyricum in 6 prevented his defeat and a possible annexation. In 9 he refused to assist Arminius and was defeated by him, but he maintained himself until 19, when he was expelled and sought refuge with the Romans. He was lodged at Ravenna and died 18 years later (Tac. *Ann.* II.44-46; II.62-63; Vell. 2.108-109; 2.129.3; Suet. *Tib.* 37.9).

11.   Nine cohorts of praetorians were established by Augustus in 27

B.C., of which three were billeted at Rome. Under the influence of Sejanus, the sole praetorian prefect, all nine cohorts were concentrated in the praetorian barracks near the Porta Viminalis by 23 and their profound importance in subsequent imperial history commenced with this event. Sejanus is ignored by Suetonius and Victor (cf. Tac. *Ann.* IV.2; Suet. *Tib.* 37.2; Dio, 57.19.6; M. Durry, *Les Cohortes prétoriennes*, Paris, 1938; A. Passerini, *Le coorti pretorie*, Rome, 1939). Augustus also established the three Urban Cohorts, a sort of police force, probably in 13, the *Vigiles* or Fire brigade, consisting of seven cohorts of paramilitary freedmen after a serious fire in 6, and a personal bodyguard of Spaniards and subsequently of Germans or Batavians, who were legally slaves and consequently their unit was termed a guild (*collegium*) rather than a cohort (Suet. *Aug.* 49).

3

1. Tiberius died on March 16, 37, having ruled for 22 years, 7 months, 7 days; at the age of 77 years, 4 months, 9 days (Dio, 58.28.5; Tac. *Ann.* VI.56; Suet. *Tib.* 73; Eutrop. 7.11). He was ill but both Tacitus and Dio state that his death was assisted as does the Epitomator (2.10), and Suetonius notes that a number of people believed this.

2. On the surname and his ancestry *vid.* Suet. *Cal.* 9.1; Tac. Ann. I.41.3; Dio, 57.5.6.

3. Cf. Suet. *Cal.* 13.1. In 29 under Sejanus' influence Tiberius banished Agrippina and Nero, Caligula's mother and brother, who died in exile (in 33 and 30) and the next year imprisoned Caligula's other brother Drusus, who died in 33 (Tac. *Ann.* VI.23; 25; Suet. *Tib.* 53, 54, 64; *Cal.* 7; Dio, 58.3.8).

4. Tacitus (*Ann.* I.41.3) also states that Caligula was born in camp, as does the Epitomator (3.1) but Suetonius demonstrates

conclusively and at length that Caligula was born at Antium (Suet. *Cal.* 8) and suggests how the error came to be widely accepted. Clearly Victor was not following Suetonius.

5.   This rhetorical use of the law of opposites is discussed by Dufraigne (*A.V.* 72). The theme recurs in *De Caes.* 17.1 and is elaborated on by the author of the *Historia Augusta* (*Sev.* 20.4-21.12). Even Julian was apparently worried by the possibility (Lib. *Orat.* 15.181; Julian, *Caesares* 312b). Victor may have been childless himself for that very reason.

6.   Cf. Tac. *Ann.* VI.20; Suet *Cal.* 10.4; *Epit.* 3.3.

7.   Cf. Dio, 59.2.4; 59.3.1; 59.6.1; *Suet. Cal.* 17. The several months refer to the period from the death of Tiberius in March, 37 until Caligula's illness in September, 37.

8.   Cf. Suet. *Cal.* 15.6.

9.   Dio (59.8) states that Caligula's change of behaviour occurred after an illness. Suetonius attributes it to an aphrodisiac (Suet. *Cal.* 50-51). The comparison of a tyrant with a wild beast is a classical commonplace; cf. Cic. *Ver.* 5.109; Ammianus, 27.6.1; Dufraigne, *A.V.* 73.

10.   For his incest with his sisters and his seduction of noblewomen while dressed as a god *vid.* Suet. *Cal.* 22.3; 24.1; 36.4; 52.2; Dio, 59.26.5; Eutrop. 7.12; *Epit.* 3.4-7.

11.   For his theatrical invasion of Germany in 39 *vid.* Suet. *Cal.* 45-46; Dio, 59.25.1-3. For his abortive invasion of Britain *vid.* R.W. Davies, *Historia* 15, 1966, 124.

12.   Cf. Suet. *Cal.* 22.2; Phil. *Leg. ad Gaium*, 119.

13.   Caligula was killed by Cassius Chaerea, a praetorian tribune, on January 24, 41 (Suet. *Cal.* 56, 58; Dio, 59.21.1; Jos. *Ant.*

Jud. 19.1.14).

14.   I translate *Quirites* as *true Romans* here.   Originally it
      indicated the original Latin and Sabine inhabitants of Rome,
      but later it described Romans in their civil capacity.   Caesar is
      said to have quelled a mutiny of the Xth legion near Rome in
      47 B.C. by addressing the soldiers as Quirites (Tac. *Ann.* I.42;
      Suet. *Caes.* 70; Dio, 42.53.3; App. *B.C.* 2.93):   cf. H.A. *Alex.*
      Sev. 52.3; 53.10 ff. *Quiris* was said to be the Sabine for lance
      and may thus have described those with the right to bear arms.

15.   Victor is thinking more of his own day here, when Pannonians
      (or Illyrians) and Germans formed the officer corps and the
      German auxiliaries had become the backbone of the army.   "In
      the middle of the fourth century soldier, *miles,* was the
      synonym of *barbarus*" (F. Lot, *The End of the Ancient World*
      and the Beginning of the Middle Ages, New York, 1961, 232).
      In fact *barbarus* just as frequently denoted German.   In general
      vid. Bird, *S.A.V.* 41 ff.   The moralizing reflections are
      Sallustian: cf. Sall. *Cat.* 2.5; 54.5; *Hist.* 48.3.

16.   Vimius (manuscript P gives *unius*) is mentioned neither by
      Suetonius (*Claud.* 10.2-3) nor by Dio (60.1.2-3), while
      Josephus calls him Gratus (*Ant. Jud.* 19.3.1).

17.   Cf. Suet. *Claud.* 38.5; Dio, 60.2.4.

18.   Cf. Suet. *Claud.* 6; 12.7.

19.   Cf. Dio, 60.1.4; Jos. *Ant. Jud.* 19.3.3.

20.   Cf. Dio, 60.1.4; Jos. *Ant. Jud.* 19.4.

21.   Cf. Suet. *Claud.* 10.7; Oros. 7.6.3-4.

22.   On the power of Fortune, a rhetorical commonplace, *vid.* Bird,
      S.A.V. 81 ff. For a similar sentiment regarding Fate *vid.* Livy,

I.42.

4

1.   For the expression cf. Sall. *Cat.* 1.1. The information derives
         via the *Kaisergeschichte* from Suet. *Claud.* 33.1-2. Cf. *Epit.*
         4.3.

2.   Cf. Tac. *Ann.* XI.28; Suet. *Claud.* 39.1; *Epit.* 4.3. The Greek
         tradition represented by Dio is much fairer (Dio, 60.2.1;
         60.3.1). Victor is influenced here by his own feelings for the
         senate (Bird, *S.A.V.* 30).

3.   Claudius limited lawyers' fees (Tac. *Ann.* XI.7), checked the
         lawless behaviour of theatregoers, restrained the excesses of
         money-lenders (Tac. *Ann.* XI.13) and punished free women
         who had relationships with slaves (Tac. *Ann.* XII.53).

4.   Cf. Suet. *Claud.* 25.13. The Druids were the Celtic priests of
         Britain and Gaul who were exempt from military service and
         taxation, possessed a monopoly of learning, including writing,
         acted as judges and executioners, and could excommunicate
         offenders. Their savage rites were incompatible with Roman
         standards (H.Last. *J.R.S.* 39, 1949, 1), but they also encouraged
         nationalist opposition to Rome. *Vid.* S. Piggot, *The Druids*,
         London, 1968.

5.   Mesopotamia was not conquered until 115, in the reign of
         Trajan. Victor is here referring to Claudius' vain attempt to
         place a Roman puppet, Meherdates, on the Parthian throne
         (Tac. *Ann.* XII.10-14).

6.   Corbulo defeated the Chauci at the mouth of the Rhine, burned
         their ships and killed their leader Gannascus, a former Roman
         auxiliary. But Claudius ordered him to withdraw to the west
         bank of the Rhine, possibly fearing another Varian disaster or

the growing reputation of his general. A colony was established at Cologne (Colonia Agrippinensis) in 50 and colonial status was granted to Trier (Augusta Treverorum). *Vid.* Tac. *Ann.* XI.19-20; Dio, 60.30.4. On the Danube frontier Vannius, who had been made King of the Suebi by Drusus, was deposed by his sister's sons, Vangio and Sido, and was allowed to settle in Pannonia. His successors, grateful for Rome's non-intervention, remained loyal allies (Tac. *Ann.* XII.29-30).

7. Mauretania Tingitana and Mauretania Caesariensis were established as provinces between 42 and 44 by C. Suetonius Paulinus and Cn. Hosidius Geta (Dio, 60.9; D. Fishwick, *Historia* 20, 1970, 467). Ptolemy was the last king of Mauretania, not Juba.

8. Cf. Dio, 60.9.6.

9. Cf. Suet. *Claud.* 17; Dio, 60.20-21; Eutrop. 7.13. For Claudius' conquest of southern Britain *vid.* S.S. Frere, *Britannia³*, London, 1978; G. Webster and D.R. Dudley, *The Roman Conquest of Britain A.D. 43-57*, London, 1965.

10. Cf. Suet. *Cal.* 19; *Claud.* 18.1; Dio, 59.17.2; 60.11.1. Dio alone notes that a famine was caused by Caligula's requisitioning of cargo ships to bridge the Bay of Naples, consequently Victor could not have taken this information from Suetonius.

11. Cf. Suet. *Claud.* 16.2, where the author views this as a sign of Claudius' inconsistency.

12. Cf. Suet. *Claud.* 25; 29; Tac. *Ann.* XI.28; Dio, 60.2.4. For Victor's attitude to women *vid.* Bird, *S.A.V.* 116 ff.

13. For Messalina, on whom Victor spends inordinate space, cf. Suet. *Claud.* 26.5; 29.5; 36.1-3; Tac. *Ann.* XI.12; 26-27; 29;

37; Dio, 60.14.1-3; 18.1-2; 31.2-4. At the age of fourteen she married Claudius, her second cousin, probably in 39 and bore him Octavia in 40 and Britannicus in 41. In 48 she went through a form of marriage with C. Silius and was subsequently executed with Silius through the machinations of Narcissus.

14.   Cf. *Epit.* 4.6. The freedmen concerned were Callistus, the secretary of petitions (*a libellis*), Narcissus, the chief secretary (*ab epistulis*), Pallas, the chief accountant (*a rationibus*), Posides, who was awarded the *hasta pura* (= Victoria Cross), Felix, appointed governor of Judaea, Harpocras and Polybius, the chief archivist (*a studiis*). Suetonius, who had held three imperial secretaryships himself, was particularly affronted by the wealth they had amassed (Suet. *Claud.* 28). Victor here may be hinting at the undue influence that Constantius' wives and flunkies had with him: cf. *De Caes.* 42.24-25; *Epit.* 42.19; Eutrop. 10.15; Ammianus, 21.16.16.

15.   For the part played in Claudius' marriage to Agrippina by the freedmen *vid.* Tac. *Ann.* XII.1-2; Dio, 60.31.8: for Agrippina's intrigues *vid.* Suet. *Claud.* 26. Agrippina (15-59) was the eldest daughter of Claudius' brother, Germanicus, and Agrippina the Elder. By her first husband, Cn. Domitius Ahenobarbus, she bore the subsequent emperor Nero. She married her uncle Claudius in 49.

16.   Tacitus compares her with Messalina in *Ann.* XII.7; 65.

17.   On the poisoning cf. Suet. *Claud.* 44.1-5; Tac. *Ann.* XII.66-67; Dio, 60.34.2; Jos. *Ant. Jud.* 20.8.1. *Epit.* 4.10. For a defence of Agrippina on the charge of poisoning Claudius *vid.* G. Bagnani, *Phoenix* 1, 1946, 15-20.

18.   The Secular Games were celebrated in 47 (Suet. *Claud.* 21.4; Tac. *Ann.* XI.11.1). Victor was bitterly disappointed that three centuries later, in his day, the 1100th anniversary passed with

little fanfare (*De Caes.* 28.2), which indicates that he was at Rome at the time (248).

19. Tacitus (*Ann.* VI.28) places the appearance in 34, Pliny (*N.H.* 10.2.5) and Dio (58.27.1) in 36, Dexippus (*H.G.M.* I. frg. 5) and the Epitomator (4.9) in the reign of Claudius. The phoenix had the plumage of a peacock and a pheasant, with a rayed crest, and was connected with Osiris. By the Romans it was used to symbolize the eternity of Rome and it appeared on coins of Constantine. In general *vid.* M.L. Walla-Schuster, *Der Vogel Phőnix in der antiken Literatur und der Dichtung des Laktanz*, Vienna, 1969, 103-111.

20. Cf. Sen. *Q.N.* 6.21.1; Dio, 60.29.7; *Epit.* 4.9; Oros. 7.6.13. The volcanic island appeared near Thera in 47. Only Victor notes the lunar eclipse.

21. Tarquinius Priscus' wife, Tanaquil, kept her husband's death a secret until she could ensure the succession of Servius (Livy, I.41.5-6). For Agrippina's intrigues and the adoption of Nero in 50 cf. Tac. *Ann.* XII.25, 68; Suet. *Claud.* 27.6; 45.1; *Ner.* 7.2.

5

1. Nero's father was Cn. Domitius Ahenobarbus (*cos.* 32), Agrippina's first of three husbands. He died in 41.

2. Nero was born on December 15, 37. He ruled from October, 54 until June, 68 while Claudius ruled from January, 41 until October, 54.

3. Cf. *Epit.* 5.2. The so-called *Quinquennium Neronis*, conspicuously absent from the accounts of Tacitus, Suetonius and Dio, has engendered considerable controversy: cf. J.G.C. Anderson, *J.R.S.* 1, 1911, 173; F.A. Lepper, *J.R.S.* 47, 1957,

95; O. Murray, *Historia* 14, 1965, 41; J.G.F. Hind, *Historia* 20, 1971, 488; M.K. Thornton, *Historia* 22, 1973, 570; R. Syme, *Emperors and Biography*, Oxford, 1971, 106-110. This notice was almost certainly in the *Kaisergeschichte* and, in my estimation, refers to Nero's first five years. For Nero's building projects cf. Suet. *Ner.* 16.1; Tac. *Ann.* XV.43.1. Most were, indeed, inaugurated after the great fire of Rome in July, 64. I take *augeo* here to mean *enhance*, which is what the Epitomator (*loc. cit.*) appears to indicate, rather than *increase in size*, which is how the author of the H.A. interpreted it (*Aur.* 21.11). As far as we know Nero did not extend the *pomerium*.

4. Cf. Suet. *Ner.* 18.1-2; Eutrop. 7.14; H.A. *Aur.* 21.11. Eastern Pontus was granted to Polemon I by Caligula in 38. It was annexed in 64 and added to Galatia and subsequently to Cappadocia. In the same period the Cottian Alps region, lying astride the Franco-Italian boundary, was annexed by Nero after the death of King Cottius II.

5. Cf. Sall. *Hist.* 1.48.14; Zos.1.6.3.

6. Cf. Suet. *Ner.* 21.2. For Nero's partiality for Greek musical contests *vid.* Suet. *Ner.* 20.2; 21.2; Tac. *Ann.* XIV.14; XV.33; Dio, 60.20-21; 63.12.2; Eutrop. 7.14. In 60 he instituted a five-yearly contest in poetry, music and rhetoric which came to be known as the Neronia.

7. Cf. Suet. *Ner.* 12; 28.3; 29.1; Tac. *Ann.* XIV.14; XV.37; Dio, 62.28.3; *Epit.* 5.5. I retain *exactor parium* (*o* and *p*) in 5.7.

8. Cf. Suet. *Ner.* 28.5; Tac. *Ann.* XIV.2; Dio, 61.11.3-4; *Epit.* 5.5. Eutropius meticulously refrains from mentioning Nero's disgusting aberrations but stresses his execution of many senatorials.

9. This righteously indignant personal intervention, coupled with his lengthy and excessive (for an abbreviator) disquisition on

Nero's vices tells us as much about Victor as it does about Nero: cf. Eutrop. 7.14 for a more genteel and balanced abridgment.

10.   Cf. Tac. *Ann.* XIV.2.

11.   E.g. Lollia, Calpurnia, Statilius, Taurus, Domitia and Lepida.

12.   Cf. Suet. *Ner.* 28.1.

13.   Cf. Tac. *Ann.* XIV.2; Dio, 61.11.3.

14.   Cf. Suet. *Ner.* 33.1; Eutrop. 7.14; *Epit.* 5.5; Oros. 7.7.9. Nero was responsible for the deaths of his stepbrother Britannicus, his first wife Octavia, his mother Agrippina, and, by accident, his second wife Poppaea Sabina (Suet. *Ner.* 33-35).

15.   Cf. Suet. *Ner.* 36.2; 37; Eutrop. 7.14. The destruction of the nobility is a customary characteristic of tyrants (Plat. *Rep.* 5676).

16.   Cf. Suet. *Ner.* 36.2.

17.   For the great fire of Rome which stated on July 19, 64 and damaged or destroyed ten of Rome's fourteen districts cf. Suet. *Ner.* 38; Tac. *Ann.* XV.38-41; Eutrop. 7.14. Although he was at Antium at the time Nero was generally blamed for it, but Tacitus sensibly expresses uncertainty.

18.   Cf. Suet. *Ner.* 43.

19.   Nero supposedly contemplated changing Rome's name to Neropolis (Suet, *Ner.* 55) but neither Suetonius nor Tacitus nor Dio mention a possible re-location of the capital, though Caligula had allegedly considered making Antium or Alexandria his capital (Suet. *Cal.* 8.12; 49.4). Rome's position as capital was clearly on people's minds in Victor's day,

particularly since the founding of Constantinople. Victor's linking of such an idea with Nero and with Rome's current enemies, the Parthians, is not gratuitous.

20.   This anecdote is only found in Victor, though it may have come from the *Kaisergeschichte*. To the Romans *regnum* was the opposite of *libertas* (Livy, II.15.3) with the result that monarchy is often called *dominatio* and subjection to monarchy *servitus*. In this passage Victor equates Nero's *imperium* with *regnum* (above). For Victor's use of negative terms denoting power and a comparison with the terms used by Eutropius and the Epitomator *vid.* Bird, *S.A.V.* 112, and for further discussion *vid.* Dufraigne, *A.V.* 84.

21.   Victor dwells excessively on Nero's vices and omits much of importance here, including the roles played by Vindex and Verginius Rufus in the overthrow of the emperor. Cf. Suet. *Ner.* 40-42; *Galb.* 9-10.

22.   Cf. Suet *Ner.* 47-49; Dio, 63.27; Eutrop. 7.15; *Epit.* 5.7. The statement that Nero was deserted on all sides was almost certainly in the *Kaisergeschichte* (cf. *Epit. loc. cit.*; Eutrop. 7.15.1) and somewhat misinterpreted by Victor, as the Epitomator makes clear. The emperor was, indeed, generally abandoned, but had four companions as he fled, a fact noted by Suetonius, Dio (who cites three) and the Epitomator.

23.   For stylistic purposes the author of the *Kaisergeschichte* had utilized the first chapter of Suetonius' *Galba* to conclude his section on the Julio-Claudians (cf. Dio, 63.29.3; Plin. *N.H.* 15.140; Eutrop. 7.15.3). Eutropius simply states: "With him the whole family of Augustus became extinct" (echoing the first line of Suetonius' *Galba*). Victor, in my estimation, chose to include the paragraph he discovered in his source but *may* have added from autopsy the note that the place for the hens still existed in his day. As Suetonius informs us, it was called "*ad Gallinas*" (The Hen Coop). White hens were supposedly

sterile (Columella, VIII.2.7), hence their suitability for religious purposes (cf. the French "*Le fils de la poule blanche*").

6

1. Servius Sulpicius Galba (3 B.C.-A.D.68) was the son of C. Sulpicius Galba and Mummia Achaica. He was consul in 33 and a favourite of Augustus, Tiberius, Livia, Caligula and Claudius. His pedigree is emphasized by Suetonius (*Galb.* 2 ff.) Tacitus (*Hist.* I.49), Eutropius (7.16) and the Epitomator (*Epit.* 6.1).

2. Galba's entry into Rome in early October, 68 was marred by his massacre of a contingent of marines (Tac. *Hist.* I.6; Suet. *Galb.* 12; Plut. *Galb.* 15). For his subsequent activities and his refusal to pay the donative promised to the troops *vid.* Tac. *Hist.* I.6-7; Suet. *Galb.* 12-16; Plut. *Galb.* 10 ff. Galba's natural frugality was exacerbated by the sad state of the treasury (due to Nero's prodigality) which he discovered after entering Rome. Suetonius, for personal reasons (his father had been one of Otho's officers) translated Galba's parsimony into greed. In effect it was Galba's subordinates, Vinius, Laco and Icelus, who were mainly responsible (Tac. *loc. cit.*; Suet. *Galb.* 14; Plut. *Galb.* 17; *Epit.* 6.2). Eutropius' brief account is much kinder (Eutrop. 7.16). Victor's use of a series of narrative infinitives here is Sallustian: cf. *Cat.* 11.4-6; *Jug.* 41.5-9.

3. Galba was murdered by Otho's supporters on January 15, 69, having ruled from Nero's death on June 9, 68. He had indeed offended Otho by adopting L. Calpurnius Piso five days before the assassination (Tac. *Hist.* I.15 ff.; I.41; Suet. *Galb.* 17-20; *Oth.* 5.2; Eutrop. 7.16; *Epit.* 6.4).

1. Cf. Suet. *Oth.* 2.3; Tac. *Ann.* I.13 .ff; Dio, 64.15.2; Eutrop. 7.17; Oros. 7.8.6. Otho was Nero's friend until the emperor seduced his wife, Poppaea Sabina, and sent him to govern Lusitania in 58. He supported Galba in 68 and expected to be named Galba's heir but when the latter selected Piso he had both killed by his praetorian supporters.

2. Otho was 37 so Victor's description is inaccurate. I believe he misrepresented what was in the *Kaisergeschichte* here: cf. *Epit.* 7.1 where the author states that Otho was shameful all his life but *especially* in his *adulescentia*.

3. Otho ruled 91 days, from January 15 to April 16. Suetonius (*Oth.* 11.3), followed by Eutropius (7.17), gives 95, which was presumably the number given in the *Kaisergeschichte*. Possibly, as Dufraigne (*A.V.* 87) suggests, the copyist of the archetype of *o* and *p* omitted an X from LXXXXV.

4. On April 6, 69 Otho beat the forces of Caecina, Vitellius' lieutenant, near Bedriacum, but eight days later the combined armies of Caecina and Valens defeated Otho's troops near Cremona, not Verona. This is probably another scribal error, made either by Victor or his copyist. Otho committed suicide on April 16 (Tac. *Hist.* II.11-50; Suet. *Oth.* 8-11).

8

1. Aulus Vitellius (*cos.* 48) was appointed governor of Lower Germany by Galba in 68. His troops acclaimed him emperor on January 2, 69. Cf. Suet. *Vit.* 12.1.

2. Titus Flavius Vespasianus (*cos. suff.* 51) commanded the *Legio II Augusta* during the invasion of Britain in 43. He was proconsul of Africa in 63 and in February, 67 Nero charged him with suppressing the Jewish rebellion which he had to a large extent accomplished by June, 68. On July 1, 69 the two

Egyptian legions acclaimed him emperor and within a few days the Judaean and Syrian legions backed their claim. In August the Pannonian and Moesian legions declared their support and invaded Italy, entering Rome on December 21st (Suet. *Vesp.* 4 ff.; Tac. *Hist.* II.73 ff.; V.10 ff.; Dio, 63.22.1a; 65.9; Jos. *Bell. Jud.* 4.10.6; Eutrop. 7.19; *Epit.* 8.3). For the rivalry of the various armies *vid.* Tac. *Hist.* II.6.4; Suet. *Vesp.* 6.3.

3.   Vespasian was born in a village called Phalacrinae (Falacrina) near Sabine Reate (Rieti) 45 miles N.E. of Rome. His family was, indeed, obscure for his father had been a tax-collector (Suet. *Vesp.* 1.1; 2.1). Both Victor and Eutropius (7.19.1) emphasize the point that Vespasian's actions ennobled him: cf. Sall. *Jug.* 63.2; 85.30; Sen. *Epist.* 44.

4.   Cf. Suet. *Vesp.* 7.3; Tac. *Hist.* III. 22-23. This refers to the second battle of Bedriacum (or Cremona) in late autumn 69, when Antonius Primus' Danubian troops defeated the Vitellians between Bedriacum and Cremona, drove them back to Cremona and sacked the city (K. Wellesley, *J.R.S.* 61, 1971, 28 ff.).

5.   Cf. Suet. *Vit.* 15.4 (who mentions the sum offered); Tac. *Hist.* III.65.3-5; Dio, 65.17.1.

6.   Cf. Tac. *Hist.* III.54.5-10 where Vitellius is said to have disbelieved an accurate report brought to him by a centurion, Julius Agrestis.

7.   Cf. Suet. *Vit.* 15.5; Tac. *Hist.* III.69-73; Dio, 65.17; Eutrop. 7.18; *Epit.* 8.4.

8.   Cf. Suet. *Vit.* 16.2.

9.   Cf. Suet. *Vit.* 16.4-17.4; Tac. *Hist.* III.84.9-85.1; Dio, 65.21.2; Eutrop. 7.18; *Epit.* 8.3-5.

10. Both Victor and Eutropius (*loc. cit.*) state that he died in the eighth month of his reign, possibly reckoning inclusively from April 16th but more probably following a statement in Suet. *Vit.* 15 *via* the *Kaisergeschichte* that he was repudiated by the Pannonian and Moesian armies in his eighth month. Vitellius was born on September 24th (or 7th) in 15 (Suet. *Vit.* 3) and died on December 20th, 69 (Dio 65.22.1) in his 55th year (despite Suet. *Vit.* 18, followed by Victor, Eutropius, 7.18 and the Epitomator, 8.5). Both manuscripts of the *De Caesaribus* actually give 75, but the *Kaisergeschichte* clearly stated 57, so this error is presumably due to a copyist's inversion (Dufraigne, *A.V.* 90).

11. The Epitomator (8.6) reproduces this statement verbatim from Victor. For a succinct discussion of the rhetorical and cultural abilities of the Julio-Claudians cf. Tac. *Ann.* XIII.3. For Victor's interest in education and culture *vid.* Bird, *S.A.V.* 71-80. Ammianus, too, made education the first prerequisite of a ruler (R.C. Blockley, *Latomus* 31, 1972, 444), as did Julian, Themistius and the *H.A.*

12. Victor's moralizing interventions are an important facet of his work and set it apart from Eutropius' *Breviarium* and the *Epitome.* For examples *vid.* Bird, *S.A.V.* 24-80.

9

1. For his rhetorical abilities, which suited a no-nonsense, military man cf. Tac. *Hist.* III.80.3; IV.3.6.

2. Cf. Suet. *Vesp.* 8.1; *Epit.* 9.5; 9.16.

3. For the clemency of Vespasian cf. Suet. *Vesp.* 12.1; 14.1-15.1; Eutrop. 7.19.2; *Epit.* 9.2. The word *satelles* is used by Tacitus to describe supporters of Sejanus (*Ann.* VI.3.2), by Victor to describe the freedmen of Claudius (*De Caes.* 4.10.3), the

supporters of Vitellius here (cf. *Epit.* 9.5), those of Commodus (17.7.4), and of Gallienus (33.31.2). For the theme of clemency cf. Sen. *De Clem.* 1.14.

4. For Vespasian's forgiveness of conspirators, as opposed to the cruelty of more tyrannical rulers (or even the severity of Constantius II) cf. Eutrop. 7.20.3. For justifiable exceptions *vid.* Suet. *Vesp.* 15; Dio, 66.16.3-4.

5. For Vespasian's good nature *vid.* Suet. *Vesp.* 22-23; Eutrop. 7.19-20; *Epit.* 9.2-4. For a similar story regarding Titus *vid.* Suet. *Tit.* 9; *De Caes.* 10.3; Eutrop. 7.21; *Epit.* 10.10. On the negative aspects of power *vid,* Plin. *Pan* VI.11.7; VII.3, i.e. it was a commonplace; cf. Adeimantus' objections in Plato's *Republic* (IV.419 ff.). Josephus affirms that Vespasian was compelled to accept power by his troops (*Bell. Jud.* 4.10.4; cf. Suet. *Vesp.* 6.1).

6. For Vespasian's superstitions and consultations of gods and auspices *vid.* Suet. *Vesp.* 5; 7; 25; Tac. *Hist.* II.78.2; IV.82; Eutrop. 7.20.3; *Epit.* 9.18.

7. For Vespasian's laws *vid.* Suet. *Vesp.* 11; Tac. *Hist.* II.82; *Epit.* 9.6.

8. Cf. Suet. *Vesp.* 16.2 ff.; Dio, 66.8.3; Eutrop. 7.19; *Epit.* 9.7. Victor alone mentions the speedy abolition of the new taxes, which may imply personal knowledge.

9. Vespasian's building projects at Rome were both numerous and substantial: *vid.* Tac. *Hist.* IV.53; Suet. *Vesp.* 8-9; Jos. *Bell. Jud.* 7.5.7; Dio, 66.15.1; *Epit.* 9.8; D. Dudley, *Urbs Roma*, Aberdeen, 1967, 25 *et passim.* The most celebrated is the Flavian Amphitheatre or Colosseum, begun by Vespasian and completed by Domitian, though Titus dedicated it in June, 80. It was 48.5 metres high, 188 metres long and held 50,000 spectators (Dudley, *op. cit.*, 142-145; N.H. & A. Ramage,

Roman Art, Englewood Cliffs, 1991, 124-128).

10.   Cf. Suet. *Vesp.* 17; *Epit.* 9.9-10. The Epitomator adds that this tunnel was vulgarly called Pertunsa Petra (The Bored Rock), i.e. with a sexual connotation. A town of the same name (now Furlo) grew up there. The Via Flaminia, built from 220 B.C. by C. Flaminius, stretched 209 miles from Rome via Fanum Fortunae (Fano) to Ariminum (Rimini). Vespasian's tunnel through the Intercisa Pass still exists about 11 km. north of Cagli.

11.   Cf. Eutrop. 7.19.5. Victor is probably thinking of his own days here, and of the abuse of the peasant farmers by state tax collectors: cf. *De Caes.* 33.13; 40.24.

12.   Cf. Suet. *Vesp.* 9.2; *Epit.* 9.11. This reformation of the senate in 73/74 by Vespasian and Titus as censors (A.W. Braithwaite, *Divus Vespasianus*, Oxford, 1927, 50-53) was of particular importance to Victor, who strongly believed that meritorious provincials should enter the senate, as he was to do about two years after writing this. The Epitomator places less emphasis on it. The information provided by Victor and the Epitomator differs in certain essentials from that given by Suetonius and presumably stems from the *Kaisergeschichte*.

13.   This information clearly stems from the *Kaisergeschichte*: cf. Eutrop. 7.19; *Epit.* 9.12-13. The Epitomator states that Vologeses I (Parthian king 51/52 - 79/80) was compelled simply by fear to make peace, but Pliny (*Pan.* XIV.1) seems to back up Victor's contention. Possibly when Vespasian refused Vologeses' request for Roman assistance against the Alans in 75 (Suet. *Domit.* 2.2.) some hostilities occurred. Victor, Eutropius and the Epitomator all erroneously state that Judaea was formed into a province at this juncture. In fact it was annexed in 6, briefly placed under the control of Agrippa II in 41, but re-annexed three years later. Only after the suppression of the Jewish revolt in 135 was it renamed Syria

75

Palaestina. The error presumably stems from the *Kaisergeschichte.*

14. Cf. Suet. *Tit.* 5.3; Dio, 66.9.2a; Oros. 7.9.3. Titus completed the capture of Jerusalem in September 70, though Masada did not fall until 72.

15. Cf. Suet. *Tit.* 6.2; *Epit.* 10.4. Titus quickly succeeded his brother-in-law, Arrecinus Clemens, as praetorian prefect, to ensure that the guard remained loyal.

16. Certain praetorian prefects such as Sejanus, Burrus, Tigellinus and Plautianus acquired enormous personal influence and power and became *de facto* vice-emperors, as Victor notes (L.L. Howe, *The Praetorian Prefect from Commodus to Diodetian*, Ph.D. Diss., Chicago, 1942, 18). The prefects obtained judicial powers in the second and third centuries and major financial responsibilities in the third century. Under Diocletian they became the chief financial ministers of the empire. In Constantine's reign they lost their military responsibilities but retained their fiscal ones over the four territorial prefectures of the empire, and in particular they were charged with collecting the *annona* which financed the army and the bureaucracy and was subject to a multitude of abuses. This became a common theme in fourth century writers.

10

1. For Titus' learning cf. Suet. *Tit.* 3.2; Plin. *N.H. praef.* 5; Eutrop. 7.21.3; *Epit.* 10.2. For his clemency cf. Suet. *Tit.* 9; Dio, 66.19.1; Eutrop. *loc. cit.; Epit.* 10.3; 9. For his generosity cf. Suet. *Tit.* 7.7; 8.4; Eutrop. *loc. cit.; Epit. loc. cit.*

2. Cf. Suet. *Tit.* 8.1; Dio, 66.19.3; *Epit.* 10.8.

3. The anecdote comes originally from Suetonius (*Tit.* 9.2-3); cf.

Epit. 10.10; Eutrop. 7.21. Dio tells basically the same story about Nerva (68.3.2). The theme that power is conferred by Fate is also in Pseudo-Sallust (*Ad Caes.* 1.1.1) and echoed earlier in the *De Caesaribus* (3.20), where Fortune is the agent. It should be noted how much of his limited account of Titus' reign is taken up by this anecdote.

4.　　　Titus' reign lasted from June 24, 79 to September 13, 81, i.e. 2 years, 2 months, 20 days (Suet. *Tit.* 11.1; Dio, 66.26.4). Eutropius (7.22) states that he ruled 2 years, 8 months and 20 days, agreeing with Victor, which leads even Dufraigne (*A.V.* 94) to posit a common source for this error. Apparently Titus died straight after the dedication of the Flavian Amphitheatre (Suet. *Tit.* 10.2; Dio, 66.26.1). Suetonius (*Tit.* 9.5; *Domit.* 2.6) notes Domitian's plots against Titus but never suggests that Titus was poisoned. Eutropius (7.22) and the Epitomator (10.15) merely state that he died of an ailment (*morbo* or *febri*), which is presumably the correct version since Domitian's numerous detractors would certainly have mentioned it had there been any suspicion of foul play. Either Victor or a scribe was responsible for this error. Titus was born on December 30, 41 (Suet. *Tit.* 1) so he was 39 when he died, as Victor states, not 41, which Suetonius incorrectly writes (*Tit.* 11) followed by both Eutropius (7.22) and the Epitomator (10.15). Either Victor was here correcting the Suetonian error he found in the *Kaisergeschichte* or he simply followed his practice of rounding out the numbers and was serendipitously accurate.

5.　　　Cf. Suet. *Tit.* 1.1; Eutrop. 7.21; *Epit.* 10.16. Eutropius presumably followed the *Kaisergeschichte* here, which retained the wording and placement of Suetonius, whereas Victor, followed by the Epitomator, showed his originality by transposing this description to the conclusion of his account of Titus and thereby neatly contrasted the two brothers.

11

1.   Cf. Suet. *Domit.* 1.2-3; Eutrop. 7.23; Plin. *Pan.* 33.4; 48.3.

2.   Cf. Suet. *Domit.* 22.1; Eutrop 7.23.4; *Epit.* 11.6.

3.   Cf. Suet. *Domit.* 13.4-5; Dio, 67.5.7; Eutrop. 7.23.2; *Epit.* 11.6; Oros. 7.10.2. The Epitomator observes that he was imitating Caligula in demanding to be addressed as lord and god. Diocletian and the tetrarchs resuscitated this usage which Caligula had begun (*De Caes.* 39.4; cf. Eutrop. 9.26).

4.   Cf. Suet. *Domit.* 2.4; 3; 10; Eutrop. 7.23.4; *Epit.* 11.2. Eutropius maintains that Domitian was, indeed, restrained in his early years. Victor and the Epitomator believe this was merely simulated, deriving their information *via* the *Kaisergeschichte* from Suet. *Domit.* 2.4.

5.   The connection here is confusing and probably the result of Victor's hasty compression of his source. For his campaigns cf. Suet. *Domit.* 6.2; 13.9; Dio, 67.6.3; Eutrop. 7.23; *Epit.* 11.2; Oros. 7.10.3. Domitian defeated the Chatti in 83, annexing the area between the upper Rhine and Danube. Two years later Oppius Sabinus was defeated and killed by the Dacians and in 86 Cornelius Fuscus lost a legion while mounting a punitive expedition in Dacia. Nevertheless in 88 Julianus won a victory at Tapae. Other operations took place against the Marcomanni, Quadi and Iazyges between 89 and 92 with mixed results. For his attempts to change the names of September and October cf. Suet. *Domit.* 13.9; Dio, 67.4.4.

6.   Cf. Suet. *Domit.* 5.1; Eutrop. 7.23.5; *Epit.* 11.3-4; Laet. *Mort. Persec.* 3.3. Domitian undertook many substantial building projects at Rome. For example he erected new temples to Jupiter Capitolinus and Jupiter Custos and rebuilt those of Janus, Castor and Apollo. He completed the Colosseum which Vespasian had begun and Titus had dedicated, and in the

Campus Martius he built an Odeum, a Stadium and a Circus. Furthermore he constructed a temple of Isis and Serapis, the Arch of Titus, a villa on the Alban Lake, a shopping centre in the Saepta, granaries, water works and, finally, he refurbished the Pantheon and the portico of Octavia. Many of these are listed by Eutropius, so they were mentioned by the *Kaisergeschichte*, but Victor ignored them and gave credit to Vespasian and Titus for beginning them all. For Victor Domitian was simply the consummate tyrant and villain, and his reign a *dominatio.*

7. Cf. Dio, 67.3.3[1]; Eutrop. 7.23.2; *Epit.* 11.6; Euseb. *H.E.* 3.17. This was a commonplace characteristic of a tyrant (Plin. *Pan.* 48.3; 90.5; 95.3; *H.A. Comm.* 18.3 ff.).

8. Another commonplace quality of a tyrant, cf. Suet. *Domit.* 19-20; Dio, 67.6.3. Victor so describes Gallienus (33.17) and Maxentius (40.20-21). Remarkably neither Eutropius nor the Epitomator accused Domitian of this.

9. Victor alone combines the two anecdotes of Domitian's fly-catching and bed-wrestling: cf. Suet. *Domit.* 3.1; 22.1; Dio, 66.9.5; *Epit.* 11.7-8. He is being humorous here: the word *palaestra* (wrestling room) meant brothel in colloquial Latin.

10. Cf. Suet. *Domit.* 3.2; 14.1; Dio, 67.14.4; 15.2; Eutrop. 7.23; *Epit.* 11.11. For the phrase "paying the penalty" used here of Domitian cf. Suet. *Vesp.* 1.1; Lact. *Mort. Persec.* 3.2; Zos. 1.6.4. This, too, had become a commonplace.

11. Cf. Suet. *Domit.* 17; Eutrop. 7.23; *Epit.* 11.12. Dio (67.18.2), with his customary precision, states that Domitian lived 44 years, 10 months and 26 days. He was assassinated on September 18, 96.

12. Cf. Suet. *Domit.* 17.7; 23.2; Eutrop. 7.23.5; *Epit.* 11.13; Lact. *Mort. Persec.* 3.2. Victor, followed by the Epitomator, is

probably responsible for injecting the erroneous notion that Domitian was buried like a gladiator, a clear reflection of Commodus (cf. H.A. *Comm.* 18 ff.; Herod. I.16.3).

13.   Cf. Suet. *Domit.* 23.1. This is ignored by both Eutropius and the Epitomator, though the latter notes that the Secular Games were celebrated in Domitian's reign, a matter which otherwise interested Victor (*De Caes.* 4.14; 28.2). For Victor's wholly negative attitude to the army, a peculiarly fourth century phenomenon, *vid.* Bird, *S.A.V.* 41-52. The conspiracy against Domitian included his wife, Domitia, his chamberlain Parthenius and the new praetorian prefects, Petronius Secundus and Norbanus. Stephanus, the steward of Domitian's niece, was the actual assassin, abetted by Parthenius' servants (Suet. *Domit.* 16-17; Dio, 67.15-18; *Epit.* 11.11; 12.2). Petronius and Parthenius were executed in 97 at the insistence of the praetorians (Dio, 68.3; *Epit.* 12.8). The disaffection of the military is revealed by Nerva's coins bearing the legend *Concordia Exercituum* and by his choice of Trajan as successor. Domitian was understandably popular with the army: he raised the pay from 225 to 300 *denarii* per year (Suet. *Domit.* 7.3; Dio, 67.3.5; G. Webster, *The Roman Imperial Army*, London, 1969, 256 ff.). He may also have given the soldiers bounties and donatives, as had Tiberius (Suet. *Tib.* 48), Caligula (Suet. *Calig.* 46), Claudius (Suet. *Claud.* 10) and Nero (Tac. *Ann.* XLI.41), but since Victor alone mentions this, it is possible that this is merely a surmise by him, based simply on his antipathy towards Domitian and the army.

14.   Cf. *Epit.* 11.15. This important passage marks the transition in Victor's source, the *Kaisergeschichte*, from its reliance on Suetonius as its main source to another primary source, in all likelihood Marius Maximus. The tribute to foreign talent is reflected in Dio (68.4.1) and Pliny (*Pan.* 6), and presumably stood in the *Kaisergeschichte*. For a full and cogent discussion *vid.* Nixon, *Caesares*, 154 ff. The passage also suggests

something about Victor's mode of composition. Although he apparently followed one written source, he felt free to add from his wide reading and numerous discussions with friends and colleagues. The allusion to Tarquinius Priscus recalls Claudius' speech on the introduction of Gauls to the senate (Dufraigne, *A.V.*, 98).

12

1.   Cf. *Epit.* 11.15; 12.1; Eutrop. 8.1. M. Cocceius Nerva was not Cretan, a personal error by Victor, but was born at Narnia in Italy and was a senior senatorial, having been ordinary consul in 71 and 90. For a full discussion *vid.* Nixon, *Caesares*, 156; Dufraigne, *A.V.*, 99; den Boer, *S.M.R.H.*, 29. The confusion of the comparative and the superlative here (*prudentius maximeque moderatum*) is a common Late Latin usage (Dufraigne, *loc. cit.*). For his selling off of imperial properties to give the impression of old-fashioned frugality *vid.* Dio, 68.2.

2.   Cf. Eutrop. 8.1; *Epit.* 12.2-3. Three more errors by Victor. Although Nerva was, indeed, worried towards the end of Domitian's reign (Dio, 67.15.5; *Epit. loc. cit.*), he was actually elevated by the praetorian prefects with the assent of most of the senate, and had not retired to Sequania. This, in the fourth century, included much of the old Germania Superior, Nerva Trajan's province, hence a possible reason for Victor's confusion (R.Syme, *Tacitus*, Oxford, 1958, 633; cf. Nixon, *Caesares*, 150 ff.; Dufraigne, *loc. cit.*). Nixon suggests that the first error may be due to a careless deduction by Victor who read in his source that a praetorian prefect was the ring-leader of the plot against Domitian (cf. Eutrop. 8.1). Despite Victor's statement and that of Lactantius (*Mort. Persec.* 18.4) Nerva did not abdicate, but died in office on January 27 or 28, 98, at the age of 65 years, 10 months and 10 days (Dio, 68.4; cf. *Epit.* 12.2; 12.11; Eutrop. 8.1). Nevertheless Dio (68.3.4) indicates that Nerva had the idea of abdicating, and Pliny (*Pan.*

6.3) represents Nerva's adoption of Trajan as tantamount to an abdication, hence this version of events in some of the sources. It was also a reflection of events in 305 when Diocletian and Maximian abdicated, which both Victor (39.48) and Eutropius (9.27-28) applauded. For other comments *vid.* Nixon, *Caesares*, 165-168.

3. The Forum of Nerva (*Forum Transitorium* or *Pervium*) was indeed a passage way from the Forum Romanum to the Subura containing a Temple of Minerva, Domitian's favourite deity and protectress. Domitian built both but Nerva may have put the finishing touches to them and dedicated them (Suet. *Domit.* 5; 15; H.A. *Alex. Sev.* 28.6; C.I.L. VI.953; D.R. Dudley, *Urbs Roma*, Aberdeen, 1967, 132-133). This may be a personal observation by Victor, based upon autopsy.

4. This is another commonplace: cf. Sall. *Jug.* 6.3; Tac. *Ann.* XIII.2.3; XV.53.5. Note how it is modified when applied by Victor to Constantine (40.2): *ardore imperitandi agitabatur.*

5. Cf. the simpler statement of Eutropius (8.1.2). The idea is to be found in Pliny (*Pan.* 10.6; 11.3). It is instructive to compare this with the much longer and rather negative account of Nerva's reign in the *Epitome*, on which *vid.* Nixon, *Caesares*, 151 ff.

13

1. Cf. Eutrop. 8.2.1; *Epit.* 13.1. M. Ulpius Traianus was born at Italica, near Seville, in Baetica in 53. He served in Syria, was quaestor, praetor and then legionary commander in Spain. Domitian transferred him to Germany in 88 and made him ordinary consul in 91. He was serving as governor in *Germania Superior* in October 97 when adopted by Nerva. Eutropius notes that his family was old rather than eminent and that his father had been the first of its members to reach the

consulship.

2.   For his qualities and reputation *vid.* Plin. *Pan.* 4.5-6; Eutrop.
       8.2.1; *Epit.* 13.2 ff; Syme, *Emperors*, 89-113; Dufraigne, *A.V.*,
       101. For a discussion of the sources of Victor, Eutropius and
       the Epitomator for Trajan's reign *vid.* Nixon, *Caesares*, 168 ff.

3.   Cf. Eutrop. 8.1. For Trajan's Dacian wars and annexation of
       Dacia (101-107) *vid.* Dio, 68.6-14. The text here is corrupt
       and I read *Sarmatisque* for *Satisque* and *Dardanis* for
       Sardonios: cf. Dufraigne, *A.V.*, 101-102; Nixon, *Caesares*,
       113,178. The Sarmatians were divided into two groups; the
       Iazyges at this period inhabited the area between Pannonia and
       the new Roman province of Dacia, whereas the Roxolani lived
       in the area of the Danube estuary. The Dardanians lived along
       the Danube in the area of Upper Moesia, now modern Serbia
       (Eutrop. 5.7) and many may have stayed north of the river as
       subjects of Decebalus. They were always wild and never
       totally pacified and Marcus Aurelius is reported to have made
       some of them soldiers (*H.A. Marc. Aur.* 21.7; Ammianus,
       29.5.22-23). The Goths, when they lived in Dacia, called their
       priests *Pilleati*: they wore bonnets when sacrificing (Jord. *Get.*
       11.71).

4.   Trajan did not conquer the nations between the Euphrates and
       the Indus, though Dio (68.29.1) states that Trajan once
       declared that if he were younger he would emulate Alexander
       in doing so. Nevertheless Trajan did conquer the nations
       between the Euphrates and the Tigris and marched south as far
       as Ctesiphon (Eutrop. 8.3; Festus, 20; Bird, *Eutropius*, 120).
       For Trajan's eastern campaigns *vid.* F.A. Lepper, *Trajan's
       Parthian War*, Oxford, 1948; Garzetti, *op. cit.*, 367-373.

5.   Cf. Dio, 68, 15.3[1]. The main Roman road along the right bank
       of the Danube had been commenced in the west by the Flavian
       emperors and was extended through Dacia to the Black Sea by
       Trajan. It probably ran from Troesmis (Iglita), a legionary

camp founded c. 107, entered Dacia at Bretcu and traversed the new province to link up with the Danube south of Aquincum (Budapest), possibly at Intercisa (*C.A.H.* XI, 1954, 233-234; L. Rossi, *Trajan's Column and the Dacian Wars*, London, 1971, 24-27).

6. Cf. Dio, 68.21.1 for a similar statement concerning the forts. On the Dacian hill-forts *vid.* L. Rossi, *Antiquaries Journal*, 1971, 30 ff. For the bridge, built by the architect Apollodorus at Drobetae (Turnu Severin), below the rapids of the Iron Gates, in c. 104 *vid.* Dio, 68.13.1. Victor repeats this statement with reference to Constantine (41.18. cf. *Epit.* 41.13; *Chron. Pasc. A.D. 328* I. p. 28). Trajan established numerous colonies e.g. Oescus and Ratiaria (Arcar) in Moesia, Ulpia Traiana (Xanten), Ulpia Novomagus (Nimègue) Tropaeum Traianis (Adamklissi), Ulpia Traiana Poetovio (Pettau) and Lopodunum (Ladenburg) and relocated several legions (G. Webster, *The Roman Imperial Army*, London, 1969, 76-82).

7. Cf. *Epit.* 13.6; 11; 13; Dio, 68.7.1; Ammianus, 16.10.15. He built the forum of Trajan (Dudley, *op. cit.*, 133-137) with its shopping centre flanking the Quirinal, the Basilica Ulpia, Latin and Greek libraries, and his celebrated column. Works begun by Domitian and completed by him include the Odeon, the Baths, the Naumachy, the Temple of Augustus, and possibly even his Forum.

8. Cf. Plin. *Pan.* 29.1. On guilds in general *vid.* S. Dill, *Roman Society from Nero to Marcus Aurelius*, New York, 1960, 251-286. On the bakers' guild cf. Gaius, 1.34; Ulp. *Frag. Vat.* 233. Guilds were strictly regulated, even before Trajan's time, by senatorial or imperial decrees (*Dig.* III. 4.1) and covered every branch of industry or social service. Trajan simply confirmed the bakers' charter, granted them privileges in return for specific and perhaps not particularly desirable duties and permanently linked them in some way to the grain supply. For similar measures taken by Aurelian with bread, salt oil, pork

84

and supposedly even wine producers *vid. H.A. Aur.* 35.2; 47; 48; Zos. I.61.3; *De Caes.* 35.7; *Epit.* 35.6.

9. Augustus found a transportation system for people and mail in existence in the eastern provinces and organized a simpler system in the west with relays of messengers. Subsequently he introduced the eastern system of stations (*mansiones*) with horses and carriages, enabling a single messenger to carry a message from his base to any other point. The cost was defrayed by the local populations and came to be a substantial burden (*I.L.S.* 214). Trajan instituted a superintendent of the post (*a vehiculis*; later *praefectus vehiculorum*) and Hadrian exonerated local authorities of personal liability for requisitions (*H.A. Hadr.* 1.7.5). But it may have been Trajan who made wider use of the postal system as an instrument of administration (H.G. Pflaum, *Essai sur le cursus publicus sous le Haut-Empire romain*, Paris, 1940, 248).

10. Cf. Ammianus, 19.11.2-3. Victor was probably working as a department head (*numerarius*) in the finance department of Anatolius in 359 (Bird, *S.A.V.,* 9-10). Anatolius was praetorian prefect of Illyricum from 357 to 359. He was born at Berytus (Beirut), was consular governor of Syria in 349, vicar of Asia in 352, proconsul of Constantinople in 354 and refused the urban prefecture in 355. He was considered efficient, strict and incorruptible, qualities which strongly appealed to Victor and Ammianus, and to Constantius (*P.L.R.E.* 59-60).

11. Another commonplace subsequently repeated by Victor (35.13-14) and reinforced in another personal intervention (24.9-11). The idea may have derived ultimately from Plato (*Leg.* 4.711b) but it is likely that Victor learned it at school.

12. Cf. Eutrop. 8.4; *Epit.* 13.4-5; 7-9; Dio, 68.6.3 ff.; Dion. Chr. 3.83; 3.115; 3.123; Plin. *Pan.* 85; 86; Bird, *S.A.V.,* 26, 135; Nixon, *Caesares*, 168-182. For the qualities required of an emperor *vid.* A. Wallace-Hadrill, *Historia* 30, 1981, 313-314.

13.   Cf. Dio, $68.15.3^2$. L. Licinius Sura, of Spanish background like Trajan, played a major part in Nerva's choice of Trajan as successor (*Epit.* 13.6). A *novus homo*, he commanded Legio I at Bonn c. 93-97, governed Gallia Belgica in 97 and that year or the next became suffect consul. He subsequently governed Lower Germany, was ordinary consul in 102 and served meritoriously under Trajan in both Dacian wars, receiving the *ornamenta triumphalia* and a statue for his work. In 107 he was again ordinary consul and afterwards was military governor of Dacia. He died in c. 110. In his honour Trajan constructed the Baths named after him on the Aventine next to the Temple of Diana. It was restored by Gordian III (*C.I.L.* VI. 1703) and again in 414 (E. Nash, *Pictorial Dictionary of Ancient Rome*², Tübingen, 1968, vol. 2, 467-468, figs. 1276-1278; Nixon, *Caesares*, 175-177).

14.   The praetorian prefect of 98.

15.   Cf. Dio, $68.16.1^2$; Plin. *Pan.* 67.8 Dio's anecdote is substantially the same as Victor's; for the relationship *vid.* Nixon, *loc. cit.*

16.   On Trajan's fondness for wine *vid.* Dio, 68.7.4; *H.A. Hadr.* 3.3; *Alex. Sev.* 39.1; Fronto, 226 N; Julian, *Caes.* 327 c. It was a standard item in the tradition about Trajan (Syme, *Emperors*, 105). The remedy for Trajan's *vinolentia* appears to have been a commonplace: cf. Euseb. *H.E.* 8.14; 11 for Maximia Daia, and *Anon. Val.* 4.11 for Galerius.

17.   Dio (68.33.3) gives 19 years, 6 months, 15 days, as does Eutropius (8.5).

18.   Cf. Dio, 68.24.1; Oros. 7.12.5. The earthquake occurred in the winter of 114-115 and only Victor associates it with Trajan's death.

19.   Victor alone of our sources states that Trajan was returning to

Italy at the request of the senate: in fact the emperor was seriously ill. He died of a stroke at Selinus, later Traianopolis, in Cilicia probably on August 8, 117 at the age of 63 (Dio, 68.33.3; cf. Eutrop. 8.5; *Epit.* 13.14; *H.A. Hadr.* 4.6). In Trajan's time Isauria was part of Cilicia, but it was separated from it by Diocletian.

20.   I have followed P.H. Damsté (*Mnemosyne* 45, 1917, 377) in transposing the last two sentences: cf. Nixon, *Caesares*, 113; Dufraigne, *A.V.*, 106. For the contentious subject of the adoption cf. Dio, 69.1.1-4; Eutrop. 8.6.1; *H.A. Hadr.* 1.1 ff.; 3.10-4.10. Dio's statement that there was no adoption (followed by Eutropius), was based upon the investigations of his father who was governor of Cilicia. On the other hand Hadrian (P. Aelius Hadrianus) was the obvious choice since he was Trajan's closest male relative, was governor of Syria and commander of the powerful eastern army. He, too, was born at Italica in Spain (*H.A. Hadr.* 1.3 should be disregarded) on January 24, 76 and upon the death of his father ten years later he became the ward of Trajan. At Trajan's death he was consul II designate. Pompeia Plotina was Trajan's wife before his accession and clearly favoured Hadrian, whose accession she almost certainly assisted for Hadrian honoured her on coins of his first two years and consecrated her at her death in 121 or 122 (Dio, 68.5; 69.1; 10; *Epit.* 42.21; Plin. *Pan.* 83; Syme, *Emperors*, 103, 126, 128).

21.   This is incorrect; it began in Hadrian's reign when he adopted L. Ceionius Commodus under the name L. Aelius Caesar (*H.A. Ael.* 1.2-2.2).

14

1.   Cf. *Epit.* 14.2; *H.A. Hadr.* 1.5; 3.1; 25.9; 26.4-5. Hadrian was, indeed, more inclined to literary pursuits and civil administration, but he had had a thorough military training and

experience (*H.A. Hadr.* 2.2-3; 14.10). For a full historiographical discussion of this chapter *vid.* Nixon, *Caesares*, 182-208.

2.   By surrendering Assyria, Armenia and Mesopotamia and making Parthamaspates ruler of Osrhoene (*H.A. Hadr.* 5.1-3; 21.11-12; Dio, 68.33.1; Eutrop. 8.6; Fronto, *Princ. Hist.* 10; Jerome, *ann.* 117, p. 197; August. *Civ. Dei*, 4.29; Jord. *Rom.* 270). It was a carefully considered plan and the rulers of these states became Roman clients, cf. *Epit.* 14.10. Hadrian's policy was that of Augustus (*consilium coercendi intra terminos imperii*: Tac. *Ann.* I.11).

3.   For Hadrian's philhellenism cf. *Epit.* 14.2; *H.A. Hadr.* 1.5; Nixon, *Caesares*, 183-184. Eutropius (8.8), the *H.A. (Ant. Pius*, 2.2; 13.4) and the Epitomator (15.3) compare Antoninus Pius with Numa, for which *vid.* Nixon, *Caesares*, 209-210; H.W. Bird, *C.J.* 81, 1986, 243-244. Nevertheless the *H.A. (Hadr.* 2.8) does quote a Vergilian oracle (*Aen.* VI.808-812) referring to Numa which Hadrian received. Here Victor employs chiasmus since the schools and teachers refer to the Greeks while the religious ceremonies and laws refer to Numa (Dufraigne, *A.V.* 107). For Hadrian's often unpleasant treatment of teachers, professors and philosophers *vid.* Dio, 69.3.3-4; *H.A. Hadr.* 15.10-13; 16.8, but *cf.* 16.9-11.

4.   The Athenaeum was probably an auditorium where rhetoricians and poets recited their works. Its location and form are unknown: *vid.* Dio, 74.17.4; *H.A. Pert.* 11.3; *Alex. Sev.* 35.2; *Gord.* 3.4. For the *H.A.'s* interest in the Athenaeum *vid.* H. Braunert, *B.H.A.C.* 1963 (1964), 9-41.

5.   Both Dio (69.11.1) and the *H.A. (Hadr.* 13.1) mention Hadrian's initiation into the Eleusinian Mysteries at Eleusis near Athens. Neither notes Hadrian's introduction of these rites at Rome, and a further statement in the *H.A. (Hadr.* 21.10) argues against it. Ceres and Libera are the Latin

equivalents of Demeter and Persephone.

6.   Hadrian was stricken with what was probably tuberculosis (and later dropsy) in c. 135. In the summer of 136 he adopted L. Ceionius Commodus Verus, subsequently called L. Aelius Caesar (*H.A. Hadr.* 23.10; *Ael.* 2.1 ff.). Victor's chronology is hopelessly confused here and his account of Hadrian's reign is flimsy and superficial. Hadrian only spent his last three years or so at his villa near Tivoli and it was his second adoptive son, Antoninus, whom he left in charge at Rome (*H.A. Hadr.* 25.5). This unflattering depiction of Hadrian probably derives from Marius Maximus (Nixon, *Caesares*, 182 ff.) *via* the *Kaisergeschichte* (cf. Eutrop. 8.6-7). For further discussion *vid.* Nixon, *Caesares*, 202.

7.   Cf. *Epit.* 14.11; *H.A. Hadr.* 19.9-13. This refers in particular to the embellishment of the Flavian Palace at the top of the Palatine, and to the celebrated villa on the south slope of a hill running down from Tivoli and covering more than half a square mile which reproduced many of the famous buildings Hadrian had visited on his tours, for example the Lyceum, the Academy, the Stoa Poikile, the Vale of Tempe and the Serapeum (Ramage and Ramage, 131-132; 170-174).

8.   For Hadrian's extravagant tastes and artistic interests *vid. H.A. Hadr.* 14.90; 17.12; 21.4; *Ael.* 5.4; Dio, 69.32; *Epit.* 14.2.

9.   Cf. Dio, 69.11.3-4; *H.A. Hadr.* 14.6. Antinous was a native of Bithynium who died near Besa in Egypt where Hadrian founded a city called Antinoopolis in his honour. Dio tells us that Hadrian first claimed in his autobiography that Antinous drowned in the Nile but then stated that the youth had sacrificed himself for the emperor because of some prophecy. For a full discussion *vid.* Nixon (*Caesares*, 199-203), who calls Victor's version of Hadrian's "retirement into a life of debauchery an absurdity and his introduction of Antinous into this setting a major chronological blunder."

10.   Victor clearly indicates what he believes.

11.   Cf. Dio, 69.20.1; *H.A. Hadr.* 24.1; *Ant. Pius*, 4.1. Hadrian was physically and mentally weakened by tuberculosis and dropsy and in 138 he formally adopted the fifty-one year Titus Aurelius Fulvus Boionius Antoninus. For a discussion of Victor's anecdote *vid.* Nixon, *Caesares*, 204-206.

12.   It is argued by Nixon (*Caesares*, 206-207) that there appear to have been only two victims at the end of Hadrian's reign, Servianus and Fuscus, and two at the beginning, but there were numerous senators under sentence of death who were reprieved by Antoninus.

13.   Hadrian died at Baiae near Naples on July 10th, 138 at the age of 62 years, 5 months and 19 days after reigning 20 years and 11 months (Dio, 69.23.1; cf. *H.A. Hadr.* 25.5-7; 11; Eutrop. 8.7; *Epit.* 14.12).

14.   According to Dio (69.23.3; 70.1.2) the senate at first refused to deify Hadrian because he had favoured unworthy individuals and had executed some of the nobility. The *H.A. (Hadr.* 25.8; cf. *Heliog.* 7.8-10) informs us in a passage probably derived from Marius Maximus (*Hadr.* 25.4) that Hadrian ordered the execution of numerous people on minor charges but they were reprieved by Antoninus. Eutropius (8.7) and Victor, both following the *Kaisergeschichte*, give slightly different versions. Eutropius merely states that the senate at first refused the deification but was prevailed upon by Antoninus: Victor adds the graphic details for reasons of artistry and plausibility, which makes him less reliable as a historian than Eutropius (Nixon, *Caesares*, 207-208).

15

1.   Manuscript *p* reads Altelio, *o* reads athelio. The *H.A. (Hadr.*

23.11 *et al* gives Helius for Aelius so, with Nixon (*Caesares*, 114), I am inclined to believe that Victor incorrectly wrote "At Helio"; cf. Dufraigne, *A.V.*, 110. After his adoption Antoninus was called Aelius. The *H.A.* (*Hadr.* 24.3-10; *Ant. Pius*, 2.3-7) gives five possible reasons for the surname *Pius*, bestowed by the senate in 138: 1) that he gave his arm to his enfeebled old father-in-law, 2) that he rescued many senators from execution, 3) that he bestowed honours on Hadrian after the latter's death, which presumably included deification, 4) that he prevented Hadrian from committing suicide, 5) that he was kind and merciful. Dio (70.1-2) and Eutropius (8.4) give the fifth reason which appears to be simply a variant of the second reason. Victor and Orosius (14.1) seem to agree that the surname was bestowed because of Antoninus' lack of vices. However, Victor had previously associated reason 1 with Antoninus' adoption by Hadrian. In all likelihood Victor found in the *Kaisergeschichte* three possible reasons given (perhaps four) and reassembled his material to use the first to explain the adoption, the second to explain the senate's final acquiescence in the deification of Hadrian, and the third (*H.A.* 5) to explain the surname *Pius*. Cf. Nixon, *Caesares*, 204-208. This section, when compared with the corresponding account of Eutropius, is important in providing us with an understanding of Victor's *modus operandi*.

2.　　Antoninus was born at Lanuvium (Lanuvio), a Latin city south of Rome on the Appian Way, on September 19, 86. His father's family came from Nîmes but both his father and grandfather had held consulships. Antoninus himself was ordinary consul in 120 and proconsul of Asia between 133 and 136. Eutropius' description of his family as eminent but not particularly long-standing (8.8.1) is more exact and demonstrates Eutropius' concern for such matters.

3.　　For his exemplary character *vid.* Dio, 69.3.1; *H.A. Ant. Pius*, 2.1 ff.; Eutrop. 8.8.2; *Epit.* 15.2 ff.

4.   The demoralizing effect of peace and leisure was a commonplace; cf. Xen. *Cyr.* 3.1.26; Plat. *Laws*, 698b; Polybius, 6.57.5; 31.25.3; Catullus, 51; Sall. *Cat.* 10.1; *Jug.* 41.1; Livy, I.19.4; I.22.2; Tac. *Agr.* 11; *Germ.* 14.2; 36.1. Victor neatly deflects it. Eutropius and the Epitomator also ignore the wars Pius fought in Britain, where he built the Antonine Wall, Mauretania, Germany, Dacia, Egypt, Greece and Judaea. Nor are natural disasters noted (*H.A. Ant. Pius*, 9.1-3). Possibly they were all omitted by the *Kaisergeschichte* since they would have spoiled the portrait of a perfect reign.

5.   A Platonic notion (Plat. *Rep.* 5.473 d). Cf. Cic. *Ad Quint. frat.* 1.1.29; Prud. *Sym.* 1.30; *H.A. Marc. Aur.* 27.7. It appears that Victor was echoing Cicero here.

6.   Cf. *Epit.* 15.3. He ruled from July 10, 138 until March 7, 161.

7.   Cf. *De Caes.* 4.14 (with note); 28.2. They were celebrated in April, 148. Victor is particularly interested in this since in 348 the celebrations were ignored, much to his dismay. In general *vid.* J. Gagé, *Recherches sur les jeux seculaires*, Paris, 1934; Dufraigne, *A.V.*, 111; Nixon, *Caesares*, 212.

8.   Cf. *H.A. Ant. Pius,* 9.10; *Epit.* 15.4.

9.   Cf. *Epit.* 15.6; Eutrop. 8.8; *H.A. Ant. Pius*, 9.6-10; Marc. Aur. *Medit.* 1.16; 6.30.

10.   Cf. *H.A. Ant. Pius*, 12.5; Eutrop. 8.10.1 M. Aurelius (for whom see below) was engaged to his cousin Faustina, Pius' daughter, in 138. He married her in 145 during his second consulship. Victor here seems to question the principle of adoption in imperial succession, presumably basing his opinion on his knowledge of almost four centuries of imperial history. As Nixon observes (*Caesares*, 212), Victor's account of Pius' reign is quite different from all the others and betrays the author's personality and interests.

16

1.   The name Boionius belonged to Antoninus Pius who derived
         it from his maternal grandmother, Boionia Procilla (*H.A. Ant.
         Pius*, 1.1-4). M. Annius Verus received the names Boionius
         and Aurelius Antoninus when he was adopted by Pius in 138.
         Victor is mistaken in writing that he came from the same town
         as his adoptive father. He was born at Rome on April 26, 131,
         to a family of Spanish origin and his grandfather was elevated
         to patrician status by Vespasian and Titus in 73 (*H.A. Marc.
         Aur.* 1.1 ff.). His family origins were traced back to Numa and
         King Malemnius of the Sallentini in Calabria by Marius
         Maximus (*H.A. Marc. Aur.* 1.6), whence they passed *via* the
         Kaisergeschichte to Eutropius (8.9).

2.   Cf. *H.A. Marc. Aur.* 1.1; Dio, 71.1.2; Eutrop. 8.11-12; *Epit.*
         16.7.

3.   Cf. *Epit.* 16.2; *H.A. Marc. Aur.* 18.4; 19.10

4.   Cf. Dio, 71.34.3; *H.A. Marc. Aur.* 19.1-9; 23.7; 29.1-3. Dio's
         account is factually the same as Victor's but he draws entirely
         different conclusions, as does the author of the *H.A. (Marc.
         Aur.* 19.10). For Victor's preoccupation with sexual conduct
         and possible misogyny *vid.* Bird, *S.A.V.*, 116-121; Nixon,
         Caesares, 199. Marcus Aurelius himself speaks with
         endearment of his wife Faustina (*Med.* 1.17). The negative
         treatment of her and of the emperor's acquiescence probably
         stems from Marius Maximus *via* the *Kaisergeschichte*. For
         further remarks *vid.* Syme, *Emperors*, 128-130, 134. For a
         similar opinion to that of Victor but in a generalized form cf.
         Plin. *Pan.* 83.4. Eutropius, following the same sources as
         Victor, normally maintains a discreet silence about such
         matters (den Boer *S.M.R.H.*, 163-164).

5.   Eutropius and the Epitomator note the death of Pius in their

respective sections dealing with that emperor. Victor, presumably for the sake of variety, retains this detail until his section on Marcus Aurelius. For similar occurrences *vid. De Caes.* 4.3; 10.5. Pius died on March 7th, 161 at the age of seventy-four, in the twenty-third year of his reign: cf. *H.A. Ant. Pius*, 1.8; 12.4-6; Eutrop. 8.8; *Epit.* 15.7; Dio, 71.1.1 (Xiph.).

6.   L. Ceionius Commodus (b. Dec. 130) was adopted by Antoninus Pius in 138 at the same time as Marcus Aurelius, who was ten years older. His name then became L. Aelius Aurelius Commodus. On coming to the throne in 161 he became L. Aurelius Varus and was immediately granted the title *Augustus* with the result that Rome had for the first time two *Augusti (H.A. Marc. Aur.* 7.5-6; *Ver* 3.8-4.1; Dio, 71.1.1; Eutrop. 8.9). In 164 Verus married Annia Lucilla, daughter of Marcus Aurelius, thus becoming M. Aurelius' son-in-law as well as adoptive brother. For the variants in L. Verus' name in the Latin sources *vid.* Syme, *Emperors*, 80.

7.   In 161 Vologaeses of Parthia seized Armenia and overcame two Roman armies. Verus arrived in Antioch in 163 but it was his generals, Statilius Priscus, who retook Armenia in 163, and Avidius Cassius who captured Seleucia and Ctesiphon in 165, and made Mesopotamia a Roman protectorate (Dio, 71.2; *H.A. Marc. Aur.* 8.6; 9.1-2; *Ver.* 7.1; Oros. 7.15.2; Eutrop. 8.10). Verus then returned to Rome to celebrate a joint triumph with M. Aurelius (*H.A. Marc. Aur.* 12.8-10; *Ver.* 7.9; Eutrop. 8.10; Jerome, *Ann.* 165, p. 205 [Helm]; Oros. 7.15.2).

8.   The scurrilous story of M. Aurelius poisoning Verus is in Dio (71.3.1) and the *H.A. (Ver.* 11.2), too. It was presumably in Marius Maximus and in the *Kaisergeschichte.* The *H.A.* condemns the *fabula* as vehemently as Victor, whereas Eutropius and the Epitomator discreetly omit it altogether. Eutropius had no time for such scabrous gossip.

9.   Verus died of an apoplectic attack at Altino, at the mouth of the Piave, in January 169 (*H.A. Marc. Aur.* 14.8; *Ver.* 9.11; Eutrop. 8.10.3; *Epit.* 16.5; Oros. 7.15.5).

10.   Cf. Eutrop. 8.11; *Epit.* 16.7; *H.A. Marc. Aur.* 8.1.

11.   In c. 166 Germans and Sarmatians crossed the Danube and fought a bitter war which lasted throughout the rest of M. Aurelius' reign. For details *vid.* A. Birley, *Marcus Aurelius*, London, 1966, 323 ff.

12.   L. Aelius Aurelius Commodus was born on August 31st, 161. He was appointed Caesar in 166 and became consul and Augustus in 177 (Dio, *Epit.* 73.1.2; *H.A. Comm.* 1.1-3.5; Herod, I.6.1; *Epit.* 17.2). Victor's chronology is inexact here: L. Verus died in January 169 (note 9 above).

13.   The same story appears in the *H.A. (Avid. Cass.* 3.5-6). It was probably in the *Kaisergeschichte* and borrowed by the *H.A.* either from that source or from Victor (Nixon, *Caesares,* 228-229).

14.   Cf. *H.A. Marc. Aur.* 2.2-3.9; 4.4; 4.9; Dio, 71.31.3; 71.35.2; Herod I.4; Eutrop. 8.12; *Epit.* 16.6-7. Among the Greek writers of his age were Lucian, Pausanias, Appian, Herodes Atticus, Aelius Aristides, Hermogenes, Ptolemaeus, Gallienus, and the emperor himself. There were fewer in Latin: Apuleius, Fronto and Aulus Gellius (Dufraigne, *A.V.*, 116). For a similar list of grammarians, rhetoricians and philosophers *vid.* Garzetti, *op. cit.*, 506-507. For architecture and the plastic arts *vid.* Ramage and Ramage, *op. cit.*, 200-216. For legal writings Scaevola and Gaius must be mentioned.

15.   Cf. *H.A. Marc. Aur.* 9.7 ff.; 10.10-12.6; 24.1; Oros. 7.15.12. The *H.A.* (10.1) notes that investigations to revise the status of dead persons had to be made within five years of the person's death. In fact M. Aurelius' law prevented any such

investigation after a person's death (*Dig.* xl.15.1). The emperor also personally examined *in camera* the evidence relating to a senator to be tried on a capital offence before submitting the case to trial, thus allowing himself the option of not proceeding. He added court days to the calendar to a limit of 230 to allow for speedier trials and judgements. Regarding the posting of bail Victor may here refer to that required of the plaintiff in order to bring an action (H.F. Jolowicz and B. Nicholas, *Historical Introduction to the Study of Roman Law*, Cambridge, 1972, 181), for it appears that the practice of posting bail (*vadimonium*) still existed in Ammianus' day (Ammianus, 30.9.4; Dufraigne, *A.V.*, 115). In general *vid.* Garzetti, *op. cit.,* 516-522.

16.   Cf. Dio, 71.19.1; *H.A. Marc. Aur.* 9.7-9. Dufraigne (*A.V.*, 115) considers that Victor confused M. Aurelius' actions with those of Caracalla (the *Constitutio Antoniniana*) but Nixon points out that the emperor actually contemplated giving citizenship to all (*Med.* I.14) and argues cogently against Dufraigne *et al.* (Nixon, *Caesares,* 247).

17.   Cf. Dio, 71.32.3; *H.A. Ant. Pius,* 9.1; *Marc. Aur.* 17.1; 23.3; *Epit.* 16.3. Central Carthage had been damaged by fire in Pius' reign and presumably Victor had personally seen M. Aurelius' reconstruction. Smyrna had also been damaged by the earthquake, as Dio notes, and was restored by the emperor. Other natural disasters, such as the flooding of the Tiber, famine, and the plague, are ignored by Victor and Eutropius and only briefly alluded to by the Epitomator (cf. *H.A. Marc. Aur.* 8.4; 11.3; 13.3; *Epit., loc. cit.*).

18.   The earthquake took place in August, 358 and is described in detail by Ammianus (17.7.1-14). Naeratius Cerealis was the uncle of Gallus Caesar, prefect of the grain supply in 328, urban prefect at Rome 352-353, consul in 358, and his niece had married Constantius. He had also been at Sirmium in 351-352. Victor may simply be using his consulship as a date here

but I am convinced this mention is a mark of honour to a powerful official whom the author respected, or from whom he hoped for advancement. For Cerealis' career *vid. P.L.R.E.* 197-198.

19. The triumphs were celebrated by M. Aurelius (27th November, 176) and Commodus (23rd December, 176). Marcomarus is otherwise unattested and should perhaps be changed to *Marcomano* (Dufraigne, *A.V.*, 115; Nixon, *Caesares,* 248). Carnuntum (Altenburg, east of Vienna) was M. Aurelius' base and headquarters for his war against the Marcomanni and Quadi. Cf. Eutrop. 8.13.1; *H.A. Marc. Aur.* 22.1 (with tribal listings).

20. M. Aurelius died on March 17th, 180. According to Dio (*Epit.* 72.34.5) he ruled nineteen years and eleven months, not eighteen as given by Victor and Eutropius (8.14). Tertullian (*Apologet.* 25) writes that he died at Sirmium but both Victor and the Epitomator (16.12) state that he died at Vienna, which is generally accepted since this derives, *via* the *Kaisergeschichte*, from Marius Maximus. For the general distress at his death cf. Herod. I.4.8; *H.A. Marc. Aur.* 18.2; 28.7; *Epit.* 16.13. Dio (71.33.4^2) retails the improbable story that the emperor was poisoned by his doctors to please Commodus.

21. Cf. *Epit.* 16.13-14; *H.A. Marc. Aur.* 18.3; 18.8. Here Victor uses the term *patres ac vulgus* for stylistic reasons: the *H.A.* opts for the more usual *senatus populusque*. On Victor's attitude *vid.* Bird, *S.A.V.*, 31; 137.

17

1. Cf. Eutrop. 8.15.1; *Epit.* 17.2-3; *H.A. Comm.* 1.7. L. Aelius Aurelius Commodus became M. Aurelius Commodus Antoninus immediately after the death of his father. His

cruelty is here indirectly contrasted with M. Aurelius' gentleness, a theme which is basically echoed by Eutropius. Dio, however, considered him weak and easily manipulated rather than naturally cruel (72.1.1).

2.   This was a rhetorical commonplace: cf. Sall. *Jug.* 85.22; Sen. *Contr.* 1.6.3; Juv. *Sat.* 8.138 ff.

3.   Cf. Eutrop. 8.15.1.   Dio (72.2.2) notes that Commodus compelled the Marcomanni, Quadi and Buri to accept peace on terms which were satisfactory to Rome.   However, both he, Herodian (1.6), the *H.A. (Comm.* 3.5-13.5) and the Epitomator (17.2-3) emphasize the emperor's indolence and preference for pleasures.   In 192 Commodus renamed all the months of the year with his own names and titles (Dio, *Epit.* 73.15.3; cf. *H.A. Comm.* 11.8-12.10).   Victor and Eutropius appear to be copying an error from the *Kaisergeschichte* by stating that the emperor gave his name to September since both Dio and the *H.A.* confirm that he gave his name to August, dislodging August to September, which would appeal to Commodus.

4.   Cf. *H.A. Comm.* 17.5-7, which notes Commodus' lack of public works and the inscription of his name on the works of others. According to the *H.A.* the Baths of Commodus were built by M. Aurelius Cleander, praetorian prefect c. 187-189, and originally named after their builder.

5.   Dio (72.1.1) and Herodian (I.8) are less negative about Commodus' character than the Latin sources.   All sources, however, agree that he had a distinct liking for gladiatorial combats: cf. Dio, 72.17.2; Herod. I.15.7; *H.A. Comm.* 5.5; 15.3; Eutrop. 8.15; *Epit.* 17.4; Oros. 7.16.2.

6.   This anecdote about Scaeva is unique to Victor.   It was probably not invented by Victor, as Dufraigne appears to indicate (*A.V.*, 117) but derived from Marius Maximus (*H.A. Comm.* 15.3) *via* the *Kaisergeschichte*.   The name Scaeva

means Lefty, clumsy or unfortunate.

7.   Dio (*loc. cit.*) and Herodian (I.15.1 ff.) state that Commodus started his "career" in the amphitheatre with beast hunts, a not ignoble pursuit for an emperor, according to Herodian.

8.   With Dufraigne (*A.V.*, 118) I believe that Victor wrote *proximus quisque; quippe*...and that the *quisque* disappeared in transmission.

9.   For his cruelty cf. *H.A. Comm.* 5.8; Oros. 7.16.4. Commodus ruled for 12 years, 9 months, 14 days (Dio, 72.22.4). Eutropius (8.15) gives 12 years, probably rounding off, as did Victor.

10.   For the poisoning cf. Dio (*loc. cit.*); *H.A. Comm.* 17.2; Herod. I.17.10; Eutrop. 8.15; *Epit.* 17.5. The attempt to poison Commodus took place during the night of December 31, 192 and the principal conspirators were Marcia, the emperor's mistress, Q. Aemilius Laetus, the praetorian prefect, and Eclectus, the chamberlain.

11.   Commodus was strangled by a young athlete named Narcissus in the early hours of January 1st, 193 (Dio, 72.22.5; Herod. *loc. cit.; H.A. Comm.* 17.3; *Epit.* 17.6).

12.   The senate did, indeed, declare Commodus a public enemy and ordered his name erased from public monuments: cf. Dio, 74.2.1; *H.A. Comm.* 20.5; Eutrop. 8.15; Oros. 7.16.4.

13.   Publius Helvius Pertinax was born in 126 and had a long, illustrious career. He had been consul (for the second time) with Commodus and urban prefect in 192 (Eutrop. 8.16; *H.A. Pert.* 4.3). Victor mistakenly gives him the *praenomen* Aulus, which appears to be a personal error on his part (H.W. Bird, *C.B.* 65, 1989, 96).

18

1.　　Cf. *Epit.* 18.3 ff.; *H.A. Pert.* 1.4; 12.1 ff.; 13.4; Dio, 74.1.1;
3.1; 3.4; 5.2; Herod II.1.3; 3.2; 4.4 ff. Victor and Eutropius
know virtually nothing about Pertinax (Nixon, *Caesares*, 249),
so their source, the *Kaisergeschichte*, provided very little
beyond what Victor states. M. Curius Dentatus and C.
Fabricius Luscinus were contemporaneous heroes of the early
third century B.C. who embodied the esteemed Roman virtues
of military prowess, incorruptibility and frugality (Eutrop. 2.9,
14; *De Vir. Ill.*33.1; 35.6, 8). For their mistaken linkage in
those sources and Claudian (*De Quart. Hon. 412-413*) *vid.* M.
Sage, *Hermes* 108, 1980, 94. Victor frequently incorporates
exempla from republican times, e.g. 3.14; 4.15; 11.12; 14.2;
33.11; 35.12; 37.2; 39.6; 42.22. Nixon (*loc. cit.*) argues that
"the early republican allusions probably go back to the
Kaisergeschichte", including this one, which may be correct,
but I am inclined to accept that some of the *exempla* were
added by Victor himself (Bird, *S.A.V.*, 100-103).

2.　　Cf. Eutrop. 8.16; *Epit.* 18.1 ff.; *H.A. D.J.* 3.7; *Clod. Alb.* 14.2;
14.6; *Pert.* 15.6 ff.; Dio (Xiph) 73.10.3; 74.8.4; Herod. II.4.4.
On March 28th, 193 Pertinax was assassinated by a group of
disgruntled praetorians who were instigated by Laetus, their
prefect. Julianus' complicity is not mentioned by Dio,
Herodian or the author of *H.A. Pert.* and may be disregarded
as part of subsequent Severan propaganda (Bird, *C.B.* 65, 1989,
95). Pertinax reigned 87 days, as Dio states, not 80 as both
Victor and Eutropius inform us. Finally, Victor again seizes
the opportunity to vilify the army (Eutropius more accurately
cites the praetorians) and indirectly contrasts it with its
republican counterpart.

19

1.　　Cf. *De Caes.* 20.1; Eutrop. 8.17; *Epit.* 19.1; *H.A. D.J.* 1.1-2.

A.D.E. Cameron (*C.R.* 15, 1965, 20-21) attributes the (*an Salvius*)? to a scribal error but since Eutropius also wrote Salvius I am more inclined to believe that this error was in the *Kaisergeschichte* (*C.B.* 65, 1989, 97). M. Didius Julianus was either the grandson or the nephew of L. Octavius Cornelius P. Salvius Julianus, the jurist and ordinary consul of 148 (cf. Syme, *Ammianus*, 92-93; Dufraigne, *A.V.*, 121, T.D. Barnes, *B.H.A.C. 1968/69*, 1970, 45-58). Victor's confusion of the two *Juliani* is probably a personal error (E. Hohl, *Historia* 4, 1955, 223).

2.   Cf. Eutrop. 8.17; Dio, 74.11; Herod. II.6.8; *H.A. D.J.* 2.6. On the day when Pertinax was assassinated the praetorians auctioned off the empire and Julianus offered more that his rival T. Flavius Sulpicianus, the urban prefect and father-in-law of Pertinax. Julianus was never prefect of the watch (P.K. Baillie-Reynolds, *The Vigiles of Imperial Rome*, Oxford, 1926, 34). The post was reserved for equestrians and Julianus was a senatorial. Victor alone makes this mistake and it appears to have been a personal error. In his day there were few distinctions between equestrian and senatorial careers. It is not completely certain when Julianus assumed office, the 28th or the 29th of March: cf. Herod. II.6.3; Ammianus, 26.6.14; Dio (Xiph.) 73.13.1; *H.A. D.J.* 3.8.

3.   Cf. Eutrop. 8.17; *Epit.* 19.1; *C.I.L.* VI.1401 = *I.L.S.* 412; *H.A. D.J.* 1.4 ff.; *Exc. Val.* 332; Herod II.6.6. Eutropius and the Epitomator seem to adhere closely to the wording of the *Kaisergeschichte* whereas Victor, here as elsewhere, elaborates for stylistic purposes.

4.   The *edictum tralaticium* of the praetors was codified between 129-138 by L. Octavius Cornelius P. Salvius Julianus and henceforth became known as the *edictum perpetuum*. It included the edicts of the *praetor peregrinus*, curule aediles and provincial governors (H.F. Jolowicz & B. Nicholas, *Historical Introduction to the Study of Roman Law*[3],

Cambridge, 1972, 357; O. Lenel, *Das Edictum Perpetuum*[3], Leipzig, 1929).

5. Character and culture are, according to Victor, the prime requirements of an emperor: *vid.* 8.7; 9.1; 10.1; 14.1; 16.1; 20.21; 39.26; 40.12; 42.1; 42.23; but cf. 39.28.

6. An edict of Hadrian, probably authored by Salvius Julianus, prescribed that parricides should be thrown to the beasts. Septimius Severus, according to the *H.A.* (*Sev.* 14.1), punished Narcissus, the murderer of Commodus, in this manner, though Dio (74.16.5) ascribes the execution to Didius Julianus (Dufraigne, *A.V.*, 121). The law of parricide covered the murder of magistrates and, of course, emperors (R.A. Bauman, *Impietas in Principem*, Munich, 1974, 218 ff.).

7. Dio (74.11.2) states that Julianus ruled 66 days, which agrees with the *H.A.* (*D.J.* 9.3) and *Chron a 354*, p. 147 M. He probably died on June 1st, 193. Eutrop. 8.17; *Epit.* 19.1; *Chron. Pasc.* 493 and Oros. 7.16 are all incorrect in maintaining that he ruled for seven months. Victor's stylistic modification of the *Kaisergeschichte* saved him from committing the same error.

8. L. Septimius Severus was governor of Pannonia when his troops acclaimed him emperor at Carnuntum in early April, 193. (Dio, 74.14.4; Herod II.9.2; *Epit.* 19.2; *H.A. D.J.* 52; *Clod. Alb.* 1.1; cf. *Sev.* 4.2; 5.1). This appears to be a personal error by Victor who confuses Severus with Niger (H.W. Bird, *C.B.* 65, 1989, 98). This Battle near the Milvian Bridge never took place. It is simply a reflection of the celebrated battle of 312 between Constantine and Maxentius. It is reported only by Victor, Eutropius (8.7) and Orosius (7.16.6) and was clearly in the *Kaisergeschichte* (Syme, *Ammianus* 106; Bird, *loc. cit.*), despite Dufraigne's supposition that it was Victor's creation and copied by the other two writers (*A.V.*, 122).

9.   Cf. Eutrop. 8.18; *Epit.* 19.3; Dio, 74.17.5; Herod II.12.7; *H.A. D.J.* 8.8; *Sev.* 5.9. Some surprisingly precise details are recorded by the Epitomator. Severus was at Interamna, 40 miles from Rome, when Julianus died.

20

1.   Victor apparently believed Severus' propaganda, *cf.* Eutrop. 8.18; Bird, *Eutropius*, 128-129. Severus confirmed Flavius Juvenalis as praetorian prefect to allay the fears of the praetorians (*H.A. Sev.* 6.5) won over the praetorian officers with bribes until he could reach Rome, when he disbanded the guard and replaced its members with men picked from the Danubian legions. Those praetorians who had helped murder Pertinax were executed (Dio, 75.1.1-2; 74.2.5-6; Herod. II.13.1 ff; *H.A. Sev.* 17.5). He thus rewarded those who had put him on the throne and simultaneously rid himself of a very suspect body of troops.

2.   Cf. *H.A. Sev.* 8.3. Apparently Severus promised to put no one to death or confiscate anyone's property without trial (Dio, 75.2.1; Herod. II.14.3), but Dio admits elsewhere that he "confiscated the property of most" (75.8.4) and executed Julius Solon (75.2.2). Pertinax was given a splendid state funeral, formally deified and endowed with a temple (Dio, 75.5.1 ff.; *H.A. D.J.* 7.8) though the senate had granted him deification even before Julianus' death (Dio, 74.17.4). The necessity of assuming the role of the avenger of Pertinax (Dio, 74.17.3; 75.1.1; 4.1 ff.; Herod. II.9.8 ff.; Eutrop. 8.18; Oros. 7.17) to offset the popularity of Pescennius Niger (Dio, 74.13.5; Herod. II.7.3; *H.A. D.J.* 4.7) was realized early on by Severus and his advisers and the elaborate funeral was presumably part of a propaganda campaign to advertise the pro-senatorial stance of the new regime.

3.   Cf. *H.A. Sev.* 17.5. Victor here confuses the *acta* of Didius

Julianus, *i.e.* his personal activities, with the *Edictum Perpetuum* of Salvius Julianus (*vid.* c. 19, note 1). The close correspondence between Victor and the *H.A.* here as well as the copying of Victor's personal error by the *H.A.* (E. Hohl, *Historia* 4, 1955, 223) has caused even the sceptical Dufraigne (*A.V.*, 122) to find it difficult not to admit the direct influence of Victor on the *H.A.* at this juncture. It is now generally accepted (Syme, *Ammianus*, 106-107).

4.   In c. 19.3 Victor had maintained the primacy of character over culture (note 5). For his emphasis on these two topics *vid.* C.G. Starr, *A.H.R.* 61, 1955-56, 583; Bird, *S.A.V.*, 71-80.

5.   For a reconstruction of Victor's background and career *vid.* Bird, *S.A.V.*, 5-15; Dufraigne, *A.V.*, IX-XV.

6.   Juvenal (*Sat.* vii. 148-149) satirizes Africa as the nurse of advocates: cf. Stat. *Silv.* iv.5, where Septimius Severus' granduncle, the celebrated orator, is praised. Severus himself, however, was the only African to become emperor (Eutrop. 8.18; T.D. Barnes, *Historia* 16, 1967, 87), which may account for the pride Victor feels for him and the extensive account of his reign. Herodian (III.15.2) considered him unsurpassed in his military accomplishments, as did the Epitomator (20.5), and the *H.A.* listed "Severus the African" among his top twelve excellent emperors (*Aurel.* 42.4).

7.   Severus died at York on February 4th, 211   (Dio, *Epit.* 77.15.2) at the age of sixty-five (Dio, *Epit.* 77.17.4), after ruling 17 years, 8 months, 3 days. Cf. Herod. III.15.3; Eutrop. 8.19; Epit. 20.1; 20.10; *H.A. Sev.* 19.1; 22.1; *Pesc. Nig.* 5.1. The *H.A.* writes that he was eighty-nine at his death, a gross exaggeration, especially as the author knew when Severus was born (*Sev.* 1.3). Severus may have been trying to deceive Albinus about his age initially to make the other think that he had a better chance to succeed (J. Balty, *Essai d'iconographie de l'empereur Clodius Albinus*, Brussels, 1966, 12-15), but it

seems more likely that the author of the *H.A.* simply fabricated on the basis of Victor's phrase *exacta aetate*.

8. Cf. *H.A. Sev.* 18.7. This *bon mot* may well have been inserted here by Victor: it was a rhetorical commonplace; cf. Sen. *N.Q.* 18.4 (citing Livy on Caesar); *Epit.* 1.28 (on Augustus) and Lydus, *De mag.* II.2.3 (on Augustus). The account of the *H.A.* seems to be an attempt to explain Victor's statement.

9. Cf. Dio, 76.16.4; Zos. I.8.4. M. Platnauer, *The Life and Reign of the Emperor Lucius Septimius Severus*, Oxford, 1918, 181-182, states: "from the principate of Severus, then, date the first laws against abortion (*Dig.* xlvii.11.4), laws protecting minors (Ulp. *Dig.* xxvii.9 - the *Oratio Severi: Cod.* iv.26.1), laws ensuring a wife's claim on money she brings to her husband at marriage (*Cod.* i.5.23.1; v.181). The rigour of certain enactments whereby children suffered for the sins of fathers was abated (*Dig.* i.2.2), and a similar mitigation was introduced in the enforcement of the *Lex Iulia Maiestatis* (*Dig.* xlviii.4.5). On the other hand, such laws as *de adulteriis* and the *Papia Poppaea* were administered with an increase of stringency (*Dig.* xlviii.5.14.3,8; Dio, 76.16.4)." Victor implies that the nobility considered Severus excessive in *corrigendis moribus* with respect to the law on abortion and the stricter enforcement of the *de adulteriis* and *Papia Poppaea*. It is more likely, however, that Severus' reputation with the senatorial aristocracy was irreparably damaged by his elimination of the supporters of Julianus, Niger and Albinus, his punishment of corrupt judges, and the favour he showed to equestrians at the expense of the senatorials.

10. The relationship between *honestas* and *voluptas* was regularly discussed by philosophers and moralists in the ancient word (Dufraigne, *A.V.*, 123-124, with citations). Victor's inclinations lean heavily towards the Stoic interpretation but there are no coherent philosophical views in the *De Caesaribus*.

11.   C. Pescennius Niger had been governor of Syria since 191 and was acclaimed emperor by his troops in April, 193. He was defeated at Perinthus, Cyzicus and Nicaea and finally crushed at Issus in late April or early May, 194. While fleeing to Parthia he was captured near Antioch and executed. On the sources *vid.* A. Birley, *Septimius Severus: The African Emperor*, New York, 1972, 172-188. Victor's error that he was killed at Cyzicus, shared by Eutropius (8.18), Orosius (7.17) and the *H.A. (Sev.* 9.1, *Pesc. Nig.* 5.8) is contradicted by the contemporary sources (Dio, *Epit.* 75.6.4 ff.; Herod. III.2.2 ff.) and may be attributed to their common source, the *Kaisergeschichte* (H.W. Bird, *C.B.* 65, 1989, 98).

12.   Decimus Clodius Albinus was governor of Britain in 193 and also made a play for the throne. Severus cleverly placated him with the title of Caesar until he could eliminate Niger in the spring of 194. In 195 attempts were made to assassinate him and he was declared a public enemy. He then seized west and central Gaul and made Lyons his base. Defeated there on February 19th, 197 he was killed and the city sacked (Eutrop. 8.18; *H.A. Sev.* 6.9; 10.1; 12.6; *Clod. Alb.* 7.1; 8.1-12.2; Dio, *Epit.* 74.15.2; 76.4.1; 6.8; Herod. II.15.1-5; III.5.2-8; 7.1-7; Birley, *op. cit.,* 189-195).

13.   Eutropius (8.18) and Orosius (7.17.2) state that Niger rebelled in Egypt and Syria, the *H.A. (Sev.* 5.8) that he seized power through the Syrian legions, reflecting a common and correct source. Victor, unfortunately, had located Severus in Syria and one mistake leads to another. Consequently he accorded the anachronistic title of *dux Aegypti* (which originated a century later) to Niger (Bird, *loc. cit.*).

14.   Eutropius (8.18) and the *H.A. (Clod. Alb.* 1.1) relate the same story, which is clearly untrue and may have been part of subsequent Severan propaganda. It was presumably in the *Kaisergeschichte* (Bird, *loc. cit.*).

15.   Cf. Eutrop. 8.18; *H.A. Pesc. Nig.* 2.1, Albinus, already Caesar, had himself proclaimed Augustus in Britain and crossed over into Gaul (Herod. III.5.2-8; 7.1-7).

16.   I read *Multorum* for *Horum*. This conforms with the text of *H.A. Sev.* 17.7, which is plainly copied from the *De Caesaribus*. For Severus' cruelty cf. Eutrop. 8.18; Oros. 7.17; Dio, 75.7.4; Herod. II.10.1; 14.3; III.4.7; 8.2.

17.   Cf. *H.A. Sev.* 14.3; 17.6; Eutrop. 8.18. He assumed the name Pertinax for political reasons (Herod. II.10.1) and dropped it when it had served its purpose.

18.   Cf. *H.A. Sev.* 17.7. I read *quidam hostium* here which conforms with *quidam ex hostibus* in the *H.A.*

19.   Cf. *H.A. Sev.* 17.7. The *H.A.* explains what Victor had left unsaid, either for stylistic reasons or because of loyalty towards the African emperor. Victor's comment that in times of civil war geographical location is a major factor in the choice of sides may be a personal reflection by him and therefore written soon after Julian had been acclaimed Augustus at Paris in February, 360. Florentius, Julian's disaffected praetorian prefect, had arrived in Sirmium by the end of that month and discussions of the situation must have taken place: cf. T.D. Barnes *Phoenix* 39, 1985, 147; Bird, *S.A.V.,* 10.

20.   Julian behaved differently in pardoning the leading people in Aquileia (except for Nigrinus, Romulus and Sabostius) who were driven by *necessitas* rather than *voluntas* to fight against him (Ammianus, 21.12.20). This passage is corrupt and I prefer to read *nihil: boni cum sanctique....* The concept that power is granted to protect rather than to punish is in Seneca (*De Clem.* 1.26.5) and in advice given to Augustus by Livia (Dio, 55.20.2), as Dufraigne notes (*A.V.,* 125-126).

21. These exact words are used by the *H.A.* (*Sev.* 17.8), which, however, omitted Victor's apology for Severus. According to E. Hohl (*Historia* 4, 1955, 227) its author did not share Victor's regional patriotism and lists forty-one senators put to death without a trial by Severus (*Sev.* 13.1 ff.).

22. In this personal intervention Victor may well be thinking of Magnentius (41.23), Nepotianus (42.6), Silvanus (42.14) and Julian. His loathing of civil conflicts parallels that of Eutropius (Bird, *Eutropius*, xxvii ff.).

23. Cf. *H.A. Sev.* 17.8; Eutrop. 8.18; Herod. III.15.2. Victor, after his personal interjection, returns to his source. The *H.A.*, which is still copying him, adds the word "almost" which is more correct since Severus was unable to capture Hatra (Dio, 76.11.1 ff.; Herod. III.9.3 ff.), and suffered some minor defeats by Albinus (*H.A. Sev.* 10.7-11.2; *Clod. Alb.* 11.1).

24. Cf. *H.A. Sev.* 18.1; Eutrop. 8.18. Abgarus was King of the Osrhoenians (Dio, 77.12.1; Herod. III.9.3), not of the Persians and was confirmed in his kingdom probably in 197. Furthermore the Persians did not overthrow the Parthians until 224 or a little later when the Sassanids replaced the Arsacids. Neither Eutropius nor the *H.A.*, when it followed its other sources (*Sev.* 9.9), makes this mistake, so it may well have been Victor's own.

25. Cf. Eutrop. 8.18; *H.A. Sev.* 9.9; 18.1; Festus, 21; Hieron. *ab Abr.* 2214. Victor here refers to the Mesopotamian or Skenite Arabs (Zos. I.8.5) whom Severus reduced in 197. They had probably been encouraged, along with the Osrhoeni and Adiabeni, by Vologaeses to use the opportunities presented by the Roman civil wars to enlarge their territories.

26. Cf. Eutrop. 8.18.4; Oros. 7.17.3; *H.A. Sev.* 9.9; 18.1; Dio, 75.1.1-3; Dufraigne, *A.V.*, 127. The latter mistakenly writes that Eutropius says nothing of Adiabene. This lay east of the

Tigris, had long been a Parthian vassal state and could only be
forced to acknowledge Roman suzerainty while the Parthians
were too feeble to resist.

27.   For the titles *vid.* Eutrop. 8.18.4; *H.A. Sev.* 9.10; Herod.
III.9.12; *I.L.S.* 417; *C.R.E.B.M.* V, 79,86, 107-109, 118-121,
131-133, 157-158, 326, 555-557, 563. They were in 195 and
198.

28.   Cf. Eutrop. 8.19; *Epit.* 20.4; *H.A. Sev.* 18.2; Oros. 7.17.7.
Here it appears that Victor, Eutropius and the *Epitomator*
followed the *Kaisergeschichte* while the *H.A.* copied Victor,
and Orosius derived his incorrect figure of 132 miles from
Eutropius. Severus restored Hadrian's Wall, which had been
damaged in the Caledonian wars when Albinus weakened its
garrison to make his play for the empire. It was 76 Roman
miles long and its western section of 31 miles was a turf
rampart (*vallum*) which Severus inspected at Carlisle
(Luguvalium), as the *H.A.* states (*Sev.* 22.4).

29.   Cf. Eutrop. 8.18; *Epit.* 20.8; *H.A. Sev.* 1.1; 18.3; Festus, 21.2;
Herod. II.9.2. Leptis Magna was in Africa Proconsularis at
this period, but after Diocletian's time it lay in Tripolitana.
Severus extended the frontier by forcing back the desert tribes
and built the *Limes Tripolitanus.* He also reconstructed the
headquarters of the *Legio III Augusta* at Lambaesis.

30.   Cf. *H.A. Sev.* 18.4 (from Victor); Zos. I.8.2.

31.   Cf. *H.A. Sev.* 18.6; Tert. *Apol.* 2.8. Brigandage had become
endemic at this period and Severus had great difficulty in
capturing the notorious bandit Felix Bulla in Italy and the latter
seemingly had contacts in high places (Dio, 76.10.1 ff.).
Victor may also be making an oblique reference to
contemporary conditions; cf. *De Caes.* 42.24-25.

32.   Cf. Eutrop. 8.19.1; *Epit.* 20.8; *H.A. Sev.* 18.5; 1.1; 3.7; *Get.*

2.2; Dio, 76.16.1-17.2; Phil. *V.S.* 2.26. The *H.A.* drew upon Victor for 18.5 but apparently shared a different source with the *Epitomator* for his other information. Dio is more cautious about Severus' cultural accomplishments but there seems little reason to doubt that he was well-educated.

33.   Cf. *H.A. Sev.* 3.2; 18.6; *Clod Alb.* 7.1; Dio, 75.7.3; Herod. II.9.4. If Victor had, in fact, read Severus' autobiography it must have been many years earlier for otherwise he would not have committed so many blunders: cf. Dufraigne, *A.V.*, 129.

34.   *Vid.* note 9. This superficial mention of Severus' very important legislation can only be explained by lack of information in Victor's source. Eutropius is silent on the matter.

35.   Cf. Eutrop. 8.20; *Epit.* 21.5; *De Caes,* 21.3; *H.A. Sev.* 18.8; *Carac.* 10.1. Julia Domna (*P.I.R.*[2] IV.I.663), second wife of Severus and mother of Caracalla and Geta, was investigated on trumped up charges of adultery by the praetorian prefect C. Fulvius Plautianus (Dio, 75.15.6). She was probably not guilty of adultery or conspiracy against her husband but may have been compelled to cause the fall of Plautianus by means of a plot which included Caracalla and his tutor, Euodus (Dio, 76.3.1 ff.). Herodian (III.11.1 ff.) accepts what was presumably the official version, a plot by Plautianus against Severus.

36.   Cf. Sall. *Cat.* 59.4. The *H.A.(Sev.* 18.9-10) reproduces Victor's account almost verbatim. Severus had long been afflicted with gout (*H.A. Sev.* 16.6) or arthritis (Herod. III.14.2) and had to be conveyed by litter on the final British campaign (Dio, 76.13.4), and plots were hatched by Caracalla against him (Dio, 76.14.1 ff.; Herod. III.15.1-2; *H.A. Carac.* 11.3-4). Caracalla was originally called Julianus Bassianus after his maternal grandfather and was born at Lyons in April, 188 (Dio, 78.6.5). His nickname Caracalla, or Caracallus, was the

name of a modified Gallic cloak which he made popular at Rome (*H.A. Sev.* 21.11; *Carac.* 9.7-8; Dio, 78.3.3; cf. Herod. IV.7.3). The *bon mot* here is one of three in Victor's description of Severus (20.6 and 20.29). All are reproduced by the *H.A.* and no other extant source, which is persuasive evidence that the *H.A.* borrowed directly from the *De Caesaribus.*

37.   Cf. Eutrop. 8.19; *H.A. Sev.* 19.1; Herod. III.15.2-3. Severus died at York on February 4th, 211 (Dio, 76.15.2), after ruling for 17 years, 8 months and 3 days (Dio, 76.17.4). The *H.A.* clearly follows Victor here, and in its account for *Get.* 2.2-4. Two particulars, however, must have come from a different source, Severus' title *Britannicus* and the gift of oil made to Rome (*Sev.* 18.2-3) which Victor mentions much later (41.19). In view of the close correspondence between *Sev.* 19.2; *Carac.* 1.1; Eutrop, 8.19.1-2 and *Epit.* 20.3 ff. the author of the H.A. possibly reverted to the *Kaisergeschichte* which appears to have contained these details: cf. A. Chastagnol, *B.H.A.C. 1966/67* (1968), 58, who argues that the *H.A.* used Eutropius. York was made the capital of Lower Britain by Severus when he divided the province and was the H.Q. of the northern command and the *Legio VI Victrix.*

38.   Cf. Eutrop. 8.18; *H.A. Sev.* 18.11. Severus' family was equestrian but a relative, C. Septimius Severus, was proconsul of Africa in 173/4 and Severus served under him as legate and presumably benefitted from his patronage. Victor possibly exaggerates Severus' humble beginnings in order to liken them to his own (cf. 20.5-6). A full account of Severus' early life and career are given in *H.A. Sev.* 1.4 ff., but some of the details are suspect.

39.   Cf. *H.A. Sev.* 18.11. Famous last words and striving for effect by the use of *sententiae* are customary in ancient historiography and a legacy of rhetorical education, but some emperors, like Vespasian and Severus, seem to have attracted

them (J. Straub, *B.H.A.C. 1963/4* (1965), 171-172).

40. Cf. Eutrop. 8.19; *Epit.* 20.3; *H.A. Sev.* 19.2. The tomb of Marcus was the *Mausoleum Hadriani* on the right bank of the Tiber, now the Castel S. Angelo, completed in 139 by Antoninus Pius, in which M. Aurelius and the Antonines were buried (S.B. Platner and T. Ashby, *A Topographical Dictionary of Ancient Rome*, Oxford, 1929, 336-338). Severus was cremated at York and his remains taken to Rome for a state funeral (Dio, 76.15.3; Herod, III.15.7; IV.2.1-11; *H.A. Sev.* 24.2).

41. Cf. *H.A. Sev.* 10.5-6; 19.1; *Get.* 2.2-4. In April, 195 Severus "adopted" M Aurelius Antoninus as his father and Commodus as his brother. He also deified Commodus (Dio, 75.7.4; cf. 76.9.4). The reasons were political, like the adoption of the name Pertinax earlier, for Severus thereby acquired a semblance of dynastic legitimacy. Caracalla assumed the name Antoninus (*H.A. Sev.* 10.3; Eutrop. 8.19) at Viminacium (Kostalac) on April 6th, 196, but Geta never received it (Eutrop. *loc. cit.*; *H.A. Get.* 6.9; Syme, *Emperors*, 60).

42. Cf. Eutrop. 8.18; H.A. *Get.* 2.4; *Carac*, 8.2. Hadrian instituted the *advocati fisci* to deal with disputes between the *fiscus* and the public. The four citations here all derive ultimately from the *Kaisergeschichte* (Syme, *Emperors*, 81) and are combined with demonstrably false details, consequently it is highly unlikely that Severus ever held this position (T.D. Barnes, *Historia* 16, 1967, 91-92).

43. Cf. Herod. IV.3.1; Dio, 77.1.4.

44. Cf. Eutrop. 8.18. P. Septimius Geta (b. March 7th, 189) died in his mother's arms, probably in December, 211, after being falsely accused of plotting against Caracalla, (Dio, 77.2.1 ff.; *H.A. Sev.* 21.6.7; *Carac.* 2.4). As Victor indicates, he was presumably named after his paternal grandfather: cf. *H.A. Sev.*

112

1.2; *Get.* 2.1. The two brothers were antithetical in character (Dio, 77, 1.4; Herod, IV.3.2-4).

45.   Cf. *H.A. Carac.* 8.5-6; *Sev.* 21.8. Aemilius Papinianus was the most celebrated of Roman jurisprudents (Jolowicz and Nicholas, *op. cit.*, 391). He was appointed in 205, dismissed probably in 211, and killed in 212 (L.L. Howe, *The Praetorian Prefect from Commodus to Diocletian*, Chicago, 1942, 71-72). The *H.A.* retails the *bon mot* with elaborations.

46.   Cf. *H.A. Carac.* 8.7; *Get.* 6.3. Dio (77.4.1a) states that Caracalla had Papinian executed to please the praetorians. The jurist had been *a libellis* (State Secretary for Justice) before becoming Praetorian Prefect (*Dig.* 20.5.12). Severus, after the fall of Plautianus in 205, created two prefects, A. Marcius Laetus and Papinian. The latter became the emperor's chief Minister of Justice. By the mid-fourth century the prefect's responsibilities had changed and it is possible that neither Victor nor his source, the *Kaisergeschichte*, understood the implications of the original anecdote in Marius Maximus. On the other hand Victor, followed by the *H.A.*, may have been right in indignantly rejecting the whole fable (Syme, *Emperors*, 149).

21

1.   Cf. *H.A. Sev.* 21.11; *Carac.* 9.7; *Macr.* 5.8; *Epit.* 21.2; Dio, 78.3.3; c. 20, note 36. Victor and the *H.A.* are the only extant sources to mention that this Gallic cloak was called an Antoniniana. It was prescribed as the regular dress for the soldiers.

2.   Cf. *H.A. Carac.* 10.6, also 5.6; 6.5 (an error); Dio, 77.13.3 ff. It was in Caracalla's reign that the name Alamanni first occurs. It denotes a confederacy of the Semnones and other tribes who originally lived west of the Elbe and settled in the *Agri*

Decumates in c. 260. In October, 213 Caracalla defeated them on the River Main. Victor alone gives the location, but it is confirmed by *C.I.L.* VI.2086.

3. Cf. Eutrop. 8.20; Oros. 7.18.2; Herod, IV.3.4. Only Victor is positive about his character and accomplishments, perhaps because Caracalla was the son of Septimius Severus. Eutropius, also following the *Kaisergeschichte*, describes Caracalla more accurately. He had his father's disposition but was somewhat harsher and more menacing.

4. Cf. *H.A. Carac.* 10.1 ff.; Eutrop. 8.20; *Epit.* 21.4. The popular story about his relationship with his mother, Julia Domna, had already appeared in Herodian (IV.9.3), but the false report that she was actually his stepmother stems from a separate historical tradition accepted neither by Herodian nor by Dio (78.24.1). The *Kaisergeschichte* was clearly responsible for this account, probably stating as fact what had appeared as rumour in Marius Maximus. The *H.A.* seems to have elaborated on the anecdote, which included the popular saying "*si libet, licet*" (Cic. *Pro Quinct.* 30.94; Vell. II.100.3. For other discussions *vid.* J. Babelon, *Impératrices Syriennes*, Paris, 1957, 65; W. Reusch, *Klio* 24, 1931, 59; Dufraigne, *A.V.*, 133.

5. Cf. *H.A. Carac.* 9.10. But the *H.A.* then criticizes his source for making this statement, observing that Commodus had already celebrated the rites of Isis (*Comm.* 9.4; *Pesc. Nig.* 6.9). Nevertheless Caracalla did construct a Temple of Serapis on the Quirinal and decorated the one of Serapis and Isis which already stood on the Campus Martius (Platner and Ashby, *op. cit.*, 283-285).

6. Cf. Eutrop. 8.20; *H.A. Carac.* 9.4; 9.9; *Heliog.* 17.8. The new road was the *Via Appia Nova*, running parallel to the Appian Way but three times as wide and giving access to the *Thermae Antoninianae* or Baths of Caracalla. These monumental baths were begun by Caracalla in 211-212, dedicated in 216 and

completed under Elagabalus and Alexander Severus (Platner and Ashby, *op. cit.*, 520-524, 560; E. Nash, *A Pictorial Dictionary of Ancient Rome II*, London, 1962, 85, 434-441, figs. 1230-1241).

7.   Cf. Eutrop. 8.20; *Epit.* 21.6; *H.A. Carac.* 7.1, Oros. 7.18.2; Herod, IV.13.3 ff.; Zos. 1.10; Dio, 78.5.1 ff. Edessa was originally the capital of Osrhoene, which became incorporated in Mesopotomia in 216 when Caracalla dispossessed Abgarus. On April 8th of 217, as he was approaching Carrhae, he was assassinated by Martialis, a praetorian soldier, who was probably instigated by his prefect M. Opellius Macrinus. Both Eutropius and Dio state that Caracalla reigned 6 years, 2 months.

8.   Cf. Eutrop 8.20; *Epit.* 21.7; Festus, 21; *H.A. Carac.* 9.1. Victor adds the touch "amid public grief" to the simpler statement in the *Kaisergeschichte* (*vid.* Eutropius). In reality Caracalla was so unpopular at Rome that he was buried quietly at night (Dio, 78.9.1).

22

1.   Cf. Eutrop. 8.21; *Epit.* 22; *H.A. Carac.* 8.10; *Macr.* 2.1; 2.5; 5.1; *Diad.* 6.9; Zos. I.10. Dio (78.14.2) implies and Herodian (IV.14.2) states that the empire was first offered to Adventus, the other praetorian prefect. M. Opellius Macrinus (Opilius and Diadumenus occur only in Victor, Eutropius, Orosius and the *H.A.*, therefore they derive from the *Kaisergeschichte*) was from Caesarea in Mauretania and was of humble ancestry. He acted as Plautianus' steward, as superintendent of traffic on the Flaminian Way and as procurator before being promoted to the praetorian prefecture in 214.

2.   Cf. *H.A. Diad.* 1.1; 6.10; *Macr.* 3.8; *Heliog.* 3.1; Dio, 78.19.1. The *H.A.* knows that Macrinus had his son called Antoninus

for political reasons (*Macr.* 3.8-9). In *Macr.* 4.2 the *H.A.* names an Aurelius Victor as a source and in 4.4 names a Festus. The former mention renders the borrowing from Victor indisputable, according to Dufraigne (*A.V.*, 135), the latter is surely a mendacious insertion of the name of another author who wrote an abbreviated History of Rome in 370.

3. Cf. *H.A. Diad.* 8.2. Dio refutes this (78.11.1-3), though he does enumerate Macrinus' faults (78.13.2; 14.1; 15.1 ff.; 27.1; 41.1 ff.) as does Herodian (IV.12.2; V.2.3 ff.). *H.A. Macr.* 11.1; 13.2 seem to be fictitious concoctions, possibly based upon Victor's cursory and reckless statement.

4. Victor's reason is insufficient and partially corrected by the Epitomator (22). Macrinus fell because of the dissatisfaction of the army and the proximity of Julia Maesa, Septimius Severus' sister-in-law, and her grandsons Elagabalus and Alexander Severus. Macrinus was defeated on June 8th, 218, captured about nine days later at Chalcedon, and killed on about the 22nd at Archelais (Dio, 78.39.1 ff.; Herod. V.4.7 ff.; *H.A. Macr.* 10.3; 15.1). He ruled 14 months less three days (Dio, 78.41.4).

23

1. M. Aurelius Antoninus, originally called Varius Avitus, was the son of Sex. Varius Marcellus and Julia Soaemias, the niece of Julia Domna and daughter of Julia Maesa and Julius Avitus (Dio, 78.30.2 ff.; Herod V.3.2 ff.). Dio, Eutropius (8.22) and the *H.A. (Heliog.* 1.4 ff.) state the Elagabalus was the *reputed* son of Caracalla: Victor and the Epitomator (23.1) incorrectly call him the actual son of Caracalla, accepting as fact the rumour spread by Julia Maesa to suborn the army.

2. Cf. *H.A. Heliog.* 2.3; Eutrop. 8.22; *Epit.* 23.2. Macrinus did not deal harshly with Caracalla's relatives and was lenient with

Julia Domna (Dio, 78.23.2). Furthermore Elagabalus' connection with the god was inherited from Julius Bassianus, his great-grandfather. The asylum story in Victor and the *H.A.* is therefore fictitious. Elagabalos (Dio, 78.31.1) or Elaigabalos (Herod. V.3.4 ff.), was the patron god of Emesa, worshipped under the form of a black conical stone. He is probably to be connected with Elâh-Gabal, the Creator God and Sun God of the region. The incorrect form Heliogabalus is only in Victor, the *Epitome* and the *H.A.* and presumably stems from the *Kaisergeschichte*, which may well be responsible for later generations knowing this emperor by his nickname rather than by his official name. He was only fourteen years old when acclaimed emperor.

3.   Cf. *H.A. Heliog.* 3.4. He transported the sacred black stone of Elagabal to Rome and built two temples for the god, one on the Palatine, dedicated in 221, the other in a suburb of the city (Herod. V.6.6-7; Platner and Ashby, *op. cit.*, 199).

4.   Cf. *H.A. Heliog.* 5.2 ff.; Eutrop. 8.22; *Epit.* 23.3; Dio, 80.11.1 ff.; 80.13.4; 80.15.3; Herod. V.5.7. Elagabalus placed his god before Jupiter, circumcised himself (or worse), had many of his companions mutilated and married a Vestal Virgin, thereby offending centuries of Roman customs. Contrary to Dufraigne (*A.V.*, 136) I read *foedarum* for *ferendarum*. Cf. *H.A. Alex.* 1.2; *Heliog.* 1.5; 64.4-5; Eutrop. 8.23; *Epit.* 23.4. However Herodian (V.7.1) writes that Julia Maesa convinced Elagabalus to adopt Alexander as Caesar in 221. For the latter's popularity *vid.* Herod. V.8.2; *H.A. Heliog.* 13.3.

5.   Cf. Eutrop. 8.22; *Epit.* 23.1; 23.5; *H.A. Heliog.* 17.1 ff.; Dio, 80.3.3; Herod. V.8.8 ff. Eutropius and the *Epitomator* inform us that Elagabalus ruled 2 years, 8 months: Dio gives 3 years, 9 months, 8 days. Victor probably rounded out the erroneous number he found in the *Kaisergeschichte*. Elagabalus died on March 13th, 222.

24

1.   Cf. Eutrop. 8.23; *H.A. Alex.* 12.1; 13.5; Dio, 78.30.3; 80.1.1;
      Herod. V.8.10. The new emperor was the son of Julia Avita
      Mammaea and Gessius Marcianus. His original name was
      Alexianus (Herod. V.3.3) and/or Bassianus (Dio, 79.30.3; cf.
      80.17.2 ff.). He was born at Arca Caesarea, near Emesa, in
      Syria on October 1st, 208 or 209. Acclaimed Augustus by the
      praetorians on March 13th, 222 he was probably recognized by
      the senate the following day. After being adopted as Caesar
      in 221, he was known as M. Aurelius Alexander. Upon his
      accession he accepted the name M. Aurelius Severus
      Alexander, which connected him with the Antonines and the
      Severi.

2.   He was twelve or thirteen years old when he became emperor
      and his youth is emphasized by both Victor and Eutropius.
      For his carefully-conceived education *vid.* Herod. V.7.5 ff.;
      H.A., Alex. 3.

3.   Cf. Eutrop. 8.23; *H.A. Alex.* 55.1; Festus, 22; Jerome, G.C.S.
      47.215; Herod. VI.2.1 ff. Victor's chronology is faulty here.
      In 230 Artaxerxes (Ardashir) invaded Mesopotamia and the
      following year Alexander marched against him and retook
      Mesopotamia in 232, though the war ended in a stalemate.
      Victor, Eutropius and Festus incorrectly cite Xerxes as the
      Persian monarch: that error was in the *Kaisergeschichte.*

4.   In 233 Alexander celebrated a triumph (*H.A. Alex.* 56.1;
      Festus, 22; *C.R.E.B.M.* VI.82-83) then hurried north to face the
      Germans who had been encouraged to raid Gaul while the
      emperor and detachments of the western army were engaged
      in the east (Herod. VI.7.6; *H.A. Alex.* 59.1-2).

5.   Cf. Eutrop. 8.23; *H.A. Alex.* 12.4; 59.4-6. For a quite different
      version cf. Herod. VI.4.7; 7.10; 8.3; Dio, 80.3.1. Alexander's
      severitas was a myth (Herod. VI.1.10; 9.8), attributable to a

play on his name (cf. *H.A. Alex.* 25.2; 59.6). The *H.A.* seems to have copied "(from which he had even earned the surname Severus)" from Victor here.

6.   Cf. Eutrop. 8.23; Oros. 7.18.8; *H.A. Alex.* 59.6; Herod. VI.9.1-8. Alexander and his mother were killed at Bretzenheim near Mainz on March 21st or 22nd, 235. The village presumably contained a garrison of British auxiliaries. The verbal similarities between Victor and the *H.A.* at this point indicate that the latter used the former, but the *H.A.* avoids Victor's error of translating Alexander directly from the east to Gaul, so presumably its author had the *Kaisergeschichte* before him too, a conclusion supported by comparison with Eutropius, *Alex.* 26.9 and Jerome, *G.C.S.* 47.215.

7.   Cf. Eutrop. 8.23; *H.A. Alex.* 25.3 ff. *Celebrio* is meaningless and should be amended perhaps to *celebrius* or *celebratione*. The building could have been the *Nympheum* (Platner and Ashby, *op. cit.*, 363; *C.R.E.B.M.* VI.63-64) or one of several undertaken or renovated by Alexander.

8.   Cf. Eutrop. 8.23; *H.A. Alex.* 26.9; Herod. VI.1.10; *Epit.* 24.4-5. Herodian and the Epitomator condemn his subservience to his mother.

9.   Cf. Eutrop. 8.23; Festus, 22; *H.A. Alex.* 26.5; *Pesc. Nig.* 7.4; Oros. 7.18.8. The celebrated jurist Domitius Ulpianus' career is difficult to determine (Dufraigne, *A.V.*, 139-140.). He was prefect of the grain supply on March 31st, 222 (*Cod. Just.* VIII.37.4) but by December 31st he had become praetorian prefect (*Cod. Just.* IV.65.4; Dio, 80.1.1; Zos. I.11.3). He was killed the following year by the praetorians. Perhaps Alexander, before he became Augustus, appointed Ulpian secretary for petitions (*a libellis*), for which *vid.* Syme (*Emperors*, 147-151). The careers of both jurists are suspect (Syme, *B.H.A.C. 1968/69*, 1970, 309 ff.).

10.   Actually he ruled for 13 years and 8 or 9 days: cf. Eutrop. 8.23; *H.A. Alex.* 60.1. Herodian's 14 years is incorrect (VI.9.8).

11.   Victor plainly realized that Alexander's reign marked a watershed for the Roman Empire: cf. *De Caes.* 1.1; 11.12-13; *H.A. Alex.* 64.1 ff. Consequently he pauses and gives the reader an insight into his way of thinking. The phraseology and sentiment, however, are Sallustian, cf. *Cat.* 8.1 ff.; 10.1 ff.; *Jug.* 67.2; Ps. Sall., *1 ad Caes.* 1.1; *2 ad Caes.* 1.1. For virtue as a defensive wall cf. Juv. *Sat.* X. 363-6. M. Cary (*A History of Rome*², London, 1954, 779) concurs with Victor in believing that the chief proximate cause of Rome's collapse in the west was "the preoccupation of the Roman garrisons in the third century with the game of emperor-making."

25

1.   C. Julius Verus Maximinus probably came from a village near Oescus, a military colony in the Treballian district of Thrace, which was incorporated in Lower Moesia by Domitian in 86. He was born in 172 or 173 and rose through the ranks of the Danubian army to become prefect of recruits (Herod. VI.8.1 ff.; Zon. XII.16; *H.A. Max.* 1.4 ff.; *Epit.* 25.1; Zos I.13; *Chron. Pasc.* 501; Syme, *Emperors*, 179-183).

2.   Cf. Eutrop. 9.1; *H.A. Max.* 8.1; *Epit.* 24.3; 25.1; Herod, VI.8.3 ff.; VII.1.1; Zos. I.13.3. Maximinus' humble origins are stressed by all writers, but Victor also lays emphasis on his lack of education. This links Maximinus with Victor's final comment in c. 24.

3.   Cf. Eutrop. 9.1; *H.A. Max.* 8.1; Herod. VI.9.5. Maximinus was acclaimed Augustus by the troops on March 21st or 22nd, 235 and accepted by the senate on March 25th (*C.I.L.* VI.2001; 2009).

120

4.   Maximinus' homonymous son was made Caesar probably in 236 (*P.I.R.*², IV, I.620).

26

1.   Cf. Eutrop. 9.1; Herod. VII.2.1 ff.; *H.A. Max.* 11.7 ff.; *Max-Balb.* 15.7. Though the *H.A.* is heavily indebted to Herodian at this juncture, its author had clearly read Victor and the *Kaisergeschichte* (or Eutropius) for he notes their apparent confusion over the length of Maximinus' reign (*Max-Balb.* 15.7), and the fact that they know of only two Gordians (*Gord.* 2.1), and chastizes them for their ignorance. The matter was registered by Dessau (*op. cit.*, 372) and perplexed Emmann (*op. cit.*, 339). Victor clarifies the length of their reign in 27.5. Maximinus won victories over the Germans across the Rhine near Mainz and subsequently against other Germans and Sarmatians across the Danube (*C.R.E.B.M.* VI.224; *I.L.S.* 488-490, 2308, 2309; *C.I.L.* III.3336).

2.   Cf. Eutrop. 9.2. In late March, 238 the governor of Africa, M. Antonius Gordianus, was proclaimed emperor at Thysdrus (El Djem in Tunisia) in an uprising of wealthy young landowners and tenant farmers, not by the army (Herod. VII.4.3 ff.; *H.A. Gord.* 7.3 ff.; cf. *Max.* 13.6). For discussion cf. Syme, *Emperors*, 175-176; Dufraigne, *A.V.*, 142; T. Kotula, *Eos* 50, 1959/60, 201; H.G. Mullens, *G. & R.* 17, 1948, 65-77 and Nixon, *Caesares*, 256 ff. The last-named observes that these two chapters are riddled with errors and that even Ammianus is confused regarding the Gordians.

3.   Victor states that Gordian I was not present when acclaimed, and was summoned, which is wrong. Herodian (VII.5.3; 6.1) and the *H.A.* (*Gord.* 8.5; cf. *Max.* 14.2), which follows Herodian here, affirm that he was at home in or near Thysdrus, which may be correct if he owned property in the vicinity. Victor's compression makes events unnecessarily vague.

Gordian's acceptance, however unwilling, of his acclamation presumably put an end to the turbulence whereby he had been acclaimed. His triumphant march to Carthage is described by both Herodian and the *H.A.* For discussion *vid.* Nixon, *Caesares*, 261-264.

4. This appears only in Victor. Two eclipses occurred in the Mediterranean in 238, on April 2nd and on September 25th. The first may have caused Gordian to have recourse to the *haruspices.* Cf. *H.A. Gord.* 20, where Gordian I consults an astrologer regarding his son's natal star, and *Gord.* 23.2, where an eclipse is mentioned predicting that Gordian III would not live long. For further discussion *vid.* Nixon, *Caesares*, 264-265.

5. The Gordians, I and II, ruled 20 days (*Chronog. A.D. 354*, p. 147M) or 22 (Zon. XII.17), whether one counts their rule from their accession on c. March 22nd to their death on c. April 12th, or from the senate's acceptance of the Gordians at Rome on or about April 1st to the date of the arrival at Rome of news of their death on c. April 22nd. The Domitius cited by Victor as instigating the praetorians' attack on the urban prefect (Sabinus) was probably the praetorian prefect of 240 under Gordian III (*Cod. Just.* I.50.1; VIII.30.2), who was possibly intriguing to gain the prefecture for himself (Howe, *op. cit.* 78). He may have been responsible for the death of Vitalianus, the deputy praetorian prefect left at Rome by Maximinus (Howe, *op. cit.* 77; E. Birley, *B.H.A.C.* 1966/67, 1968, 43-51). Herodian writes that Sabinus was killed in the riots which followed news of Gordian I's acclamation reaching Rome (VII.7.4; cf. *H.A. Max.* 15.1; *Gord.* 13.7 ff.). He mentions two other disturbances, one when the deaths of the two Gordians reached the capital, leading to the election of Pupienus and Balbinus (VII.10.1 ff.) and another instigated by two senators, Gallicanus and Maecenas, who murdered some praetorians who had entered the senate house in civilian dress (VII.11.1 ff.). For a full discussion of the sources *vid.* Nixon,

Caesares, 265 ff.; P.W. Townsend, *Y.Cl.S.* 14, 1955, 49 ff.

6.   Cf. Herod. VII.6.3-4; *H.A. Max.* 14.4; *Gord.* 9.7-8; 10.4. Gordian I was following established precedent in promising a substantial donative to the praetorians. He also promised to banish informers, retry those unjustly condemned, restore exiles and give the people distributions of money.

7.   Here again Victor openly demonstrates his antipathy for the military: cf. 3.14-15; 11.9-11; 18.2; 33.13; 34.1; 34.7; 36.1; 37.3 ff.; Bird, *S.A.V.*, 41-52.

8.   Cf. Herod. VII.10.1 ff.; 12.1 ff.; Zos I.14; *H.A. Max.* 20.1-3; 32.3; *Gord.* 10.1-2; 22.1; *C.I.L.* XIV.3902; *I.L.S.* 1186. The board with shared powers was the *vigintiviri* who were elected to conduct the war against the Danubian army and administer Rome on behalf of Gordian I (Victor's chronology is confused). Both the praetorian and the urban prefect had been killed soon after the news of Gordian's accession had reached Rome and mob violence had given Rome the appearances of a captured city. To restore order the *vigintiviri* (board of twenty) held a conscription of recruits (mentioned again by Victor in the next chapter). Then news of the death (on c. April 12th) of the two elder Gordians reached Rome and the senate chose two of the *vigintiviri* as *Augusti* to oppose Maximinus (Herod, VII.10.1 ff.). Victor knows of only two Gordians, refers to Pupienus and Balbinus as *Caesares* and gives D. Caelius Calvinus Balbinus (*P.I.R.*[2] II.C.126) the erroneous *nomen* Caecilius. On Balbinus and M. Clodius Pupienus Maximus *vid.* Syme, *Emperors*, 163-178.

27

1.   M. Antonius Gordianus II (*P.I.R.*[2] I.A. 834), the son of Gordian I, was serving on his father's staff when the latter was acclaimed. He received the rank of Augustus, presumably

through his father (*C.R.E.B.M.* VI, pp. 4, 247), and died leading his force of irregulars who were crushed by Capellianus and the *Legio III Augusta* (Herod. VII.9.7). Zosimus (I.16.1) mistakenly ascribes his death to a shipwreck. Howe (*op. cit.*, 87) observes that the praetorian prefecture is given only by Victor "in a badly garbled account." It was a figment of his imagination. The *Kaisergeschichte*, however, was responsible for confusing Gordian II with Gordian III: cf. Eutrop. 9.2; Oros. 7.19.3-5.

2.   The enthusiasm felt for Gordian III is here transferred to Gordian II (Herod. VII.10.7 ff.; *H.A. Max.* 20.2; *Gord.* 22.5-6; *Max-Balb.* 3.3; 9.4-5). The mistake may be Victor's for the Chronographer of A.D. 354, following the same source, registers three Gordians (E. Hohl, *Klio* 27, 1934, 154 ff.).

3.   Cf. Herod. VII.11-12 (who mentions both gladiators and recruits); *H.A. Max.* 20.6; *Max-Balb.* 9.1-2. According to Herodian a riot, started by Gallicanus and Maecenas after the acclamation of Gordian III as Caesar, pitted the senate, the people, young recruits and gladiators against the praetorians, and a large part of the city was burned. In the *H.A.* this riot is erroneously said to have occurred after Pupienus Maximus had departed to fight Maximinus at Aquileia. Victor's phrase *inter implana urbis atque ipso sinu* may be a reflection of Sall. *Cat.* 52.35 or Tac. *Hist.* III.38.

4.   Cf. Herod. VII.12.8; *H.A. Max.* 13.3-4. The Maximini were at Sirmium (Mitrovica) in Pannonia Inferior when the Gordians were acclaimed.

5.   Cf. Herod VIII.5; Eutrop. 9.1; *Epit.* 25.2; *H.A. Max.* 23.4 ff.; 33.2-4; *Max-Balb.* 11.1 ff.; Oros. 7.19.2. Herodian, followed by the *H.A.*, states that the Maximini were killed on about June 24th by their own troops after the lengthy siege at Aquileia had reduced them to starvation and because the families of the *Legio II Parthica* were at the senate's mercy on Mt. Alba near

Rome. Pupienus was at Ravenna at that time.

6.   Cf. *De Caes.* 26.1; Eutrop. 9.1; Oros. 7.19.2; *H.A. Max-Balb.* 15.7; Herod. VII.4.1. Their reign had lasted from about March 22nd, 235 until they were declared *hostes publici* (public enemies) on April 1st or 2nd, 238, *i.e.* a little over three years.

7.   Cf. Eutrop. 9.1; *Epit.* 26.2; *H.A. Gord.* 22.5; *Max-Balb.* 14.2 ff.; 15.7; Herod. VIII.8.3 ff. According to Herodian, followed by *H.A. Max-Balb.,* they were killed outside the palace by the praetorians who could not accept senatorial predominance. They died probably on July 29th, 238 when the praetorians acclaimed the son of Gordian I's daughter, M. Antonius Gordianus III, who was born at Rome on January 20th, 225 and was only thirteen years old (Herod. VIII.8.8; Eutropius calls him just a boy).

8.   For the Quinquennial Games or *Neronia vid.* c. 5, note 6. They were revived by Domitian in 86 (Suet. *Domit.* 4) and if the intervals between had been properly observed those in Gordian's reign should have occurred in 240 or 241, though political considerations could always cause changes. The extension and confirmation of these games were necessary since Maximinus had confiscated public funds for games and festivals (Herod. VII.3.5) and Gordian's advisers perhaps felt that their reinstatement would gain popular support. Victor here states that the Quinquennial Games, the opening of the gates of the Temple of Janus and Gordian's departure for the east took place in the same year. Cf. Eutrop. 9.2.2; Oros. 7.19.4 (where Orosius demonstrates his dependence on Eutropius and the fact that he had *not* read Victor); *H.A. Gord.* 26.3; Festus, 22. This is unlikely since Victor was severely compressing his source and even omitted Gordian III's marriage to Tranquillina (Eutrop. 9.2; *H.A. Gord.* 23.6; Zos. I.17).

9.   The Persians under Ardashir had captured Carrhae and Nisibis

and overrun Mesopotamia probably soon after Maximinus' accession. In 241 Sapor (Shapur) seized Hatra and subsequently conquered Osrhoene and threatened Syria (A.T. Olmstead *C.Ph.* 37, 1962, 250-253). In 243 C. Furius Sabinius Aquila Timesitheus, Gordian's father-in-law and praetorian prefect, recovered Carrhae, Resaina and Nisibis, retook Mesopotamia and was making for Ctesiphon when he died of disease that autumn (Eutrop. 9.2; Oros. 7.19.5; *H.A. Gord.* 26.3).

10.   Cf. Eutrop. *loc. cit.*; Oros. *loc. cit.*; *Epit.* 27.1-3; Festus, 22; Ammianus, 23.5.17; *H.A. Gord.* 29.1 ff.; Zos. I.18. M. Julius Philippus, the Arab officer who replaced Timesitheus, manufactured a shortage of supplies for which he blamed the nineteen-year-old emperor and had him killed near Zaitha in late February or early March, 244 (P.W. Townsend, *op. cit.,* 130 ff.; S.I. Oost, *C.Ph.* 53, 1958, 106-107; K.T. Erim and J. Reynolds, *J.R.S.* 59, 1969, 56 ff.; Dufraigne, *A.V.,* 148).

28

1.   The new emperor was born at Traconitis, an Arabian village s.w. of Syria, which Philip made into a city called Philippopolis. It is now named Shabba. He was the son of an Arab chief, Marinus, and made his son, M. Julius Severus Philippus (b. 235 or 236), Augustus in 246 or 247 (Cf. Eutrop. 9.3; *Epit.* 28.3; Oros. 7.20.1). Soon after seizing power Philip made peace with Sapor (Zos. I.19.2; Zon. XII.19; Sync. 683), ransomed Roman prisoners still in Persian hands, but retained control of Mesopotamia and Armenia (J., Guey, *Syria* 38, 1961, 261-274; T. Pekary, *Syria* 38, 1961, 275-283; M. York, *Historia* 21, 1972, 310 ff.). He was in Rome by July 23rd, 244 (*I.L.S.* 505).

2.   This is the only mention of public construction at Rome by Philip. It is identified by Platner and Ashby (*op. cit.,* 258)

with the *Naumachia Philippi*, which was possibly a restoration of Augustus' naumachy completed by 247-248 for the millennial celebrations. In Victor's day it was perhaps simply a reservoir though in 248 it may have served both purposes.

3. Cf. Eutrop. 9.3; *Epit.* 28.3; Oros. 7.20.2; *H.A. Gord.* 33.1-3. The Secular Games celebrating Rome's one thousandth anniversary were held in 248, probably in April. They lasted three days and three nights and included theatrical performances on the Campus Martius, diverse gladiatorial combats and the display of numerous rare animals. To gain popular favour Philip chose to follow Claudius' precedent of a hundred-year *saeculum* rather than Augustus' of a hundred and ten years and used the animals collected by Gordian for his Persian triumph.

4. Flavius Philippus (Ammianus, 19.12.9) was consul in 348 and disgraced in 351. Victor is here expressing his Roman patriotism and is not alone in linking this discontinuance of the Secular Games, a major Roman tradition, with Rome's decadence (Zos. II.7.2). By Diocletian's day Rome was no longer the imperial capital (Bird, *S.A.V.*, 60-65). In 348, during the reign of Constans in the west, Victor was probably at Rome and this outburst may well have been inspired by autopsy and personal resentment.

5. Cf. *H.A. Alex.* 24.4; 39.2; *Heliog.* 32.6; A. Chastagnol, *B.H.A.C.* 1964/65, 1966, 49 ff.; *R. Ph.* 41, 1967, 85-97. Even though Philip supposedly banned male prostitution, it apparently still flourished under Constantius II despite Constantine's severe legislation in 326 on sexual offences: *vid.* Lib. *Or.* 38.8 ff.; 39.5 ff.; 53.6 ff. For Victor's strict views on sexual morality *vid.* Bird, *S.A.V.*, 116-121. Victor's rather banal observation that "people seek more avidly whatever is dangerous and forbidden" is echoed in *H.A. Alex.* 24.4, which led Chastagnol to conclude, correctly I believe, that the author of the *H.A.* had the *De Caesaribus* open before

him when writing that passage.   Dufraigne, too (*A.V.*, 150) concurs.   The commonplace remark is also to be found in Sallust (*Jug* 1.5; *Hist.* 48.17) and Tacitus (*Hist.* III.54.3).

6.   The old Etruscans were widely viewed in the Roman world as immoral voluptuaries. They were also regarded as experts in foretelling the future from the entrails of sacrificial beasts (*haruspices*), and Claudius I had instituted a college of sixty of them to perform regular services for the state.   In 318 Constantine forbade *haruspices* from entering private homes, in 319 he termed such divination "a wrongful usage of the past," and in 320 he contemptuously referred to it as a "superstition" (R. MacMullen, *Constantine*, New York, 1969, 130).   He was clearly not alone in being sceptical of their powers: cf. Cic. *De Div.* II.28 ff.; 71 ff.   For the importance of a sense of decency (*pudor, pudicitia*) *vid.* Sen. *De matr. fr.* 78; *De Ben.* 1.11.4.

7.   Cf. Eutrop. 9.3; *Epit. 28.2; Chronog. A.D. 354*; Zos. I.21-22; Zon. XII.19.   C. Messius Quintus Decius Valerianus was governor of Moesia Inferior in 234, and of Tarraconensis in 238 (B. Gerov, *Klio* 39, 1961, 222 ff.; Syme., *Emperors*, 196), and was urban prefect in 248 (*F.H.G.* IV.598).   He was both experienced and Pannonian, so Philip despatched him as *Dux Moesiae et Pannoniae* to reassert his authority in the Danubian provinces where T. Claudius Marinus Pacatianus had been acclaimed emperor by the troops sometime after April 21st, 248. The Goths and other tribes used the opportunity provided by the revolt to invade, but by the end of 248 Decius had seemingly restored the situation (Jord. *Get.* 91-92; Dexippus, *frg.* 18 in *F.H.G.* III.675; *I.L.S.* 510). Decius' popularity with the army led to his acclamation probably in mid-June, 249. He appears to have sought an arrangement with Philip, who may have been in bad health, but Philip distrusted him (Zon. *loc. cit.*).   A battle took place near Verona probably in September, 249, when Philip was killed (F.S. Salisbury and H. Mattingly, *J.R.S.* 14, 1924, 3-4; L. Fronza, *Annali Triestini* 21, 1951,

227).

8.   Cf. Eutrop. 9.3; *Epit.* 28.1; 28.3; John of Antioch, *frg.* 148, in
     F.H.G. IV. 597-598; Oros. 7.20.4; Zos. I.22.4; Zon. XII.19.
     Zosimus and Zonaras incorrectly state that the younger Philip
     died with his father; but it is unlikely that the thirteen-year-old
     would have accompanied his father. The Chronographer of
     A.D. 354 states that the reign lasted 5 years, 5 months and 29
     days. It began in late February or early March, 244 and ended
     in September, 249.

29

1.   Cf. Eutrop. 9.4; *Epit.* 29.1. Decius was born in c. 190 in
     Budalia, a village near Sirmium, and because a "rare and
     almost unique specimen, a Danubian senator and consul"
     (Syme, *Emperors*, 196; Syme discusses Decius' background
     and career at some length).

2.   This statement is contradicted by Zos. I.22.1, but supported by
     Fronza (*loc. cit.*). For the phenomenon of "the reluctant
     usurper" *vid.* Syme., *Emperors*, 198.

3.   Cf. Eutrop. 9.4; *Epit.* 29.2; Oros. 7.21.3; Ammianus, 31.5.16.
     Q. Herennius Etruscus Messius Decius, the emperor's eldest
     son, was born c. 220-230 and appointed Caesar by his father
     in the summer of 250.

4.   Decius sent his son to the Danubian region soon after making
     him Caesar to deal with an invasion of Moesia by Goths and
     Carpi (Lact. *De Mort. Persec.* 4.3). During his brief reign
     Decius built the Decian Baths on the Aventine (Eutrop. 9.4;
     Platner and Ashby, *op. cit.*, 526-527), restored the Colosseum
     after a fire (*ibid.*, 6), and perhaps constructed the *Porticus
     Decii* (*ibid.*, 421).

5. Cf. Zos. I.20.5; 21.3; 22.2. He states that Iotapianus revolted in the east against Philip and was easily crushed. The revolt was probably caused by the heavy taxation imposed and rigorously exacted by Iulius Priscus, Philip's brother and *Rector Orientis*. Zosimus is supported by Polemius Sylvius (37-38) who locates the revolt in Cappodocia. Syme (*Emperors*, 202) observes that the usurper's name "may show a claim to ancestry from the rulers of Commagene, two princes of that family being called Iotape." For the revolt and its dating (248 or 249) cf. G.M. Bersanetti, *Laureae Aquincenses memoriae V. Kuzsinsky dicatae* II (*Diss. Pann.* II.11, 1941) 265-268; G.E.F. Chilver, *J.R.S.* 38, 1948, 166. Victor alone remarks that Iotapianus claimed descent from Alexander (*P.I.R.*[2] IV.I.49) and it is unclear whether that refers to Alexander the Great, which I am inclined to believe, or Alexander Severus, which Dufraigne considers more likely (*A.V.*, 152).

6. Cf. Zos. I.23.1; Dexippus, *frg.* 16a. In late 250 or early 251 the Goths crossed the Danube at Oescus and besieged Philippopolis, which T. Iulius Priscus (not Lucius), the governor of Thrace and Macedon, was defending. A second group under Kniva moved eastwards to Novae, where Trebonianus Gallus, governor of Moesia Inferior, blocked his advance (*Sync.* I.705; Jord. *Get.* 101-102). The king veered south to invest Nicopolis where Decius defeated him but not decisively. The emperor was subsequently beaten at Beroea. Priscus, placed in jeopardy by Decius' defeat, made a pact with Kniva (cf. Dexippus, *frg.* 18; Jord. *Get.* 18) and allowed himself to be proclaimed emperor in 251 (Polemius Sylvius, 39-40). He probably perished when Philippopolis was sacked by the Goths (Ammianus, 31.5.17).

7. Cf. *Epit.* 29.5; *H.A. Tyr. Trig.* 20. While Decius and his son were fighting the Goths Julius Valens Licinianus seized power at Rome in March, 251. He was a senatorial and presumably supported by the senate but his popularity with the people, if

it existed, may have been caused by the austerity of Decius'
reign, which contrasted sharply with the munificence of Philip.
The usurpation lasted only a few days for he seems to have
issued no coins (Dufraigne, *A.V.*, 152; cf. L. Fronza, *Annali
Triestini* 23, 1953, 331-332).

8.   Priscus may already have been dead by the time the senate,
        ignorant of the fact, proclaimed him a public enemy (*P.I.R.*[2]
        IV.I.489).

9.   Cf. Eutrop. 9.4; *Epit.* 29.3; Dexippus, *frg.* 16a; Jord. *Get.* 103.
        Along with Dufraigne (*A.V.*, 152) I correct *Bruti* to *Abryti*,
        which both Dexippus and Jordanes mention. Abrytus (Aptaat)
        lies in the Dobrudja near Adamklissi.   In June Kniva led
        Decius into a trap in a marshy area near Abrytus where both
        Decii fell in battle, the younger first (Salisbury and Mattingly,
        op. cit., 15; F. Lammert, *Klio* 34, 1942, 125-126).   Zosimus
        (I.24.1) blames Gallus for their deaths and Victor was perhaps
        following the same tradition, but Gallus may have been
        suspected because he benefitted from this.   Decius was
        acclaimed probably in June, 249 and died c. July 1st, 251, i.e.
        he ruled two years (Salisbury and Mattingly, *op. cit.*, 20),
        which accords with Eusebius (*H.E.* 7.1.1).   The Epitomator's
        error (*menses triginta*) is possibly due to a misreading of xxx
        for xxiv.

10.   Cf. Eutrop. 9-4; *Epit.* 29.3; *H.A. Aur.* 42.6; Zos. I.23.3; Lact.
        De Mort. Persec. 4.3; Jord. *Get.* 103; Dexippus *frg.* 16a.   The
        story of the illustrious deaths of the Decii is probably due to
        the fact that their name recalled that of the two Republican
        heroes, P. Decius Mus and his son. The elder gained a victory
        for Rome against the Latins in 340 B.C. by devoting himself
        and the enemy to the gods and charging to his death (Livy,
        VIII.9) and his son did the same at Sentinum in 295 B.C.
        (Livy, X.28; Diod. 21.6.2).   Victor returns to the theme in 34.2
        with the *devotio* of Claudius.   Because of Decius' persecution
        of the Christians the Christian tradition, epitomized by

Lactantius, is less kind.

30

1. Cf. Eutrop. 9.5 (who mistakenly conflates Gallus and Hostilianus); *Epit.* 30.2-2. C. Vibius Trebonianus Gallus, governor of Moesia Inferior in 250-251, was born c. 206 of a senatorial family from Perusia (Barbieri, *Albo*, 1759). At the beginning of July, 251 the remnants of the troops on the Lower Danube acclaimed him since he was the only one capable of saving them, and the senate, which had little choice in any case, readily accepted one of their own. He quickly made peace with the Goths, who were fortunately marching homewards, not only allowing them to keep their booty and prisoners but also promising an annual subsidy. He then hastened to Rome where he found Decius' younger son, C. Valens Hostilianus Messius Quintus, who perhaps already held the rank of Augustus. He apparently adopted Hostilianus (Zos. I.25.2), possibly to prevent strife, and promoted his own son, C. Vibius Afinius Veldumnianus Volusianus, to the rank of Caesar. Hostilianus died between August and November, 251, apparently of the plague, though Zosimus suspected that he was murdered (I.25.3). Volusianus then was appointed Augustus to replace Hostilianus. Victor, Eutropius and the *Epitomator* were unaware that Hostilianus was Decius' son: it was not in the *Kaisergeschichte*. In general *vid.* H. Mattingly, *Num. Chron.* 6.6, 1946, 36 ff.; C. Préaux, *Aegyptus* 32, 1952, 152-157.

2. Cf. Eutrop. 9.5; *Epit.* 30.2; Oros. 7.21.5; *H.A. Gall.* 5.2 ff.; Zos. I.26.3; Zon. XII.21; Euseb. *H.E.* 7.22.1; Jord. *Get.* 104,106. The nature of this plague cannot be identified with certainty, but its symptoms were described by Cyprian of Carthage as violent diarrhoea and vomiting, an ulcerated throat, burning fever and gangrene of the extremities (F. F.

132

Cartwright, *Disease and History*, New York, 1972, 20-21). It seems to have spread from Ethiopia to the whole empire, lasted sixteen years and wrought havoc with Valerian's troops in the East. At Rome it caused the minting of coins with the legend *Apoll[ini] Salutari*. Victor remarks that Gallus and Volusianus won favour by carefully burying the poorest people. Presumably it was done to arrest the spread of the disease, but only Victor considered it significant enough to mention.

31

1. Cf. Eutrop. 9.6; *Epit.* 31.1; Zos. I.28.1; Jord. *Get.* 105. M. Aemilius Aemilianus was born at Girba on the island of Meninx off the N. African coast near the Lesser Syrtis in 206 (*Epit.* 31.1-3) or 213 (Zon. XII. 22). He was of Moorish ancestry (*Epit. loc. cit.*; cf. Zon XII.21). Soon after the death of the Decii he succeeded Gallus as governor of Moesia, reorganized the army there and gained some success against the Goths (Zos. I.28.1). In gratitude for this and possibly because he promised them the tribute money intended for the Goths his troops acclaimed him emperor probably in July, 253.

2. Cf. Eutrop. 9.5; *Epit.* 31.1; Zos. I.28.6; Zon XII.21-22. Aemilianus' sudden march into Italy surprised Gallus and Volusianus. They hastily gathered what troops they could and met Aemilianus at Interamna (Terni) just north of Rome, but their troops killed them either in the expectation of rewards from Aemilianus or through fear of Aemilianus' superior forces. Victor, Eutropius and the Epitomator give accounts that are so close here that it is evident that they are following the same source but the Epitomator adds further details which indicates he is using the *Kaisergeschichte* independently or using a supplementary source.

3. Another example of Victor's antipathy towards the army. Zosimus (I.28.6) says the soldiers considered Gallus negligent,

which may be due to Aemilianus' propaganda, but Thrace and Asia Minor did suffer while Gallus spent most of his time at Rome (Zos. I.27.1). Dalmatia, Dacia, Moesia and Sardinia, along with the East, were quick to recognize the usurper (G.M. Bersanetti, *R.F.C.* 76, 1948, 258-260).

4. Cf. Eutrop. 9.5; Jord. *Get.* 106; *Rom.* 258. The Chronographer of 354 gives 2 years, 4 months, 9 days. Victor implies that the three month reign of Aemilianus is included in the two years, unless he used *nam* in an adversative sense. The *Kaisergeschichte* presumably gave a round figure of two years: cf. Eutrop. 9.6; *Epit.* 31.2.

5. Victor alone states that the senate first declared Aemilianus a public enemy before formally accepting him and that he died of a disease. In fact his troops killed him at Spoletium in Umbria, just north of Interamna, or at "Pontem Sanginarium" between Narnia and Otriculum, presumably because he had lost their goodwill (Zos. I.29.1; *Epit.* 31.2). The senate presumably played no part in these events beyond a formal acceptance which it could not withhold (Bersanetti, *op. cit.*, 263-264). Note Victor's sad comment on the weakness of the nobility.

32

1. Cf. Eutrop. 9.7; Oros. 7.22; Euseb. - Hieron. *Chron. CCLVIII Olymp.*, CCLVIII Olymp., 220; Jord. *Rom.* 287. P. Licinius Valerianus was born before 200 (cf. *H.A. Val.* 5.1; Mal. *Chron.* 12.298) and was probably consul before 238 (Zos. I.14). Under Decius he held an important post at Rome (Zon. XII.20) and may have fought against the Goths in 251 (*H.A. Val.* 5.4). In the summer of 253 Valerian was a commander in Raetia and Gallus ordered him to collect the Rhine legions and march against Aemilianus. Upon hearing that Gallus and Volusianus had been murdered, his troops proclaimed him emperor (Bersanetti, *op. cit.*, 247 ff.; E. Manni, *R.F.C.* 75, 1947, 106-

117).

2.   Cf. *Epit.* 32.1; *H.A. Val.* 5.7. Valerian belonged to the ancient
        Licinian *gens* and was an aristocrat. Victor's statement that
        Valerian "was pursuing a military career as was still the
        custom" seems to be based upon his belief that Gallineus
        issued an edict precluding senators from military service
        (33.34). In effect the role of the nobility in the military had
        declined from the reign of Septimius Severus (C.W. Keyes,
        *The Rise of the Equites in the Third Century of the Roman
        Empire*, Princeton, 1915, 49 ff.).

3.   Cf. Eutrop. 9.7-8; Festus, 23; Oros. 7.22.1; Jord. *Rom.* 287.
        Zosimus (I.30.1) and the Epitomator (32.2) write that Valerian
        raised Gallienus to the rank of Augustus. P. Licinius Egnatius
        Gallienus was born possibly in 218 (*Epit.* 33.3; cf. *De Caes.*
        32.4; Eutrop. 9.8) and became Augustus (not Caesar) soon
        after August 29th, 253 *I.L.S.* 531; *C.I.L.* VIII, 2482; *R.I.C.* V
        (1), 71, No. 39; 72; *Epit.* 32.2; *H.A. Val.* 2.2). The error of
        Victor and Eutropius that Gallienus was appointed Caesar
        probably derives from the *Kaisergeschichte* which may have
        used the inexplicit term *imperator* (Festus, 23). Victor's term
        adulta aestate should mean high summer, i.e. July or August
        (Tac. *Ann.* II.33) but it might indicate early September before
        the autumn rains begin. The Tiber overflowed its banks on at
        least twenty-three occasions between 241 B.C. and A.D. 589,
        providing an omen of impending disaster for Otho in spring,
        69 (Tac. *Hist.* I.86). For the Tiber and its flooding *vid. R.E.*
        VIA, 792 ff.; *s.v. Tiberis*.

4.   It was not normal for the Tiber to overflow in September,
        allowing oracle-mongers (assisted by hindsight no doubt) to
        say that the fickleness of the river, which originated in Etruria,
        predicted the fickleness of Gallienus, whose *gens* hailed from
        Etruria. Gallienus was thirty-five in 253 (*Epit.* 33.3), *i.e.* he
        could be termed either *adolescens*, as here and in Eutropius, or
        iuvenis.

5.   A gross exaggeration: cf. *De Caes.* 33.1-2; Eutrop. 9.8.

6.   Cf. Eutrop. 9.7; *Epit.* 32.5. The chronology of this period is confused (G. Walser and T. Pekary, *Die Krise des römischen Reiches*, Berlin, 1962, 28 ff.; T. Pekary, *Historia* II, 1962, 123 ff.; R. Remondon, *La crise de l'Empire Romaine*, Paris, 1964, 276 ff.; T.D. Barnes *Phoenix* 26, 1972, 140; Dufraigne, *A.V.*, 156-157). Sapor (Shapur) attacked Mesopotamia and Syria in 253 and probably early the following year Valerian was in the East fighting the long, indecisive war with him. Probably in the summer of 260 he was captured at Edessa by Sapor, perhaps through treachery (cf. Zos. I.36.5-7; Zon. XII.23; *H.A. Val.* 1.2; *Petr. Patr. frg.* 13.). He was in the seventh year of his reign when captured according to *Epit.* 33.3 (*i.e.* 260), the sixth according to Victor and *H.A. Gal.* 21.5 (*i.e.* 259). Two late sources (Lact. *De Mort. Persec.* 5.6; *Petr. Patr. frg.* 13) state that he was flayed after his death. For the explanation that he was stripped of his royal clothing and covered with an asses skin to humiliate him and the Romans *vid.* J Gagé, *Syria* 42, 1965, 343-388. Victor errs in saying Valerian died soon after his capture. Eutropius (*loc. cit.*), the *Epitome* (32.5-6), Zosimus (I.36.2) and Lactantius (*loc. cit.*), all write that Valerian died in captivity (after being used as a mounting stool, according to the *Epitome*), and Eutropius and the *Epitome* add that he grew old in captivity. He was probably in his mid-sixties when captured (cf. Dufraigne, *A.V.*, 157).

33

1.   Cf. Eutrop. 9.8. Between 254 and 258 Gallienus fought five campaigns on the Rhine and was successful both militarily and diplomatically for by 258 coins proclaimed him GERMANICUS MAX V and RESTITUTOR GALLIARUM (G. Elmer, *B.J.* 146, 1941, 19).

2.   Cf. Eutrop. 9.8.1; *H.A. Tyr. trig.* 9.1; Zon. XII. 24. The dating

of Ingenuus' (not Ingebus) revolt and the Battle of Mursa (Eszek) is controversial: for a summary of modern views *vid.* Dufraigne, *A.V.*, 157-158. I follow that of J. Fitz (*Ingenuus et Regalianus*, Brussels-Berchem, 1966, 24; supported by T.D. Barnes, *Phoenix* 26, 1972, 160-161). In the summer of 258 (*H.A. Tyr Trig.* 9.1) Gallienus learned that Ingenuus, his commander in Pannonia and Moesia, had rebelled. He therefore marched into Illyricum (a general term including Pannonia) that autumn and defeated Ingenuus at Mursa in Pannonia Inferior later that year or perhaps early in 259 (Fitz, *op. cit.*, 41). Victor, or his source, may have confused the death of Valerian, elder son of Gallienus, in 258 (*P.I.R.*[2] L. 184)) with the capture of Valerian the Augustus in 260.

3. Cf. Eutrop. 9.8.1; *H.A. Tyr. trig.* 9.1; 10.1-2; *Epit.* 32.3. In 259 Gallienus reorganized the Danube frontier defences, settling some Marcomanni in Pannonia and some Roxolani elsewhere. He then learned of the Alamannic invasion of Italy and left Regalianus in charge while he marched his main army to Italy to deal with the Alamanni. Meanwhile the Roxolani attacked the Danubian region and caused the remaining troops to acclaim Regalianus. He held out at Carnuntum (near Haimburg) for several months before being killed by his own troops (*H.A. Tyr. trig.* 10.2), not by Gallienus who was in Italy, in 260, after which the Iazyges and Quadi also invaded the defenceless provinces (Fitz, *op. cit.*, 17-71; Dufraigne, *A.V.*, 158).

4. Cf. Eutrop. 9.8; *Epit.* 33.1; *H.A. Gall.* 1.1; *Tyr. trig. passim;* Oros. 7.22.13; Julian, *Caes.* 313 c; Ammianus, 14.1.9. The Latin sources, many of whom derive wholly or in part from the *Kaisergeschichte*, condemn Gallienus as incapable, indolent and wicked. The extant Greek sources, however, give a different picture. Zosimus (I.36.1 ff.) has no word of reproach for him and Zonaras (XII.25) praises him highly. The vilification of Gallienus may have been due to senatorial fabrication (A. Alföldi; *Z.F.N.* 38, 1928, 156 ff.; L. de Blois,

The Policy of the Emperor Gallienus, Leiden, 1976, esp. 26, 205-215). P. Licinius Cornelius Saloninus Valerianus, the younger son of Gallienus, was made Caesar in 258 and killed in Gaul in 260, just before Postumus proclaimed himself Augustus (*P.I.R.*² L.183; Barnes, *op. cit.*, 171).

5.   Cf. Eutrop. 9.8.2; *H.A. Gall.* 1.2; *Tyr. trig.* 30.1; Oros. 7.22.7-8; Zon. XII.24; Zos. I.37. The Goths, Borani and Heruli repeatedly invaded Macedonia, Greece, Pontus and Asia between 254 and 268. They attacked Thessalonica and Athens, plundered Ephesus, Chalcedon and Prusa and razed Nicomedia and Nicaea. The Persians (not Parthians as the *Kaisergeschichte* states, cf. Eutrop., *loc. cit.*) had attacked Mesopotamia and Syria in 253 and had occupied Mesopotamia since 256. They were eventually defeated at Carrhae in 262 by Odenathus and the Palmyrenes (Victor's bandits), who were ruled after Odenathus' assassination by his widow Zenobia (whose name Victor disdainfully ignores though it was in the *Kaisergeschichte*, cf. Eutrop. 9.13). For Zenobia *vid.* Barnes, *op. cit.*, 177. For Victor's sentiment being modified and used by the *H.A.* cf. *Tyr. trig.* 30.1. The Alamanni broke the Rhine frontier and invaded central Gaul and northern Italy probably in 259 and 260 before being defeated by Gallienus near Milan (de Blois, *op. cit.*, 6). The Franks, a German confederacy of Bructeri, Chamavi, Salii and others, make their first appearance in history here. They took advantage of Gallienus' weakening of the Rhine legions in c. 258 to invade Gaul and subsequently crossed the Pyrenees and entered Spain where they devastated Tarraco (Tarragona); cf. Oros. 7.22; Zos. I.30.2; Zon. XII.24; F.J. Wiseman, *Roman Spain*, London, 1956, 71-72. One group, the Bavares, even raided Mauretania (*I.L.S.* 2767, 9006). For the loss of Dacia cf. Eutrop, 9.8; Festus, 8; Oros. 7.22. All depend on the *Kaisergeschichte* which exaggerated the loss. Gallienus probably gave up Dacia Inferior and concentrated on holding Dacia Superior, which was not lost until about 271 under Aurelian (D. Tudor, *Historia* 14, 1965, 377-380; de Blois, *op. cit.*, 5; den Boer, *S.M.R.H.*, 203-204).

6.   Cf. Eutrop. 9.9, which probably reflects the common source, and Sall. *Cat.* 10.1; Tac. *Hist.* I.2-3; IV.47.7, which Victor may be echoing here as he strives for rhetorical effect. The *H.A.* (*Gall.* 4.9) seems to follow Victor's account but the subsequent phrase *saeviente fortuna* (*Gall.* 5.6) may be an imitation of Sallust. On this *vid.* den Boer, *S.M.R.H.*, 100.

7.   Cf. *H.A. Gall.* 5.5-6; Zos. I.26; 37.3; Oros. 7.22.1-2. The plague had been devastating Rome since 251 but Victor uses its occurrence to excoriate Gallienus. The theme of despair during this period was in the *Kaisergeschichte* (cf. Eutrop. 9.9) but Victor's phrase *desperatio animi* is unique, at least in extant sources (den Boer, *S.M.R.H.*, 97).

8.   Cf. *Epit.* 33.1; *H.A. Gall.* 21.3; *Tyr. trig.* 3.4; 8.9; 9.1. For similar descriptions of Nero and other "bad" emperors cf. *H.A. Ver.* 4.4 ff.; *Comm.* 3.7; Suet. *Nero*, 26; *Otho*, 2.1; Tac. *Ann.* XIII.25; Dio, 61.8.   The description derives from the *Kaisergeschichte* and is greatly exaggerated or mainly fabricated: cf. the restrained comment of Eutropius (9.1.1) and the silence of Zosimus and the Greek sources.   Cornelia Salonina Augusta (*P.I.R.* [2] II. C 1499), Gallienus' wife, was prominently displayed on the emperor's coinage until his death in 268. The Marcomanni, situated in Bohemia at this period, invaded Pannonia in 254 (Zos. I.29). When they threatened to invade again in 258 Gallienus reached an agreement with their king, Attalus, whereby the Marcomanni received a strip of land in Pannonia Superior and agreed to defend the Roman border, while Gallienus received Attalus' daughter, Pipa, as a concubine, and perhaps hostage (Fitz, *op. cit.*, 11,36 ff.; cf. den Boer, *S.M.R.H.*, 80).

9.   Victor, in his search for cause and effect, ingenuously considered Gallienus' conduct responsible for the numerous invasions and usurpations of the period. Cf. Oros. 7.22.9, where Orosius ascribes the responsibility to a vengeful Divine Providence.

10. Cf. Eutrop. 9.9; *Epit.* 32.3; Oros. 7.22; *H.A. Gall.* 4.3; *Tyr. trig.* 3.1-9; Zos I.38.2; Zon XII.24. M. Cassianius Latinius Postumus (*P.I.R.*[2] II. C 466; Barnes, *op. cit.*, 166-167), military commander on the Rhine in 258, killed Gallienus' younger son, Saloninus, and rebelled at Cologne in 260. He established himself as independent emperor, gained the allegiance of Spain and Britain, organized a Gallic senate and even dreamed of ruling the whole empire. Eutropius, the *H.A.* and Orosius thought highly of him: this was presumably the view of the *Kaisergeschichte.*

11. Cf. Eutrop. 9.9; *Epit.* 32.4; *H.A. Gall.* 4.3; *Tyr. trig.* 3.2-3.7; 4.1-5.1 ff.; 6.1 ff.; Oros. 7.22.10; Zos. I.38.3. Postumus ruled successfully for nearly ten years, reorganizing the defences of Gaul and countering attacking by the Germans (P. van Gansbeke, *R.B.N.* 98, 1952, 5-30; *id. Latomus* 14, 1955, 404-425; H. Schoenberger, *Latomus* 15, 1956, 222-224) and Gallienus (de Blois, *op. cit.,* 6-7). Ulpius Cornelius Laelianus revolted at Mainz with the aid of *the Legio XXX Ulpia Victrix* probably in 268. He was defeated by Postumus at Mainz in late 268 or early 269, but his refusal to allow his troops to sack the city cost him his life (Barnes, *op. cit.*, 161-167; Dufraigne, *A.V.*, 160-161, de Blois, *loc. cit.*). For the various forms of Laelianus' name and the historiographical consequences *vid.* Barnes, 161; T. Damsholt, *C. & M.* 25, 1964, 141.

12. Cf. Eutrop. 9.9; *H.A. Tyr. trig.* 5.3; 8.1 ff.; 31.2; Oros. 7.22.10. M. Aurelius Marius Augustus was acclaimed emperor presumably after the deaths of Laelianus and Postumus in December, 268 or early 269. Evidence from coins indicates that he ruled for longer than the two or three days given in the sources, which derive ultimately from the *Kaisergeschichte.* The *H.A.* is clearly wrong in locating him after Victorinus but may have retained a piece of authentic information by describing him as energetic (*strenuus*), for the army would have chosen such a man. The statement that he was a former

blacksmith in Victor and the *H.A.* (simply *opifex* in Eutropius) was also in the *Kaisergeschichte* (cf. Syme, *Emperors*, 251-252).

13.   C. Marius (c. 157-86 B.C.) was of equestrian origin and rose through the ranks of the army to be consul seven times. There is no evidence he was ever a blacksmith, though his family reputedly earned their livelihood by their own hands (Vell. II.11.1; Plut. *Marius*, 3; Juv. *Sat.* VIII.245-246). He boasted of his humble origins (Sall. *Jug.* 85). Doubtless this later Marius would find it convenient propaganda to invent such family connections (Dufraigne, *A.V.,* 161; cf. den Boer, *S.M.R.H.*, 76-77). The general sentiment here, as elsewhere, is Sallustian (cf. Sall. *Jug.* 1-4; *Cat.* 2.3 ff.) and Victor may well have had Sallust's portrait of C. Marius in mind (cf. Sall. *Jug.* 85; 114).

14.   Cf. Eutrop. 9.9; *H.A. Tyr. trig.* 6.3; Oros. 7.22. M. Piavonius Victorinus defeated Marius probably in the spring of 269 and ruled for approximately two years (cf. Dufraigne, *A.V.*, 162). The quartermasters' plot was in the *Kaisergeschichte* (cf. Eutrop. *loc. cit.*) and may have been authentic but the story of Victorinus' lechery resembles that told of Carinus (*De Caes.* 39.11; *Epit.* 38.7-8; cf. *H.A. Car.* 16-17) and may have been fabricated.   On the other hand the account of Attitianus' vengeance probably deserves credence (den Boer, *S.M.R.H.*, 78).

15.   This is a unique passage, according to den Boer (*S.M.R.H.*, 77) without parallel in classical literature. I am convinced that Victor's outburst of righteous indignation is based upon personal experience. Corruption in the commissariat was hardly a recent phenomenon (cf. Tac. *Agr.* 19.5) but in the third century corruption had invaded all aspects of the bureaucracy (*Cod. Theod.* XIII.2; XVI.3,5,7; XXXII.1; Alföldi, *Conflict*, 28 ff.; E.A. Thompson, *A Roman Reformer and Inventor*, Oxford, 1952, *passim*). The *actuarius* or

quartermaster was in charge of a specific function in the commissariat (Ammianus, 15.5.3; 20.5.9; 25.10.7). The *annona* (annual taxes in kind) was collected by curial officials (*procuratores* or *susceptores*) who were elected by city councils. They worked in groups to make collections from village headmen (*praepositi pagorum* or in Egypt *exactores civitatis*) and were liable for the full amount due, which was probably assessed initially by the *actuarii*, hence their power over civic and village officials. The *actuarii* then picked up supplies (*pittacia*) from the *mansiones publicae* and distributed them to the troops. A law of Valentinian (*Cod. Just.* XII.38) made the *actuarii* responsible for supplies not delivered within thirty days of the appointed date, implying that their graft was widespread and notorious. To further encourage honesty they were raised to the rank of *perfectissimus* after ten years of blameless service (*Cod. Theod.* VIII.1.10). In general *vid.* Jones, *L.R.E.* I.456-459, 526, 626 ff.; 672; Dufraigne, *A.V.*, 162.

16.   Cf. Eutrop 9.10; *H.A. Tyr. trig.* 5.3; 6.3; 7.1; 24.1; 25.1; 31.1; *Aur.* 32.3; 39.1; *Claud.* 4.4; Oros. 7.22. Victoria was presumably a rich member of the Gallic nobility, hence her influence after her son's death in procuring the acceptance of her relative C. Pius Esuvius Tetricus, governor of Aquitaine, as emperor. He was living at the provincial capital Bordeaux (Burdigala) when proclaimed, in his absence, probably in early 271 by the troops at Cologne, for there would be no significant forces at Bordeaux. His son was made Caesar and subsequently given senatorial rank at Rome by Aurelian. Victor, Eutropius and the *H.A.* imply that he was in power during Gallienus' reign, another error imported from the *Kaisergeschichte*.

17.   Cf. Eutrop. 9.10; *H.A. Gall.* 7.4 ff. Gallienus celebrated his *Decennalia* in the autumn of 262 and a triumph over the Persians for Odenathus' successes in 264. They are confused by the *H.A.* which, however, may provide some authentic

details derived from Dexippus at this point. Victor here indulges in rhetorical hyperbole, again at Gallienus' expense, an idea picked up by the *H.A. (Gall.* 9.1).

18. Cf. *Epit.* 33.2; *H.A. Gall.* 5.1; 5.7; 9.1; 14.6; *Tyr. trig.* 9.1. The *H.A.* (in *Gall.* 5.1; 5.7; 9.1) seems to have been influenced by Victor's personal comment made conspicuous here by *uti mos est* (as is customary). M'. Acilius Aureolus rebelled in 261 but was won over by Gallienus (Barnes, *op. cit.,* 149). While Gallienus fought the Goths and Heruli in the Thracian-Macedonian border area in 267/8 Aureolus, Gallienus' cavalry commander, who was left in charge of operations against Postumus in Raetia and was based at Milan, again rebelled in 268. This was not because of Gallienus' negligence and indolence (*vid.* de Blois, *op. cit.,* 26).

19. Cf. *Epit.* 33.2; *H.A. Tyr. trig.* 11.3-4; Zos. I.38; I.40; Zon. XII.24. Gallienus defeated Aureolus at Pons Aureoli (Pontirolo), some 20 miles N.E. of Milan, which indicates he marched along the *Via Postumia* from Aquileia to Verona, not from Rome as Victor states. He then drove Aureolus to his base in Milan and besieged him there. The *H.A.* erroneously assigns the victory at Pontirolo to Claudius, whether through mendacity or confusion, for Aureolus was declared a public enemy by Claudius and died while he was in command.

20. Cf. Eutrop. 9.11; *Epit.* 33.2-3; *H.A. Gall.* 14; Oros. 7.22.3; Zos. I.40; Zon. XII.25; Sync. 1.707. It was probably in August, 268 that a conspiracy of high-ranking officers was formed against Gallienus, including Aurelius Heraclianus, the praetorian prefect, Marcianus, senior commander against the Goths, M. Aurelius Claudius, cavalry commander and next emperor, L. Domitius Aurelianus, the future emperor, and Cecropius., prefect of a squadron of Dalmatian cavalry who actually killed Gallienus soon after August 28th (Barnes, *op. cit.,* 181).

21.   Victor's account of the plot against Gallienus is found in no other source and appears to be a doublet of the plot against Aurelian (35.8) on which all the sources agree (Dufraigne, *A.V.*, 163). But the Epitomator (33.2) does mention the plot of Aureolus, so it may have been in the *Kaisergeschichte*, which, according to Syme (*Emperors*, 205), expurgated Claudius' involvement.

22.   Cf. *H.A. Gall.* 14.6-9; Zos. I.40, which give a fuller, very similar and presumably more accurate account. The assassin was known and went unpunished because he, like Claudius, was part of a successful conspiracy. Victor, relying on the *Kaisergeschichte*, may not have known this. If he did, he was guilty of exonerating Claudius for personal reasons. Claudius was the supposed ancestor of Victor's emperor and probable patron, Constantius II (H.W. Bird, *C.J.* 66, 1971, 252-254).

23.   This pessimistic reflection is Sallustian and had become traditional: cf. Sall. *Cat.* 1.3 ff.; 7.3; 10.4; Livy, *praef.* 9; Tac. *Hist.* I.2; I.12.4; Dufraigne, *A.V.*, 164. For an intriguing discussion of this whole passage *vid.* den Boer, *S.M.R.H.*, 79-86.

24.   Cf. Sall. *Cat.* 52.11.

25.   This is another rhetorical commonplace: cf. Diod. Sic. I.2; Tac. *Ann.* III.65.1; *Agr.* 1.1. History was intended to elevate public morality.

26.   Victor alone informs us that Gallienus was deified on the orders of Claudius. The *H.A. (Gall.* 15.2) gives a quite different version and Gallienus' name was erased from many monuments. According to P. Damerau (*Kaiser Claudius II Gothicus, Klio* Beih. 33 (N.F. 20), 1934, 45-47) Victor's account is either exaggerated or fabricated, but it is further discussed and fully supported by den Boer (*S.M.R.H.*, 79 ff).

27.   This story is also in *Epit.* 34.2 but in no other extant
        source. It was probably in the *Kaisergeschichte* (*vid.* note 21),
        which presumably followed the official Constantinian version
        of Claudius' accession (*vid.* note 22). Claudius may actually
        have been kept at or despatched to Ticinum (Pavia), twenty
        miles south of Milan, when the actual assassination of
        Gallienus occurred. It is unlikely that he was a simple tribune,
        and he probably held the *tribunatus maior* of the *protectores*,
        i.e., he commanded the imperial staff officers training corps
        which was at this juncture quartered at Ticinum (Bird, *loc. cit.*;
        cf. Dufraigne, *A.V.*, 165).

28.   A mixture of Pythagorean/Platonic and Stoic ideas of
        immortality: cf. what Victor says about Constantine (41. 14-
        15). The passage is fully discussed by Dufraigne, *loc. cit.*
        Nevertheless the sentiment may have been borrowed (by
        memory) from Sallust: cf. *Jug.* 4.4; *Cat.* 14.4. Ammianus
        echoes Victor's reproaches of Gallienus in general (21.16.9;
        23.5.3; 30.8.8), but his use of a Greek source or sources
        favourable to the emperor compelled him to modify the picture
        somewhat (21.16.10; cf. Zon. XII.25).

29.   I follow Olivarius in reading *perducto* for *perduci*, as does
        Dufraigne (*A.V.*, 42). The passage bears a close resemblance
        to Suet. *Tib.* 75.1, where events at Rome following Tiberius'
        death are described, but Victor may have been influenced by
        the description of what happened at Rome after Sejanus' fall
        (Tac. *Ann.* V. 9.3; Suet. *Tib.* 61; Dio, 58. 11.5) and the word
        satelles is used by Tacitus to describe a supporter of Sejanus
        (*Ann.* VI. 3.2).

        The *H.A.* (*Gall.* 15) gives a different version of events and
        only mentions a mutiny of the troops who were appeased by
        their customary donative. The treasury lawyer so maltreated
        was presumably punished thus in an act of vengeance for his
        particularly dishonest or vicious activities. The Gemonian
        Steps, or Steps of Sighs, led to the summit of the Capitoline

from the Forum between the Temple of Concord and the prison (*carcer*). Criminals executed in the latter had their bodies thrown out onto the steps where they were subjected to desecration before being dragged down in the Tiber. For a somewhat different translation and interpretation *vid.* den Boer, *S.M.R.H.* 85. He believes that Victor could not have invented these details, which shows that this passage is historically reliable.

30. Some senators clearly detested Gallienus (de Blois, *op. cit.*, 78) and there is seldom a shortage of people willing to join in riots and bloodletting. No emperor, however, could allow such activities to continue for long, whether the army actually demanded it to be stopped or not. But it should be noted that Gallienus was very popular with the rank and file of the army and went to extreme lengths to remain so. (*H.A. Gall.* 15; Zos. I.41; de Blois, *op. cit.*, 26-119; esp. 117).

31. Cf. *De Caes.* 32.2; 37.5; Victor is the only author to mention this edict and although it is lent some support by epigraphic evidence (A. Bellezza, *Atti della Academia Ligure di Scienze e Lettere*, 17, 1960, 157-158) its existence has been thrown into doubt by many scholars such as Bellezza, Syme (*Emperors*, 241), Seston (*Dioclétien*, 317) and Warmington (in Parker, *A History of the Roman World A.D. 138-337*, 395). It does appear, however, that Gallienus abolished the exclusive right of senators to obtain the officer ranks of *Tribunus Laticlavius* (senior legionary tribune) or *Legatus Legionis* (legionary commander); for these *vid.* G. Webster, *The Roman Imperial Army*, London, 1969, 116-117). It was an attempt to break the links between the rich senators and the army and thereby prevent senators from electing their own emperors (de Blois, *op. cit.*, 206), and to make the army more professional and efficient. But Victor may have exaggerated the edict and its effects. For a full discussion *vid.* den Boer, *S.M.R.H.*, 85; Dufraigne, *A.V.*, 165-167; de Blois, *op. cit.*, 40, 57, 75, 82, 87, 117, 206, with bibliography.

32.   Cf. Eutrop. 9.11; *Epit.* 33.3; *H.A. Gall.* 21.5. Gallienus' sole
        rule dates from the capture of Valerian, probably in the
        summer of 260 (c. 32, note 6), until the late summer of 268,
        i.e. eight years, as Eutropius and the Epitomator state. On the
        dating cf. Dufraigne, *A.V.*, 167; Barnes, *Phoenix* 26, 1972,
        180-181.

34

1.   Cf. Eutrop. 9-11; *H.A. Gall* 15.3; *Claud.* 1.1-2.8; Oros. 7.23.1;
        Zos. I.41;46; *Syn. Sathas*, p. 39; Ammianus, 31.5.17. All the
        sources praise Claudius warmly. This passage, however, is
        another instance of Victor's prejudice against the soldiery
        (Nixon, *Caesares*, 299).

2.   Cf. *De Caes.* 29.5 and note 10; *Epit.* 34.3-4; Ammianus,
        16.10.3. The *devotio* of Claudius II, who had been "adopted"
        as an ancestor by Constantine (Syme, *Emperors*, 204, 234),
        and the comparison of him with the republican heroes of that
        name had become a tradition in the fourth century (Dufraigne,
        A.V., 168). Claudius actually died of the plague at Sirmium
        (Eutrop. 9.11; *H.A. Claud.* 12.2; Zon. XII. 26; Zos. I.46; *Sync.*
        p. 720; Malalas, p. 299).

3.   Cf. *Epit.* 34.3. The Sibylline verses were the utterances of the
        Cumaean Sibyl collected in early times for later consultation
        and entrusted to the *Quindecimviri sacris faciundis* (Livy, V.
        13.5). For their sale to Tarquinius Priscus *vid.* Plin. *N.H.*
        13.88; Dion. Hal. 4.62. 1-6; Lact. *Inst.* 1.6.10-11. They could
        only be consulted at the instigation of the senate (Tac. *Ann.* I.
        76.2; VI. 12), usually in times of public danger (*H.A. Aur.* 18.5
        ff.). The last known consultation occurred in 363 (Ammianus,
        23. 1.7) and the collection, associated in the post-Constantine
        period with militant paganism, was officially burned sometime
        between 395 and 408 (Rut. Namat. 2.52). Claudius defeated
        the Alamanni near Lake Benacus (Lago di Garda) in 268/9 and

the following year beat the Goths at Doberus in Macedonia and again at Naissus (Nish) in Moesia, before dying of the plague probably in late August, 270. The first victory is only mentioned in the *Epitome* (34.2), but confirmed by epigraphic and numismatic finds. The successes are reported by Zosimus (I. 42-46) and by the *H.A.* (*Claud.* 6-12), though the latter's account is highly suspect (*vid.* P. Damerau, *op. cit.*, 62-75; P. Goessler, *Klio* 35, 1942, 107). The Epitomator provides one piece of evidence not in Victor, the identity of the *princeps senatus* in 269/70, T. Pomponius Bassus, twice consul and urban prefect (*C.I.L.* VI. 31747). The person is authentic, the *devotio* story is almost certainly an invention of the Constantinian age (Syme, *Emperors*, 234). It was probably in the *Kaisergeschichte* as a variant but spurned by Eutropius and the *H.A.* The latter seems to have been using Dexippus at this juncture (*Claud.* 12.6; Damerau, *op. cit.*, 81). In 34.5 I read *vitam* for Pichlmayr's *vita*.

4.   Julian, in his dying words, stated that the aim of a just government (*imperium*) was the welfare and safety of its citizens (Ammianus, 25.3.18), a theme to which Ammianus returns in similar words when discussing Valentinian's character (30.8.14). The idea was, of course, Platonic (*Rep.* I. 342 ff.) and presumably a regular topic in the schools.

5.   For the importance of the judgement of history and its moral purpose, which is quite traditional, *vid. De Caes.* 33.26; *Epit.* 3.6; Tac. *Ann.* III. 35.1; IV. 38; *Agr.* 1.1; Livy, I.1; Diod. Sic. 1.2; Bird, *S.A.V.*, 88.

6.   There is a substantial *lacuna* in both manuscripts at this point, which argues for their dependence on a common ancestor (Nixon, *Caesares*, 115). Victor is here referring to Constantius Chlorus, Constantine the Great, Constantius II and Julian. All were supposed descendants of Claudius Gothicus, a relationship noted by Eutropius (9.22), the *H.A.* (*Claud.* 1.1; 1.3; 9.9; 13.2) and Zonaras (XII. 26). The *lacuna* would

probably contain a brief account of Claudius' deification and honours, Quintillus' elevation and death, and the acclamation and early exploits of Aurelian (H.W. Bird, *C.J.* 67, 1972, 360).

7.   The person referred to here by Victor was probably Zenobia of Palmyra (Bird, *loc. cit.*). Aurelian defeated her in two major campaigns in 272 and 273 before attacking the Persians, to whom she was fleeing for assistance. She was reputedly very beautiful. Cf. Eutrop. 9.13; *H.A. Aur.* 28.4; 35.4; 41.9; *Tyr. trig.* 30; Zos. I. 55.

8.   Cf. Tac. *Ann.* XV. 48. Victor was fond of such melancholy *topoi*; *vid.* c. 28, note 5.

35

1.   L. Domitius Aurelianus was born c. 215 in that area of Moesia which later became Dacia Ripensis (*Epit.* 35.1; *H.A. Aur.* 3.1-2). He was acclaimed emperor at Sirmium in autumn, 270. After capturing Palmyra in 273 he may have made a brief, punitive sortie into Persian territory for he adopted the titles *Parthicus Maximus* and *Persicus Maximus* (*C.I.L.* VI. 1112; VIII. 9040; XII. 5456, 5549, 5561; *I.L.S.* 577) and issued coins with the legend *Victoria Partica* (*R.I.C.* V, p. 291, no. 240). The campaign aroused little interest: only Victor and the *H.A.* mention it (*Aur.* 28. 4-5; 35.4; 41.9).

2.   Victor errs here chronologically. Aurelian first drove the Vandals out of Pannonia, then learned that the Alamanni and Juthungi were devastating northern Italy (Winter, 270/71). After an initial defeat at Placentia (Piacenza) he destroyed their armies at the Metaurus, at Fanum Fortunae (Fano) and near Ticinum (Pavia). Cf. *Epit.* 35.2; *H.A. Aur.* 18.3; 21.1; Zos. I. 49. 1-2; Dexippus, *F.H.G.* III. 685-6; *Petr. Patr.* frg. 10.3. There is some confusion among the sources as to the identity of the Germanic peoples who invaded Italy; *vid.* A. Alföldi,

Bull. Inst. Arch. Bulg. 16,1950, 21-24; Dufraigne, *A.V.*, 170.

3. Once again Victor inverts the order of events. After the defeat of the Gallic legions, they were incorporated in Aurelian's army and under Probus drove the Franks, Saxons and Alamanni out of Gaul (*H.A. Prob.* 12. 3-4; L. Homo, *Essai sur le règne de l'empereur Aurélien*, Paris, 1904, 116-121).

4. Cf. Eutrop. 9.13; *H.A. Tyr. trig.* 24. 2-3; *Aur.* 32.3; Oros. 7.23; Zos. I. 61; Polem. Silv. *Chron. Min.* I, ed. Mommsen, p. 522. Tetricus was threatened from within by his own senior officers, especially Faustinus (mentioned only by Victor and Polemius Silvius), who appears to have been the military commander at Augusta Treverorum (Trèves), and externally by Franks, Saxons and Alamanni. In view of his subsequent treatment he presumably arranged to defect to Aurelian when the latter marched into Gaul in late 273. When the Gallic and central armies clashed at Catalaunum (Châlons) Tetricus deserted.

5. Cf. Eutrop. 9.13; *Epit.* 35.7; *H.A. Tyr. trig.* 24.5; 25.4; *Aur.* 39.1. Though the anachronistic title *corrector Lucaniae* is used by Victor, the Epitomator, Eutropius and the *H.A.* it is clear that it stems from one source, the *Kaisergeschichte* (W.H. Fisher, *J.R.S.* 19, 1929, 132; cf. Dufraigne, *A.V.*, 170-171). In Victor's day, as in that of the author of the *H.A.* (*vid. Tyr. trig.* 24.5), the title *corrector totius Italiae*, which had not been employed for such a long time, would not be readily understood and this possibly explains the anachronism (A. Chastagnol, *Historia* 4, 1955, 174). The evidence of *H.A. Tyr. trig.* 24.5 may stem from Dexippus or from the Greek source it used in common with Zosimus after Dexippus had ended (Fisher, *op. cit.*, 126-129). Tetricus probably ruled from 270 to 273, about three years: cf. J. Lafaurie, *B.S.F.N.* 1974, 517-525; Dufraigne, *A.V.*, 170, who accept Victor's figure.

6. Cf. Eutrop. 9. 14.1; *Epit.* 35.4; *H.A. Aur.* 38. 2-4. It was while Aurelian was engaged in Northern Italy with the German

150

invaders that serious disturbances broke out at Rome (*H.A. Aur.* 18.4; 21.5; 50.5; Zos. I.49). Felicissimus, the *procurator* or *rationalis* of the mint, would be held responsible for the debasement of the coinage and possibly for the sacrilege involved in desecrating the emperor's image on the coinage (R. Turcan, *Latomus* 28, 1969, 948-959) and he revolted against Aurelian (in Polem. Silv. *Chron. Min.* ed. Mommsen I, p. 522, he is called *tyrannus* or usurper). The insurgents used the mint, located on the Caelian hill and seemingly well-fortified, as a stronghold. In view of the number of combatants killed, the nobles subsequently executed and Aurelian's reputation afterwards for cruelty it appears that an extensive faction, possibly including the former supporters of Quintillus, may have joined Felicissimus.

7.   Cf. Eutrop. 9.15; *H.A. Aur.* 39.2; 39.6 (also *ibid.* 1.3; 10.2; 25.6; 28.5; 35.3; 48.4; *Tac.* 9.2; *Quad. tyr.* 3.4); Zos. I. 61. Aurelian was clearly a devotee of *Sol Invictus*, the Unconquered Sun-God, but his main concern in erecting this temple and establishing a college of priests was political. Particular deities, such as Jupiter, Apollo, Serapis, Mithras *et al.*, were becoming recognized as manifestations of a superior deity, the Sun-God. Aurelian sought to romanize the Solar cult and make it a common bond of unity (cf. F. Cumont, *Les religions orientales dans le paganisme romain*[4], Paris, 1929, 106 ff.; (Homo, *op. cit.*, 184-195). The temple stood on the campus of Agrippa, was richly endowed and contained the spoils of Palmyra (Platner and Ashby, *op. cit.*, 491 ff.). It was apparently intended to be the centre of worship for the whole empire for some of Aurelian's coin bear the legend *Sol Dominus Imperii Romani* (*R.I.C.* V. 301, nos. 319-322).

8.   Cf. Eutrop. 9.15; *Epit.* 35.6; *H.A. Aur.* 21.9; 39.2; Zos. I. 49; Oros. 7.23; Malal. XII, p. 229; *Chron. Pasc. ann. 273*, p. 508; *Chron. Min.* ed. Mommsen, I, p. 229; II. p. 148. In view of the recent Germanic attacks on Italy in 259, 268 and 270 (the Alamanni reached Rome in the first) Aurelian began work on

a new city wall in 271 with the help of the senate and city corporations. It generally stood 26 feet high, 12 feet wide, with gates, posterns and artillery towers, and had a circuit of around 12 miles. Completed under Probus, it was designed to withstand predatory attacks by raiders like the Alamanni rather than protracted sieges by professional armies (I.A. Richmond, *The City Wall of Imperial Rome*, Oxford, 1930).

9. Cf. *Epit.* 35.6; *H.A. Aur.* 35.2; 48.1 ff.; Zos. I. 61. Despite *H.A. Alex.* 26.1 Aurelian was probably the first to establish regular free distributions of pork analogous to those of bread. In addition, he probably instituted regular distributions of salt and oil, thereby systematizing earlier exceptional grants (Plin. *N.H.* 31.89; Dio, 49. 43), and may have wished to include wine, if we can believe the *H.A.* (*Aur.* 48.1). The pork distributions continued until at least 306 (Zos. II.9). Aurelian's alimentary system represents the maximum effort ever made by the state in favour of the Roman populace and had to be modified by his successors the following century (*De Caes.* 41.19; *Cod. Theod.* XIV. 17.5; 19.1. It was paid for probably by the booty brought back from the east and the restoration of the revenues from the eastern provinces.

10. Cf. *H.A. Aur.* 39.3-5; 37.7. *Calumniae fiscales* (*fiscales molestiae* in 41.20) were charges made against individuals by agents of the *fiscus* (imperial treasury) for revenue purposes, but there were, of course, cases of extortion and blackmail (cf. Suet. *Domit.* 9). *Quadruplatores* were public informers who originally received one fourth of the property of those against whom they laid charges of *maiestas* (treason) provided that the prosecution succeeded. The rest of the property went initially to the *aerarium*, later to the *fiscus*. When the informer's fee increased before Nero's reign (Suet. *Ner.* 10) the term *quadruplator* was generally replaced by *delator*. For a description of such an informer *vid.* Tac. *Ann.* I.74. Aurelian's cancellation of debts in 274 by the burning of public records was presumably modelled on Hadrian's action in 118 (Dio,

69.8.1; *H.A. Hadr.* 7.6; *C.I.L.* VI.967) which M. Aurelius followed in 178 (Dio, 71.32.2; *H.A. M. Aur.* 23.3). Hadrian and M. Aurelius, both philhellenes, were probably influenced by the actions taken in 594-93 B.C. by Solon to relieve distress in Attica. For Victor's surprise and delight at Aurelian's reforms *vid.* Nixon, *Caesares*, 300.

11.   Cf. Eutrop. 9.15; *Epit.* 35.8; *H.A. Aur.* 35.5-36.6; Zos. I.62. 1; Zon. XII.27; Lact. *De Mort. Persec.* 6.2. Zosimus and Zonaras call the secretary responsible for the forgery Eros, the *H.A.* has Mnestheus which is probably a corruption of the Greek word for *notarius, menutes.* The actual assassin was an officer named Mucapor (*De Caes.* 36.2; *H.A. Aur.* 26.2; 35.5). Aurelian died near Perinthus in the autumn of 275 (Barnes, *op. cit.*, 173, 181; Syme, *Emperors*, 243, with a curious error in note 3, Victor has Coenofrurium).

12.   Cf. *H.A. Aur.* 40.2-3; *Tac.* 1.1; 2.1 ff.; 14.5; *Epit.* 35.10. The *Kaisergeschichte* probably noted that the brief reigns of Tacitus and Florianus were like a short interlude (*interregnum*) between Aurelian and Probus. Victor, through fraud or more likely through misconception, developed the theme of an extended *interregnum* (E. Hohl, *Klio* II, 1911, 284, 316). The *H.A.*, following Victor here, simply elaborated (Syme, *Emperors*, 237 ff.). The situation was unlike that of 268 when Gallienus was killed through a plot of high-ranking officers who were on the spot and agreed on a successor. Aurelian's death was an accident and the officers involved had no successor in mind. Several possessing the best qualification, like Probus, were scattered over the empire while those at Coenophrurium were disqualified by being implicated in Aurelian's assassination for he was popular with the rank and file (*De Caes.* 35.12; *H.A. Aur.* 37.1 ff.; 50.5; *Tac.* 2.4-5; Zos. I.62). The army resolved the problem (Zos. XII.28), not the senate, as the Latin authors would have us believe, by choosing a candidate it found acceptable, who would hardly be a civilian (Syme, *Emperors*, 245). For Victor's surprise at the

actions of the army *vid.* Nixon, *Caesares*, 300. He was, of course, quite mistaken.

13. I read *simul ac* for *simulata*. Cf. 36.1; *Epit.* 35.10; *H.A. Tac.* 1.1; 2.1; 2.6. An *interrex* was originally appointed by the senate at the death of a king to rule provisionally until the next king had been chosen. Under the Republic an *interregnum* was proclaimed when there were no senior magistrates in office (*i.e.* consuls or dictators). This would occur *e.g.* if both consuls died in office or if elections could not be held. Successively appointed *interreges* governed until new consular elections could be held. Livy (I.17) informs us that the practice originated at the death of Romulus, before Numa Pompilius came to the throne. The *interregnum* of 275 is attested by coins (*R.I.C.* V. p. 361), as well as by the Latin sources, but its duration was short, not more than two months, while the army decided and Tacitus, who was in Campania, was informed and travelled to Rome for his investiture (Zos. I.63; Zon. XII.28; *H.A. Tac.* 7.5; Syme, *Emperors*, 237; Barnes, *op. cit.*, 173-174; 181; cf. Dufraigne, *A.V.*, 173).

14. This is the major statement of Victor's philosophy of history, supplemented by 24.9 ff. and 38.5 ff. The cyclical conception of the universe is traditional and both Stoic and Pythagorean: *vid.* Tac. *Ann.* III.55; Cic. *De Rep.* 6,22,24; *De Nat.* 2.51; Virg. *Buc.* 4; Bird, *S.A.V.*, 86 ff. The term *praeceps dari* is Tacitean: cf. Tac. *Ann.* VI.17.4.

15. A *topos* already used by Victor with respect to Trajan (13.7; Dufraigne, *A.V.*, 174).

36

1. Cf. Eutrop. 9.16; *Epit.* 36.1; *H.A. Tac.* 2.1 ff.; 4.1 ff. M. Claudius Tacitus, who was supposedly 75 years old (Zon. XII. 28), was acclaimed emperor in November or December, 275.

He had been ordinary consul in 273 (*C.I.L.* VIII. 18844) and was again in 276, possibly for the third time (*P.I.R.*[2] II. C. 1036). The notion that the senate chose Tacitus as emperor and the joy its members felt is elaborated upon by the *H.A.* (*Tac.* 3.1 ff.; 12.1). It appears to be merely a reflection of Victor's account, from whom the whole fabricated tradition of a senatorial candidate derives (Syme, *Emperors*, 238).

2.   Cf. Eutrop. 9.16; *Epit.* 36.1; Oros. 7.24; *H.A. Tac.* 13.4; 14.5; 16.1; *Prob.* 13.3; Zos. I.63, 65; Zon. XII.28; *Cons. Constant a* 275; 277. Tacitus was assassinated at Tyana (Kiz Hissar) in Cappadocia (the Epitomator confuses the death-place of Tacitus with that of Florianus) probably in June, 276, after he and his praetorian prefect, Florianus, had defeated the Goths from Lake Maiotis who had penetrated as far as Cilicia. Tacitus had considered it expedient to execute Mucapor and some of those involved in Aurelian's murder, (*H.A. Tac.* 13.1) but not all, for others remained to be punished by Probus (*H.A. Prob.* 13.2; Zos. I.65; Zon. XII.29).

3.   Cf. Eutrop. 9.16; *Epit.* 36.2; *H.A. Tac.* 9.6; 13.6; 14.1; 17.4; *Prob.* 13.3; Zos. I.63.1; Zon. XII.28. M. Annius Florianus was not Tacitus' brother, an error made by Victor who confused Claudius/ Quintillus with Tacitus/Florianus (Barnes, *op. cit.*, 158). The *H.A.* (*Tac.* 14.1) merely perpetuated Victor's error and the theme that Florianus seized power without consulting the senate or soldiers, which is ludicrous. The Greek sources state that he was Tacitus' praetorian prefect and was recognized by the senate (clearly after acclamation by Tacitus' army) and by the European and African parts of the empire, evidence supported by coins and inscriptions (*P.I.R*[2]., I.A. 649).

37

1.   Cf. Eutrop. 9.16-17; *Epit.* 36.2; *H.A. Tac.* 14.2; *Prob.* 10.8;

13.4; Zos. I.64.1; Zon. XII.29; Malal. 12.301; *Chron A.D. 354*, p. 148. M. Florianus' tenuous reign is corroborated by the legends on his coins: *Perpetuitas*; *Securitas*; *Victoria Perpetua* (*R.I.C.* V. i. p. 319 ff.). His soldiers, possibly suborned by Probus (Zos. *loc. cit.*), assassinated him at Tarsus, in Cilicia, probably in early September, 276, after a reign of two-and-a-half months (J. Lafaurie *B.S.A.F.* 1965, 139 ff.).

2.   M. Aurelius Probus was born at Sirmium (Sremska Mitrovica) in Pannonia Inferior (*De Caes.* 37.4; *H.A. Prob.* 3.1; 21.2), on August 19th, 232, and was acclaimed probably in June, 276. He presumably held a senior command in the East (*Prob.* 7.4; 8.7; 9.1 ff.) for he was supported by the troops in Syria, Palestine and Egypt (Zos. I.64.1; Zon. XII.29; *H.A. Prob.* 10.1). Victor is wrong in stating that Probus was acclaimed emperor in Illyricum, probably confusing the place of his acclamation with that of his birth.

3.   Hannibal (247-183 B.C.), considered one of the world's greatest generals (Nepos, *Hann.* 1.1), managed to weld together an effective army out of the most diverse elements (Polyb. 9.19; 9.21-26; 11.19; 15.15.3-16.6; 23.13.1-2; Livy, 21.4; 21.23). Victor, an African, was clearly proud of the great Carthaginian hero, who must have been a common subject of discussion in the province, but other fourth century writers also mention Hannibal with approbation, e.g. Ammianus, 15. 10.10-11; 18.5.6; *H.A. Pesc. Nig.* 11.4.

4.   Cf. *H.A. Prob.* 20.2; Nepos, *Hann.* 7.1. After peace was signed between Rome and Carthage in 201 B.C., Hannibal, still commanding a large army but precluded from using it for military purposes, apparently employed it in planting olive trees and performing other agricultural tasks. Victor alone draws the parallel between Probus and Hannibal, but the point he makes about not allowing soldiers to be idle is echoed by the *H.A.* twice (*Prob.* 9.2; 20.2) and may reflect conditions in the third and fourth century, at least in Victor's opinion. J.

Schwarz (*Chronique d'Egypte* 14, 1970, 381-386) argued that the name of Hannibal should be replaced by that of Marius, but his arguments are not convincing (Dufraigne, *A.V.*, 176).

5.   Cf. Eutrop. 9.17.2; *H.A. Prob.* 18.8; Hieron. *Chron. A.D. 280.* Domitian, in an attempt to protect Italian viticulture and produce more grain and other crops, forbade the planting of new vineyards in Italy and ordered half of those in the provinces cut down (Suet. *Domit.* 7.2). Probus possibly rescinded Domitian's edict (though probably it had simply lapsed) and promoted viticulture, particularly in the Danube region near Sremska Mitrovica (Sirmium) in the Fruška-Gora range. The information derives from the *Kaisergeschichte* (Syme, *Emperors*, 224; T.D. Barnes, *C.Q.* 20, 1970, 202-203).

6.   Cf. Eutrop. 9.17; *H.A. Prob.* 13.5; 16.2; 17.2; *Tac.* 3.4; Oros. 7.24.2; Hieron. *Chron.* p. 223; Zos. I.66.1; Zon. XII.29. Between 277 and 279 Probus and his generals expelled the Franks from northern Gaul, the Alamanni from central Gaul and the Burgundians and Vandals from Raetia and Illyricum. Victor's anti-military sentiment is again evident here.

7.   Cf. Eutrop. 9.17; *Epit.* 37.2; *H.A. Prob.* 18.4; *Quad. tyr.* 7.1; Oros. 7.24.3; Hieron. *Chron.* p. 224; Zos. I.66.1; Zon. XII.29. Proculus is noticeably absent from Victor's account, but is in Eutropius, the Epitomator and the *H.A.*, which led Syme, (Ammianus, 56) to suggest adding *Proculoque cum* after *Bonoso* as an emendation. Not necessary. Victor may simply have omitted Proculus through carelessness or for stylistic balance. As Dufraigne points out (*A.V.*, 177), these were merely names to Victor. Saturninus, a Moor, had himself proclaimed emperor by his troops in Syria, where he was serving as a military commander, but was murdered by those same troops at Apamea, possibly in 278. Bononsus seems to have been the commander on the Rhine after Probus had cleared the Germans out of Gaul. He and Proculus had themselves acclaimed at Cologne, probably in 280 and were

rapidly suppressed. In general, *vid.* J.H.E. Crees, *The Reign of the Emperor Probus*, London, 1911, 113 ff.; G. Vitucci, *L'Imperatore Probo*, Rome, 1952, 58-68, Syme, *Ammianus*, 4; Barnes, *Phoenix* 26, 1972, 150, 168, 171-172. The latter two emphasize that nothing in the *H.A. Quad. tyr.* except the bare names should be regarded as anything but fiction.

8.   Cf. Eutrop. 9.17; *H.A. Prob.* 20.4-5; 22.4. Probus crushed a rebellion in Britain (Zos. I.66; Zon. XII.29), stamped out brigandage in Pamphylia and Lycia (Zos. I.69-70; cf. *H.A. Prob.* 16.4) and put down an insurrection in the Thebaid (Zos. I.71; *Prob.* 17.4-6; Vitucci, *op. cit.*, 54-60). Eutropius probably follows the *Kaisergeschichte* closely here whereas Victor characteristically attempts stylistic change. The *H.A.* (*Prob.* 20.2) elaborates, having Probus state "that a soldier should not eat free rations". This clearly came from the pen of a writer, not the mouth of a general (Vitucci, *op. cit.*, 80). It is hardly likely that an emperor acclaimed by his army would make such a statement. Presumably it stems from the senatorial tradition which was favourable towards Probus and hostile to the military.

9.   Cf. Eutrop. 9.17; *Epit.* 37.1; 37.4; *H.A. Prob.* 21.2-3; 22.2; Zos. I.71.5; Zon. XII.29; Petr. Patr. *Exc. Vat.* 179; Barnes, *Phoenix* 26, 1972, 167. Probus was killed by his troops probably in September, 282, as he was using them to alleviate the flooding caused by the first heavy rains of the season. The Latin sources indicate he was killed in a simple mutiny, the Greek sources link his death with a revolt by Carus. The *H.A.* knows both traditions (*Car.* 6.1; Dufraigne, *A.V.*, 178), but rejects the second (*Prob.* 20.1), preferring that of the *Kaisergeschichte*, which it clearly follows here, for it mentions an iron tower omitted by Victor, notes the marshes and ditch ignored by Eutropius, and names the River Save which is not in either Victor or Eutropius. Victor's *paulo cis sextum annum* (a little less than six years) is a simple error by the author (Vitucci, *op. cit.*, 130). Eutropius, Zosimus and Orosius

158

    (7.24.2) give 6 years, 4 months; the *Chron A.D. 354*, p. 148
    M. gives 6 years, 2 months, 12 days.

10.   This "highly significant passage" (H. Mattingly, *C.A.H.* XII,
    318) is rather a reflection of fourth century thought than an
    exact estimation: cf. Alföldi, *Conflict*, 99 ff.; C. Starr,
    A.H.R. 61, 1955/56, 579 ff.; Bellezza, *op. cit.*, 149 ff;
    Dufraigne, *A.V.*, 178. Victor is deluded in believing that an
    improvement in the powers and prerogatives of the senate
    occurred under Tacitus and ended with the death of Probus.
    Unable to adduce any positive evidence he resorts to rhetoric
    in blaming the senate for its sloth and addiction to luxury.
    Similar denunciations are to be found in Sallust (*Jug.* 4; *Cat.*
    10.2 ff., 52.3; Ps. Sall. *Ep. II ad Caes.* 10.9) and Tacitus (*Ann.*
    VI.27). The theme of a senatorial resurgence in the reigns of
    Tacitus and Probus proved engaging to the author of the *H.A.*
    (*Tac.* 18.1; *Prob.* 13.1;). Both accounts are fabrications
    (Vitucci, *op. cit.*, 91 ff.; Syme, *Emperors*, 240-241). For
    Gallienus' edict *vid.* c. 33, note 31.

                                    38

1.   Victor varies his biographical structure here by leaving his
    discussion of Carus' background until the death of Carinus and
    the end of the dynasty (39.12). Cf. Eutrop. 9.18; *Epit.* 38.1-2;
    H.A. Car. 4.1-5; 5.4; 7.1; Oros. 7.24. M. Aurelius Carus was
    appointed praetorian prefect by Probus (Howe, *P.P.*, 83) and
    was serving as military commander in Raetia and Noricum.
    According to Greek sources (Zon. XII.29; John of Antioch,
    F.H.G. IV, p. 600, Frag. 160; Petr. Patr. *Exc. Vat.* 179) his
    soldiers compelled him to accept the throne. He was born at
    Narbo (Narbonne) in southern Gaul, not at Narona in
    Illyricum, and consequently was not one of the Danubian
    officers (P. Meloni, *Il Regno di Caro, Numeriano e Carino*,
    Cagliari, 1948, 11-13; T.B. Jones, *C.P.* 37, 1942, 193-194;
    H.W. Bird, *Latomus* 35, 1976, 123-127). He probably rebelled

in August or September, 282 and simply announced to the senate his own acclamation and the fact that he had made his sons Caesars.

2.   Cf. Eutrop. 9.18-19; *H.A. Car.* 7.1; 8.1; 9.4; Zon. XII.30. Carus left his elder son, Carinus, as governor in the west and quickly defeated the Quadi and Sarmatians in Pannonia before continuing to confront the Persians under Vahram II in Mesopotamia (Iraq). This had, indeed, been a regular bone of contention between the two empires, as Victor shrewdly observes. First annexed in 115 by Trajan it was promptly given up by Hadrian. In 165 L. Verus again made it a Roman protectorate. The Parthians recaptured it in 195, but Septimius Severus recovered it for Rome shortly afterwards. In 230 the new Persian Empire under Ardashir overran it though Severus Alexander once more regained it. Under Maximinus Thrax it was lost again, but recovered by Gordian III. Finally the Persian seized it in c. 260 when they defeated Valerian and retained it until 283 when Carus recaptured it. Victor, perhaps through haste, omits Carus' victory over the Quadi and Sarmatians, though it was clearly in the *Kaisergeschichte*: cf. Eutrop. 9.18; *H.A. Car.* 8.1.

3.   Cf. Eutrop. 9.18; *Epit.* 38.3; *H.A. Car.* 8.1; 8.5 ff.; Festus, 24; Zon. XII.30. In 283, after recovering Mesopotamia, Carus marched south and captured Coche (Veh Ardashir), which Ardashir had built c. 230-240 to replace Seleucia, destroyed by the Romans in 165. It stood on the west bank of the Tigris across from Ctesiphon (Matthews, *R.E.A.*, 140-143). Carus afterwards crossed the Tigris and seized Ctesiphon, the Persian capital, forcing Vahram II, who was faced by a rebellion of his brother in Persia, to make peace. He was then (summer, 283) killed supposedly by a bolt of lightning but more probably succumbed to a plot by the Danubian officers led by Diocletian (Diocles), who wished to return with all speed to the Danube. On the chronology on his death *vid.* Bird, *op. cit.*, 123-127. For the unreliability of the *H.A.* at this point *vid.* Syme,

Emperors, 26, 50, 218-219; Barnes, *op.cit.*, 152.

4.   Cf. Eutrop. 9.18; Festus, 24; *H.A. Car.* 9.1-3. The similarities in the versions of Victor, Eutropius, Festus and the *H.A.* regarding Carus' death indicate use of the *Kaisergeschichte* (cf. Enmann, *Kaisergeschichte*, 396; T.D. Barnes, *C.Q.* 64, 1970, 198-203). Victor is to be distinguished from Eutropius, Festus and the Epitomator by virtue of his personal comments and attitude towards fate (cf. 3.20; 24.8 ff.). The *H.A.*, however, takes a strong stand against such fatalism and appears at this juncture to level its attack firmly against Victor. The notion of the ineluctability of fate is Ciceronian: cf. Cic. *De Nat.* 3.6.14; *De Div.* 2.20. On the oracle *vid.* J. Straub, *Studien zur Historia Augusta*, diss. Berne, 1952, 123-132.

5.   Cf. Eutrop. 9.18; *Epit.* 38.4-5; *H.A. Car.* 12.1; Zon. XII.30-31; John of Antioch, *F.H.G.* IV. Frag. 161. Though he may have suffered a minor defeat by the Persians (Zon. *loc. cit.*), M. Aurelius Numerius Numerianus extricated his army and although suffering from trachoma had almost reached Chalcedon (which lies opposite Byzantium/Constantinople) when he was murdered, probably in early November, 284. His father-in-law, L. Flavius Aper, was made the scapegoat but it is more likely that Diocletian, commander of the imperial bodyguard, was the ringleader of the plot (T.B. Jones, *A.J.P.* 59, 1938, 338-339; Bird *op. cit.*, 125-130).   Three other praetorian prefects, Sejanus, Plautianus and Timesitheus, had had their loyalty to the ruling family confirmed by similar marriage arrangements.   In addition Diocletian, who benefited directly from the deaths of Numerian and Aper, subsequently erased Numerian's name from monuments: hardly the act of an avenger (W. Seston, *Dioclétien et la Tétrarchie*, Paris, 1946, 48; cf. Meloni, *op. cit.*, 133 ff.; T.B. Jones, *C.P.* 35, 1940, 302-303.

1.　　Cf. Eutrop. 9.19; *H.A. Car.* 13.1; Zon XII.31. C. Aurelius Valerius Diocletianus was apparently commander of Numerian's *protectores* not *domestici*: the latter is an anachronism (Jones, *L.R.E.*I, 53;II,636;III,195; M. Woloch, *Hermes* 96, 1969, 758-760). Before the formation of the *domestici* the imperial bodyguard were called *protectores* and comprised a select corps of centurions and staff officers who carried out administrative tasks and the instruction of other ranks.   Jones thinks the *domestici* were founded under Constantine, accepting the testimony of the *H.A.* which he believes was written under Constantine. Woloch opts for the reign of Constantius II, for the earliest unequivocal evidence we have for *domestici* is from 354 (Ammianus, 14.10.2) and 357 (*C. Theod.* XI.1.38). Both Victor, Eutropius and the *H.A.* note Diocletian's good sense and astuteness (cf. Eutrop. 9.26). He was acclaimed emperor near Nicomedia on November 20, 284.

2.　　Cf. Eutrop. 9.26; *H.A. Car.* 17.1; Ammianus, 15.5.18. The *H.A.*'s description refers to Carinus, but is clearly borrowed directly or indirectly from the description of Diocletian in the *Kaisergeschichte.* Augustus introduced emperor worship into Roman religion. He was regarded in the east as the successor of the divine oriental and Hellenistic monarchs from the beginning of his reign. In the west he fostered a modified form of the cult in order not to violate Roman tradition. After his death he was deified, following the precedent of Julius Caesar. Except for spasmodic attempts to bring about abrupt changes by Caligula (Suet. *Calig.* 22) and Domitian (Suet. *Domit.* 13; Dio, 67.5.7), emperor worship apparently developed in step with the growing consciousness of an imperial power created and blessed by the gods.   Thus respect for the personality of the emperor was gradually replaced by an obligation to respect the idea of a ruler personified by the reigning emperor. Furthermore, *adoratio* had been paid to effigies of the emperors long before Diocletian, so his action in assuming the pose and garb of a divine monarch was merely the culmination of a lengthy process (A. Alföldi, *Röm. Mitt.* 49 1934, 67; 50, 1935, 75 ff.). Cf. *H.A. Elag.* 23.4; *Alex.* 4.2. For an example of *adoratio* (Diocletian and Maximian at Milan in 291) *vid. Pan.* 3.11.

3.   Cf. Claud. *In Eutrop.* 1.181: "Asperius est nihil humili cum surgit in alto." This is the second occasion that Victor has invoked Marius as an example of a humble man rising to a position of great power (cf. 33.11). Sallust writes that Marius acted contrary to established custom in enlisting men lacking property qualifications (*capite censi*) in *Jug.* 114, and describes him as a self-made man, eager for glory (*Jug.* 63.1), who was subsequently driven headlong by ambition (*Jug.* 63.6), a sentiment echoed by Seneca (*Ep.* 94.66). On Marius as a Roman hero-figure and various interpretations of his work and character over a period of six centuries after his death *vid.* T.F. Carney, *Mosaic* 1, 1967, 34-38.

4.   For the arrogance of the nobility cf. Sall. *Jug.* 5.1;64.1; *Cat.* 52: for a defence of its rights similar to that of Victor cf. Tac. *Ann.* II.33.3. It is noticeable that *novi* like Tacitus, Victor and Eutropius are staunch defenders of the nobility and its prerogatives, but Tacitus and Victor realize that the nobility itself is responsible to a great extent for its own downfall (cf. Tac. *Ann.* I.7.1; II.38; *De Caes.* 31.3; 37.7; R. Syme, *Tacitus*, Oxford, 1958, 566 ff.). Alföldi (*Conflict*, 98 ff.) dismisses Victor as a senatorial lackey who gives us a perverted picture of imperial history, but Starr (*op. cit.*, 579 ff.) corrects this impression and notes that Victor pays less attention to the nobility than a reader of Tacitus or Suetonius would expect and emphasizes the senate less than his contemporary, Eutropius. Even Alföldi (*Conflict*, 105) admits that Victor is aware of the senate's faults and does not gloss over them.

5.   Cf. Eutrop. 9.26; *H.A. Car.* 13.1; *Elag.* 35.4; Lact. *De Mort.*

Persec. 7.1 ff. Eutropius gives us the most balanced assessment of Diocletian but Victor shows a remarkable awareness of the importance of circumstances; cf. *De Caes.* 20.11; 38.2. They were soon to have a profound influence on his own life and career.

6.   Cf. *Epit.* 38.6; Zos. I.73.2; John of Antioch, *F.H.G.* IV.601, Frag. 163. Victor apparently describes M. Aurelius (Sabinus) Julianus as *corrector Venetiae*, an anachronism (Jones, *L.R.E.*, 45). John of Antioch indicates he was a (praetorian) prefect, which is rejected by Stein (*P.I.R.*[2] A.1538) and Howe (*P.P.*, 94) on the grounds that Aper and Aristobulus were prefects at this time. Julianus may have been *corrector Italiae regionis Venetiae et Histriae* (A. Chastagnol, *Historia* 12, 1963, 348-349), but he could simply have been a military commander in Illyricum for he must have had an army and he did control the mint at Siscia (Siszek) in Pannonia Superior (*R.I.C.* V. pt. II, 579, 593-594). He rebelled perhaps in autumn, 284, but was easily crushed by Carinus near Verona by the following spring. For the hypothesis, based upon the confusion of the sources, that there were two usurpers named Julianus at the point, Sabinus and M. Aurelius, *vid.* Dufraigne, *A.V.*, 182.

7.   I have made the obvious emendation of *Margus* for *Marcus.* Cf. Eutrop. 9.19-20; *Epit.* 38.7-8; *H.A. Car.* 16.1 ff.; 18.1-2; Zon. XII.30; Petr. Patr. *Exc. de Sent.* 269, 181 B; Jord. *Rom.* 295; *Chron. A.D. 354* (*Chron. Min.* I, p. 229). Probably in the summer of 285 Carinus and Diocletian faced each other across the River Margus (Morava) in Moesia (Serbia) near Belgrade. Carus' army was larger and initially successful but some of his officers were disaffected and he was assassinated by a tribune whose wife he had allegedly seduced. It appears more likely that Diocletian had suborned the tribune through Aristobulus, Carinus' praetorian prefect and consul, who retained both offices under Diocletian (Howe, *P.P.*, 84). Diocletian presumably offered rewards and a general amnesty at this point and it is presumably to this that *De Caes.* 39.14 refers, not to

the time immediately after the murder of Aper.

8.   For Carus' birthplace *vid,* c. 38 note 1: cf. Dufraigne, *A.V.,* 182. *Epit.* 38.1 incorrectly gives two years for Carus' reign. The chronographer of A.D. 354 (*loc. cit.*) states that Carinus ruled 2 years, 11 months, 2 days: Eusebius (*H.E.* 7.30.22) and Zonaras (XII.30) give them a little under three years: *Chron. Pasc.* gives three years. If the period included Carus' reign, i.e. it began in August or September, 282, it would extend Carinus' reign to July or August, 285: cf. Meloni, *op. cit.,* 170.

9.   Cf. Eutrop. 9.20; *H.A. Car.* 7.1; 12.2-13.2. the source of these three accounts is the *Kaisergeschichte* which may have derived its information from an "official" version of events published in Diocletian's reign. Cf. Dufraigne, *A.V.,* 182. It is wholly improbable that either Aper or Diocletian was unaware of Numerian's death. The latter may have died a natural death which Aper was concealing until the army was met by Carinus, so as to avoid the sort of coup which occurred. If Numerian was assassinated Diocletian was surely privy to the plot. He was certainly capable of vigorous and violent action (O. Seeck, *Geschichte des Untergangs der antiken Welt I*, Stuttgart, 1921, 3-4; cf. E. Costa, *Diz. Epigr.* II, s.v. Diocletianus, 1793-1794, for a completely different and quite naive assessment.

10.   This statement must refer to events which occurred after the Battle of Margus (*vid.* note 7). T. Claudius Aurelius Aristobulus, praetorian prefect and consul under Carinus, not only kept his positions under Diocletian (Ammianus, 23.1.1), but became proconsul of Africa from 290 to 294, then urban prefect in 295 (cf. *P.L.R.E.,* p. 106). It should be noted that Aper's death had left Diocletian with no praetorian prefect and Carinus' death allowed Diocletian to step into a vacant consulship. On Diocletian's clemency *vid. Pan.* 3.5.3, the official line which is supported somewhat for his early years by *H.A. Car.* 15.6 and even by Lact. *De Mort. Persec.* 11.8.

But the action which Victor represents as a demonstration of his noble character may have been simply a shrewd move to eliminate his rival.

11. With Schott I have amended *humani* (in *o humanum*) to *humanam*. Victor again abandons his source to make a personal interjection and the Latin immediately become "idiosyncratic and difficult" (V.S. Sokolov, *V.D.I.* 86, 1963, 216); cf. 40.29-30. In all likelihood Victor had been at Rome in 350 when the usurper Magnentius occupied the city (*De Caes.* 28.2) and later that June, when Nepotianus seized control for twenty-eight days before being crushed and killed by Magnentius' forces. The results were devastating, particularly for the upper-classes (*De Caes.* 41.24-26; Eutrop. 10.9 ff.; Zos II.42 ff.). The part played by foreigners (*i.e.* non-Italians) in Rome's greatness is emphasized by Victor earlier (11.12). Here he is being more precise and indicates the semi-civilized Illyrians such as Maximian. Lactantius, admittedly a denigrator of Diocletian for religious reasons, intimates that Diocletian had many killed because of their possessions and wealth (*De Mort. Persec.* 7.11).

12. Cf. Eutrop. 9.20; Oros. 7.25.2; Zon. XII.31; *Pan.* 2.4.3; 6.8.3. The Gallic peasantry of north and east Gaul, impoverished by German depredations and government exactions, seized the opportunity presented by Carinus' departure to rise up in rebellion. *Bagaudae* is probably a Celtic word denoting vagabonds. Their leaders, Aelianus and Amandus, represented as "emperors" on coins, were possibly former soldiers, the rank and file were not. After establishing their headquarters on a peninsula of the Marne, just upstream from its confluence with the Seine, they raided the neighbouring districts and even attacked some cities. Maximian suppressed their rustic bands by 286 but the movement could not be stamped out because the social causes remained and further outbreaks occurred in 369, 406 and sometime prior to 439 (Ammianus, 28.2.10; Zos VI.2.5; *Chron. Min.* I.475-476; A. Dimitrev, *V.D.I.* 3-4, 1940,

101-114; R. MacMullen, *Enemies of the Roman Order*, Cambridge, Mass., 1966, 192 ff., 198, 211-213, 216, 232, 266, 357).

13.   Cf. Eutrop. 9.20; 9.27.1; *Epit.* 40.10; *H.A. Elag.* 35.4; Lact. *De Mort. Persec.* 8.2; *Pan.* 2.9.3; 2.10.1; 3.6; 6.9.2. Diocletian, realizing that he could not manage the empire alone, chose a younger fellow officer and loyal friend, M. Aurelius Valerius Maximianus, who came from near Sirmium, to be Caesar (not Augustus) probably on July 21st, 285 at Milan. He was raised to the rank of Augustus probably on April 1st, 286 (Barnes, *New Empire*, 4).

14.   The assumption of the titles Jovius and Herculius seemingly symbolized Diocletian's pose as the earthly counterpart of Jupiter Optimus Maximus, and Maximian's as Hercules, Jupiter's agent in ridding the world of evils (Jones, *L.R.E.* I,38). It also demonstrated the *de facto* seniority of one of two legally equal Augusti. Finally, these grandiose titles possibly served to efface the obscure origins of the new rulers. The use of the term *auxilia* here is misleading. The *Joviani* and *Herculiani* were crack legions established by Diocletian and probably belonged to the imperial *comitatus*. The new *auxilia*, subsequently called the *auxilia palatina*, were corps of a different kind and are to be distinguished from the old *auxilia*. Many bore fancy names like *Petulantes*, *Cornuti* or *Brachiati*, but some were named after warlike Gallic or German tribes like the *Nervii* or *Batavi* (Jones, *L.R.E.*I,97-98). Later they became the mainstay of the Roman army (cf. H.M.D. Parker, *J.R.S.* 23, 1933, 175-189; W. Seston, *Historia* 4, 1955, 284-296; D. van Berchem, *L'armée de Dioclétien et la réforme constantinienne*, Paris, 1952).

15.   Cf. Eutrop. 9.20; Zon. XII.31; *Pan.* 2.4.3. Victor's simple statement is chronologically deceptive. Not only did Maximian quickly crush the *Bagaudae* in spring, 286, but also

he defeated the Alamanni and Burgundii on the Upper Rhine and the Eruli and Chaibones near Cologne on the Lower Rhine, which took several years. Furthermore Constantius, Maximian's praetorian prefect, won a notable victory across the Rhine and caused a Frankish chief, Gennobaudes, to swear allegiance to Rome, in return for which he was recognized as King of the Franks.

16.   Cf. Eutrop. 9.21-22; Oros. 7.25.3; *Pan.* 4.12.1. M. Aurelius Carausius, a native of Menapia, which lies between the Meuse and the Scheldt, was commissioned by Maximian in late 285 or early 286 to protect the shores of Gaul and Britain from Saxon and Frankish pirates. He commanded a Roman fleet based at Boulogne (Gesoriacum/Bononia) and his knowledge of the North Sea and its coasts together with his obvious expertise in seamanship made him remarkably successful. Nevertheless the booty he seized was seldom returned to provincial authorities and most of it was used to build a bigger fleet.   Maximian learned of this and ordered Carausius executed but the latter was warned and in self-defence had himself proclaimed Augustus and transferred his fleet to Britain probably late in 286. He still controlled Boulogne and most of N.W. Gaul. T.D. Barnes has made a convincing case for the independent use of the *Kaisergeschichte* in these passages by Victor and Eutropius (*The Sources of the Historia Augusta*, Brussels, 1978, 93) and even Dufraigne (*A.V.*, 184) admits that they follow a common source here.

17.   Cf. *De. Caes.* 39.33-37; Eutrop. 9.22-23; 9.24-25; *Epit.* 39.3-4; Festus, 25; Oros. 7.25.4, 8. For the Persians *vid. inf.*, note 25. The Quinquegentiani were a Berber confederacy which broke through the Numidian and Mauretanian frontiers in the 280s. Driven back in 289 they soon resumed their incursions. In 297 Maximian, with a large army, pushed them first into their mountain retreats, devastated their villages and lands, killed large numbers of them, then forced the rest into the Sahara. On March 10, 298, he marched triumphantly into Carthage

(Williams, *Diocletian*, 75). We are not sure who Julianus was: possibly a chief of the Quinquegentiani. He was not the Julianus of *Epit.* 39.3. For a discussion with bibliography *vid.* Dufraigne, *A.V.*, 184.

18.   Cf. *De Caes.* 39.38; Eutrop. 9.23; *Epit.* 39.3; Oros. 7.25; Pan. 8.5.2; Jord. *Rom.* 298, 300 M.; Zon XII.31; Malal. 12.308 f. All the literary sources make Achilleus the leader of the Egyptian revolt but coins reveal a L. Domitius Domitianus as Augustus at Alexandria in 297. He was dead by December of that year but Aurelius Achilleus, with the title *corrector*, held out until c. March, 298. After savage reprisals Diocletian divided Egypt into two provinces and reformed the administration: cf. Barnes, *New Empire* 11-12, 211; *Constantine*, 17-18; Williams, *Diocletian*, 81-83; Dufraigne, *A.V.* 184.

19.   Cf. Eutrop. 9.22; *Epit.* 39.2; Oros. 7.25.4; Lact. *De Mort. Persec.* 7.2; *Chron. Min.* I.229; *Chron. Pasc.* 512; *Pan.* 8.3; *I.L.S.* 642. Despite the confusing statements of Eutropius and the Epitomator, which were almost certainly caused by compression, Maximian became Augustus in 286. Only Victor and the Epitomator give Galerius the *cognomen* Armentarius: it is not on inscriptions or in the official documents of the period. It means herdsman, and was possibly a barrack-room sobriquet retailed by the *Kaisergeschichte*, which Victor, Eutropius and the Epitomator followed independently here. On March 1st, 293 Flavius Julius Constantius was appointed Caesar at Milan and probably that same day C. Galerius Valerius Maximianus acquired the same office at Nicomedia (Izmid) in Bithynia (cf. Seston, *Dioclétien*, 88 ff.). For their titles *vid.* Williams, *Diocletian*, 58-60, Seston, Dioclétien, 210 ff.; Jones, *L.R.E.*I,38; Barnes, *Constantine*, 11. For the families of the tetrarchs *vid.* Barnes, *Constantine*, 8-9; *New Empire*, 30-38. Barnes does not accept the tradition, derived from the *Kaisergeschichte*, that the Caesars divorced their wives to marry into the imperial families. In 11 B.C. Tiberius

was compelled by Augustus to divorce his wife, Vipsania, and marry the emperor's daughter, Julia. This was possibly noted early in the *Kaisergeschichte* (cf. *De Caes.* 2.1; Eutrop. 7.10; *Epit.* 1.23; 2.1) but only Victor had the historical perspicacity to use it as an *exemplum* at this juncture.

20. Diocletian was born in Dalmatia, Maximian near Sirmium in Pannonia Secunda, Constantius was probably Illyrian or Pannonian and Galerius either came from near Serdica in Dacia Mediterranea (formerly Thrace), where he died, or more probably from Romulianum near Bononia (Vidun) on the Danube in Dacia Ripensis (Syme, *Emperors*, 222 ff.). The term Illyricum is here used in a general sense to denote the Pannonias, the Moesias, the Dacias south of the Danube, and Dalmatia. Victor again breaks his narrative to dwell upon a school of generals and to moralize on the qualities of the tetrarchs who served the empire well at this critical juncture because they possessed practical abilities and resourcefulness and worked harmoniously for the good of the state (Syme, *Emperors*, 211). For similar comments cf. *H.A. Tyr. trig.* 10.14-16; *Prob.* 22.3; *Car.* 18.3-4. The author of the *H.A.* was perhaps influenced by Victor in carrying the notion of a school of generals back to the reign of Valerian (Syme, *Emperors*, 212). The *concordia* of the emperors is a favourite theme of their propaganda (J. Straub, *Vom Herrscherideal in der Spätantike*, Stuttgart, 1939, 43). On its importance and how difficult it was to maintain cf. Ammianus, 26.2.8; Tac. *Ann.* IV.4; Jones, *L.R.E.*I,41.

21. Victor is, in part, alluding to the Julio-Claudian and Severan periods, but in particular to the murders of Constantine's relatives during and after his reign, including that of Constantine II by Constans, events which had occurred during the author's lifetime.

22. Cf. Lact. *De Mort. Persec.* 7.1; 8.3; *Eutrop.* 10.1; Julian, *Or.* 2; 3.51d; Praxagoras, *F.H.G.* IV, p. 2; *H.A. Car.* 18.3.

Diocletian controlled the East, including Egypt and Libya, Maximian governed Italy, Africa, Sicily, Sardinia and Spain, Galerius held Illyricum, i.e. those provinces south of the Danube from the Black Sea to the River Inn, and Constantius was in charge of Gaul and Britain, though the last named had to be reconquered. Despite Julian and Praxagoras, Spain was not placed under Constantius' authority, though in the 360s it was attached to the prefecture of the Gauls (Dufraigne, *A.V.*, 185). Both Victor and Eutropius fail to mention Spain. This division of the empire was made partially for military and administrative purposes, but in the main it was an admirable safeguard against rebellion as long as the four emperors remained loyal to one another. All depended on their harmony, which Diocletian secured by his moral dominance (Jones, *L.R.E.*I,41).

23.   Until Diocletian's reorganization Italy had enjoyed a privileged position in fiscal matters, *i.e.* it possessed immunity from general provincial taxation. In 297-8 Italy was divided into eight districts, each governed by a senatorial or equestrian *corrector*. It was also organized, in actuality if not officially, into two dioceses, Italy north of the Apennines, including Raetia and the Cottian Alps (*regio annonaria*), and the Suburbicarian diocese of peninsular Italy, Sicily, Sardinia and Corsica (Jones, *L.R.E.*I,45, 47; III, 4, note 16). Diocletian made the former subject to regular provincial taxation (Jones, *L.R.E.*I,61-66), though it had always been liable to irregular indictions (Tac. *Ann.* I.71). Galerius' attempt to make the *regio suburbicaria* similarly subject to taxation in 306 was a major cause of the acclamation of Maxentius (Lact. *De Mort. Persec.* 26.2; *Pan.* 12.16.2). By 540 Justinian had finally abolished all distinctions between Italy and the provinces (Jones, *L.R.E.*I,65; III,8).

24.   Cf. Lact. *De Mort. Persec.* 7.2 ff. This refers to the fiscal reforms of Diocletian in 297. Lactantius, a professor of rhetoric but also a contemporary, paints a horrendous picture

of the mounting cost of the imperial bureaucracy and armies. The ministers of the imperial retinues had possibly quadrupled, there were twice as many provincial governors, additional diocesan officials, up to twenty military commanders (**duces**) with all their attendant staffs. Furthermore, the army had approximately doubled its number of legions since the Severan period (Jones, *L.R.E.*I,51-60). All of this put an extra burden on the taxpayers. But Victor, an imperial bureaucrat, is perhaps correct in stating that Diocletian's system was initially bearable. It was fairer than the irregular indictions it replaced, but abuses had become endemic by the time of Constantius II (Ammianus, 21.16.17). Nevertheless, it did work efficiently under Julian (Ammianus, 16.5.14; 25.4.15; *Pan.* 11.9). For Victor's views of the bureaucracy *vid.* Bird, *S.A.V.*, 52-59.

25.   Cf. Eutrop. 9.24-25; Oros. 7.25.9; Lact. *De Mort. Persec.* 9.5; Jord. *Rom.* 301; Festus, 25; Zon XII. 31. Verbal similarities coupled with distinct differences in detail between Eutropius and Festus indicate that Festus, (as well as Victor and Eutropius), was at this point following the *Kaisergeschichte* (T.D. Barnes, *B.H.A.C. 1968/69*, 1970, 21). Narses, son of Sapor, became king of Persia in 293 and made an initial but unsuccessful attack on the Romans. Three years later he invaded Armenia, captured those parts of Mesopotamia ceded to Rome in 287 by Vahram, and marched into Syria. In spring, 297 Galerius (Maximian) and his Armenian allies were beaten near Callinicum, south of Carrhae (Harran) in Mesopotamia. Eutropius, Festus, Orosius, Jerome and Ammianus (14.11.10) inform us that on his return to Antioch Galerius was publicly humiliated by Diocletian (Valerius), which may have been a later invention or exaggeration (cf. Eadie, *Festus, 146-148;* Barnes, *Constantine*, 17; *id. Phoenix* 30, 1976, 182-186; Williams, *Diocletian*, 80). Galerius gathered a new army of Danubian troops and Gothic and Sarmatian mercenaries during the balance of 297, and the following year he avoided the normal route across the Mesopotamian plains which suited the Persian cavalry and

marched into Armenia to ensure it remained loyal and to strike from the north. Narses followed and was utterly defeated and his family and harem captured. The King fled but was forced to submit to humiliating peace terms after Galerius had overrun Media and Adiabene and captured Ctesiphon. The booty and victory were so impressive that Ammianus recalled them nearly a century later (22.4.8; 23.5.11; 24.1.10). Peace came in 299 and lasted almost forty years. Roman territory was regained, parts of Armenia annexed and Nisibis became a Roman fortress city (Eadie, *loc. cit.*; Barnes, *Constantine*, 18; Williams, *Diocletian*, 84-86; Dufraigne, *A.V.*, 187). At the end of Constantine's reign war with Persia again erupted (*De Caes.* 41.16) and the Persians besieged Nisibis and overran parts of Mesopotamia three times between 337 and 350. In 357/358, after an uneasy truce, negotiations between Sapor II and Strategius Musonianus, praetorian prefect of the East, broke down and in spring 359 Sapor invaded Roman Mesopotamia and captured Amida and other Roman fortress cities (Ammianus, 17.5 ff.; 18.4 ff.). The Persians' demands are well illustrated by Ammianus in a letter from Sapor to Constantius and it is to these demands and the war which had just broken out that Victor refers. Before Constantius could act against the Persians Julian was proclaimed emperor in Gaul in early 361 and Constantius was forced to turn his troops towards Europe. His death in November left the Persian War to Julian (Matthews, *R.E.A.*, 3, 39-66; R.C. Blockley, *Phoenix* 42, 1988, 244-260). After Julian's death in June, 363 'similar demands were made on Jovian (Ammianus, 25.7.9).

26.   Cf. Eutrop. 9.23; *Pan.* 5.21.2; 6.8.8.   The Panegyrics, Diocletian's official version, underline the emperor's clemency. Eutropius says the siege of Alexandria lasted eight months: *vid.* note 18. For Africa at this juncture *vid.* note 17.

27.   Cf. Eutrop. 9.22.2; Oros. 7.25.6; *Pan.* 4. In 290 Carausius received recognition from the central government, a temporary expedient as was later demonstrated.   In 293 Constantius

captured Boulogne (Gesoriacum) and expelled Carausius'
forces from Gaul (*Pan.* 8.6-7). Meanwhile Carausius and his
successor, Allectus, began the coastal defences from Norfolk
to the Isle of Wight known as the Saxon Shore. In the west
they fortified Lancaster and Cardiff against piratical attacks by
the Picts of Scotland and the Scotti of Ireland. Carausius was
assassinated in 293 by his *rationalis* (finance minister) or
praetorian prefect, Allectus. In 296 Constantius and his
praetorian prefect, Asclepiodotus, attacked Allectus
simultaneously with two fleets and armies, but it was
Asclepiodotus' army which, after landing near Winchester and
marching north-east, defeated Allectus near Farnham (Barnes,
New Empire, 11; *Constantine*, 15-16; Williams, *Diocletian*,
74).

28.   Cf. Eutrop. 9.25; Oros. 8.25.12; *Pan.* 4(5).1; 8(5)5; Jord. *Rom.*
299; *Get.* 16.91; *Chron. Min.* I.230, 295; Ammianus, 28.1.5;
Lact. *De Mort. Persec.* 13.2; 18.6. The Carpi were defeated
and transferred to the depopulated areas of northern Pannonia
Inferior by Diocletian in 296. Aurelian had already settled
many of them there in 272 (*H.A. Aur.* 30.4). The Marcomanni,
however, were defeated in 299 (Barnes, *Phoenix* 30, 1976, 176,
187; William, *Diocletian*, 76-77; P. Brennan, *Chiron* 10, 1980,
562 ff.).

29.   The legislation and behaviour of Diocletian and the tetrarchs
in their early years is praised even by Christian writers (Eus.
H.E. 13; Lact. *De Mort. Persec.* 9.11), but Lactantius gives a
different picture in 7.1 ff. Diocletian abolished the previous
chaotic system of taxation, with its mass of unwieldy and
inequitable local practices, which had grown up over the
centuries. He replaced it with a system of land tax and poll
tax for the whole empire, based upon land and human
resources which, however, still took into consideration local
variations in custom (Jones, *L.R.E.I*,61-66, 68-70;II,819-821).

30.   The *frumentarii* were, in the early principate, minor army

officials in charge of the military grain supply (*annona militaris*). Together with the *speculatores* (scouts and intelligence agents attached to each legion) the *frumentarii* acted as couriers, envoys and gatherers of intelligence (Dio, 78.17.1-2). Diocletian probably established them as secret police (W.G. Sinnigen, *C.J.* 57, 1961, 66), though it was under Hadrian that we first hear of them acting in this capacity and supervising the imperial postal system (*H.A. Hadr.* 11.4; *Max.-Balb.* 10.3; *Macr.* 12.4; *Claud.* 17.1; *De Caes.* 13.5-6). Because of their functions as secret police and collectors of the *annona* they acquired an evil reputation. The *agentes in rebus* (or *rerum*) were apparently organized by Diocletian, even though we first hear of them in 319 (*Cod. Theod.* VI.35.3), and they were then officially controlled by the *magister officiorum*, an office established by Constantine before 320 (*Cod. Theod.* XVI.10.1). Probably, like the *frumentarii* whom they replaced, they were initially under the praetorian prefects. Jones (*L.R.E.* I,581) considered that they did not normally carry out police functions except as inspectors of the postal system and that only under Constantius II did they achieve notoriety as secret police. Nonetheless Julian rebukes two of them as informers (*delatores*) after Constantius' death (Ammianus, 22.7.5; cf. Zos. II.55) and there was no less need for this service among his predecessors (Sinnigen, *op. cit.,* 70). Victor is here emphatic and informed: they appear to have been established to ferret out information and denounce their victims, and undoubtedly some abused their powers.

31.   Cf. Lact. *De Mort. Persec.* 7.1 ff. for a totally different, albeit biassed, point of view. The *annona urbis*, a monthly dole of grain to the citizens at Rome, was instituted in 58 B.C. by Clodius. By the fourth century approximately 150,000 citizens still receiving the dole were entitled to 50 oz. of coarse bread daily (Jones, *L.R.E.* II,696). Diocletian made the southern region of Italy (*regio suburbicaria*) responsible for supplying the capital with pork, beef, wine, wood and lime. Grain for the bread still came from Egypt, Africa and Sicily. For a

discussion of sources *vid.* Jones, *L.R.E.*III,215-221. Severe inflation and a shrinkage of the tax base in the third century, coupled with a substantial increase in government expenditure caused Diocletian between 296 and 301 to make attempts to stabilize the currency, fix prices on all commodities and services, and provide rations, clothing and arms for all soldiers and civil servants. He also revamped the entire tax system of the empire (*vid.* note 29).

32.   Victor uses the term *honestiores* here in a technical sense to mean the upper ranks of society, i.e. senators, decurions, civil servants and soldiers, to be distinguished from the common people, *humiliores*. To Victor, "an intellectual, cultural and social snob" (Nixon, *Caesares*, 411), the term may also have indicated a class of people more honest than the common folk. Diocletian and Constantine established extremely severe penalties for those guilty of corruption (*Cod. Theod.* I.12.2; I.16.7; I.32.1; X.4.1) or those transgressing the Edict on Maximum Prices (N. Lewis & M. Reinhold, *Roman Civilization* II, New York, 1966, 466). Victor's claim that virtues began to increase because of these measures is negated by the continuous fulminations and harsh laws of Diocletian's successors against corruption and the rapacity of their functionaries (Alföldi, *Conflict*, 28-47; Jones, *L.R.E.*I,467-468).

33.   A cautious allusion to the tetrarchs' support of paganism and harsh persecution of Christians. It may also be an indirect criticism of the Christian emperors for their indifference to Rome's ancient religion and promotion of the new and, for Victor, alien faith.

34.   At Rome Diocletian built the magnificent Baths which still bear his name and have been converted into the celebrated Museo Nazionale on the modern Piazza della Repubblica (for which *vid.* S. Aurigemma, *Le Terme di Diocleziano ed il Museo Nazionale Romano*, Rome, 1955). In addition he was responsible for the design and much of the construction of the

Basilica of Maxentius, the reconstruction of the Curia in the Forum, the *cellae* of the Temple of Venus and Rome, and the design of the Circus of Maxentius and repairs to many other buildings (D.R. Dudley, *Urbs Roma*, Aberdeen, 1967, 24, 43, 88, 202-203; N. Ramage and A. Ramage, *Roman Art*, New Jersey, 1991, 252-257). In the provinces Diocletian built palaces at Split, Palmyra and Nicomedia and imperial baths at Trier. The building projects at Nicomedia, Trier and Milan were meant to enhance the new imperial capitals and were, indeed, costly (Lact. *De Mort. Persec.* 7.8-10). Carthage is cited here and again in 40.19 perhaps because of Victor's affection for his native province. He may also have lived and studied there. It was never an imperial capital but was one of the empire's major cities and probably benefitted from Diocletian's building schemes for coins of the period bear the legends *AUCTA KART.* or *FEL KART.* (Sutherland, *R.I.C.* VI, 411 ff.).

35.   Cf. Eutrop. 9.26-27; Lact. *De Mort. Persec.* 7.1 ff; 8.1 ff. Lactantius, a contemporary of Diocletian who vividly recalled the persecution of his fellow Christians instigated by that emperor, is understandably biassed. Victor and Eutropius, however, despite their evident admiration for Diocletian (*De Caes.* 39.1; 39.8; 39.15; 39.26 ff.; 39.32; 39.44; 39.48; Eutrop. 9.26; 9.28), find it impossible to omit his evident faults and those of the partner he chose. There seems no reason to doubt Maximian's cruelty, severity and crudity, or his loyalty to Diocletian (Williams, *Diocletian*, 44-45).

36.   Cf. Lact. *De Mort. Persec.* 26.3. Though the number of praetorian cohorts at Rome in 306 remained as before, ten (*Ann. Epig.* 240, 1961, 60), Diocletian probably reduced their effective personnel substantially. But the prestige of the city and its turbulent mob prevented him from eliminating the guard entirely. Galerius may have attempted to abolish the guard when he abolished the tax exemption of Suburbicarian Italy in 306 (*vid.* note 23). Constantine finally did disband the

praetorians soon after capturing the city in 312 (*De Caes.*
40.25; M. Durry, *Les cohortes prétoriennes*, Paris, 1938, 89,
394). The last part of Victor's statement is unclear. Dufraigne
(*A.V.*, 189) thinks that the *vulgi in armis* may refer to ordinary
troops quartered at Rome. Possibly Victor is referring to the
vigiles and urban cohorts, for both disappeared in the early
fourth century and in the 350s, when Victor was at Rome, the
city prefects had no troops at their disposal (Jones, *L.R.E.*II,
693). It is difficult to understand how the reduction of troops
at Rome had any influence on Diocletian's decision to retire.
The copyist may have made an error in punctuation for it
appears that the phrase *quo quidem plures volunt imperium
posuisse* more naturally refers to what follows than to what
precedes.

37.   Cf. Eutrop. 9.27-28; *Epit.* 39.5; Oros. 7.25.14; Lact. *De Mort.
Persec.* 10.1; 17.1 ff.; 18.1; 19.5-6; Euseb. *H.E.* 8.13; Zos.
II.10.5; Zon XII 32. After celebrating his *Vicennalia* and a
joint triumph with Maximian at Rome on November 20th, 303
Diocletian, then about sixty years old (Barnes, *New Empire*,
30-31) embarked upon a winter journey to Nicomedia and fell
ill *en route.* He reached Nicomedia in summer, 304 but his
health had deteriorated and he nearly died. He had partially
recovered by March 1st, 305, but Galerius visited him that
month and probably helped to convince him to step down. A
suitable occasion was presented by the *Vicennalia* of Maximian
(April 1st to May 1st, 305) and on May 1st, 305 Diocletian
retired from office at Nicomedia and took up residence at Split
in Dalmatia, while Maximian unwillingly abdicated at Milan
and retired to Lucania. The reasons given by our sources for
Diocletian's abdication vary. Zosimus agrees with Victor,
Eutropius attributes it to old age and lack of vigour, Lactantius,
a contemporary, to religious prognostications, old age, sickness
and pressure from Galerius, Eusebius to a serious illness
visited upon him as a punishment by God. There is no
evidence that Diocletian envisaged a fixed term of office for
the emperors until ill-health and pressure from Galenius forced

a decision on him (N. H. Baynes, *J.R.S.* 38, 1948, 112). It is possible that the word *valentior* should read *valentioribus*, i.e. he gave up the administration of the state to those who were more vigorous. This would correspond to Eutropius' *stationem tuendae republicae viridioribus iunioribusque mandarent* and Lactantius' *se invalidum esse, requiem post labores petere, imperium validioribus tradere* (*De Mort. Persec.* 19.3).

38.   The abdication must have been a common topic of discussion in the following half-century. Victor and Eutropius, following the *Kaisergeschichte*, and *Pan.* 7.15.4 are full of admiration for Diocletian's unique act: *Pan.* 6.9.2 is more reserved. Even Lactantius, however, is compelled to acknowledge Diocletian's efforts and accomplishment in preserving the state (*De Mort. Persec.* 18.15).

40

1.   Cf. Eutropius. 10.1-2; *Epit.* 40.1; Oros. 7.25.15; Zos. II.8.1; *An. Val.* 3.5. Armentarius, a nickname for Galerius, is only mentioned by Victor and the Epitomator. Constantius was assigned Britain, Gaul and Spain, Galerius received the Danubian provinces and Asia Minor. Of the two new Caesars Flavius Valerius Severus was to administer Italy, Africa and perhaps Pannonia, while C. Galerius Valerius Maximinus (Daia) was given the diocese of Oriens (Barnes, *New Empire*, 197; cf. *id.*, *Constantine*, 26; Williams, *Diocletian*, 192). Eutropius mistakenly states that Constantine gave up Italy and Africa: these two provinces had already been assigned to his Caesar, Severus, by Diocletian and Galerius. Both new Caesars were Illyrian and nominees of Galerius, the former a low-born drinking buddy of his, the latter his nephew (Syme, *Emperors*, 212), and their new titles, Valerius and Galerius Valerius, are indicative of the connection.

2.   Constantine's ambition is emphasized by Eutropius (10.5) and

Zosimus (II.8.2-3).

3.   Cf. *Epit.* 41.2; Lact. *De Mort. Persec.* 24.1-8; Euseb. *Vit. Const.* 1.20.2; *Anon. Val.* 2.4; Zos. II.8.3; Zon. XII.33. The Epitomator's statement that Galerius detained Constantine in Rome is an obvious error, but he alone notes that Crocus (or Erocus), an Alamannic king, supported Constantine's bid for power. The account that Galerius sent Constantine to his father and that the latter subsequently fought against the Picts in *Anon. Val.* is supported by *Pan.* 7.7 of 310, but the romantic version of Constantine's escape soon became accepted and was presumably in the *Kaisergeschichte.*

4.   Cf. *Epit.* 41.2; Lact. *De Mort. Persec.* 24.8; Euseb. *Vit. Const.* 1.21.1; *Anon. Val.* 2.4; *Pan.* 7.8.1; Zos. II.9.1. I have omitted *vel parentem* from the text. The copyist responsible for the *De Caesaribus* and the *Epitome,* seeing the word *parentem* in the latter and considering that a subtle distinction may have been implied, probably added the superfluous *vel parentem* (A. Cameron, *C.R.* 15, 1965, 20-21; cf. Dufraigne, *A.V.,* 191.

5.   Constantius died at York (Eboracum) on July 25th, 306 and Constantine was acclaimed Augustus by the troops (Eutrop. 10.13; 10.2.2; Epit. 41.3; Lact. *De Mort. Persec.* 24.8-9; *Anon. Val.* 2.4; Zon. XII.33; Zos. II.9.1; *Chron. Min.* I, 231, 235; Socr. 1.2.3; *Pan.* 6.5.3; 7.2.3; 7.7.4; 7.8.2). Constantine (Flavius Valerius Constantinus) was Constantius' son by his first wife Helena, a woman of humble origin. Galerius only accepted him as Caesar, but Maximian reappointed him as Augustus in c. September, 307.

6.   Cf. Eutrop. 10.2; *Epit.* 40.2; Oros. 7.28.5; Lact. *De Mort. Persec.* 26.1 ff.; *Anon. Val.* 3.6; Zos. II.9.3 ff. M. Aurelius Valerius Maxentius, son of Maximian, was passed over like Constantine in the settlement of Nicomedia in 305. He was living near Rome when he learned of Constantine's acclamation. On October 28th, 306 he had himself proclaimed

emperor by the disaffected senate and praetorians with the support of the populace and was recognized in Italy, Sicily, Africa (except for 308-309), Sardinia and Corsica (Barnes, *New Empire,* 12-13; Williams, *Diocletian,* 195). Victor, and Lactantius maintain that the populace was involved. The praetorians, already reduced in numbers by Diocletian and threatened with abolition by Galerius, needed popular support for their choice and it was readily forthcoming because of Galerius' move to abolish tax exemptions for Rome and Suburbicarian Italy. Maxentius, being close at hand, probably offered himself as the champion of their cause.

7.   Cf. Eutrop. 10.2-3; *Epit.* 40.3; Lact. *De Mort. Persec.* 26.5 ff; Zos. II.10.1; *Anon. Val.* 3.6; *Pan.* 7.10.5; 9.3.4; 12.3.4; Euseb. *Vit. Const.* 1.26. According to Zosimus Severus marched from Milan, probably in early 307, and besieged Rome. His troops, however, who had served under Maximian, were readily bribed to desert. Severus fled to Ravenna where Maximian, who had resumed his position as Augustus, besieged him in turn and eventually induced him to surrender and renounce his position. Thereafter Severus was taken to Rome as a hostage and then to Tres Tabernae, thirty miles from Rome on the Appian Way, where he was interned in a state villa. When Galerius invaded Italy Severus was executed or forced to commit suicide and was buried in Gallienus' tomb (Barnes, *Constantine,* 30; Williams, *Diocletian,* 195). Victor and Eutropius inform us, erroneously, that Severus died at Ravenna, so the account must have been in the *Kaisergeschichte* (Nixon, *Caesares,* 321). The Epitomator, however, has the correct version (cf. Zos. II.10.2; *Anon. Val.* 4.10) so he must have used a different source here. For a somewhat different conclusion *vid.* Dufraigne, *A.V.,* 191-92.

8.   Cf. Eutrop. 10.4; Lact. *De Mort. Persec.* 27.1 ff.; 29.2; *Pan.* 12.3.4; *Anon. Val.* 3.7; Zos. II.10.3 ff.; Zon. XII.34; *Chron. Min.* I.231. Victor is chronologically confused here, as is Zonaras. It was in November, 308 that Valerius Licinianus

181

Licinius was proclaimed Augustus at Carnuntum (near Altenburg), the capital of Pannonia Superior. Licinius (born c. 265) was from New Dacia and an old friend of Galerius. The latter invaded Italy and encamped at Interamna (Terni), north of Rome, in 307. It was there that his troops were tampered with by Maxentius, probably with Maximian's help, and Galerius was forced to retreat to avoid Severus' fate. Victor again commits a minor error, either through compression or because he confused Galerius' campaign and experiences with those of Severus.

9.   Galerius died, possibly of cancer of the bowels and genitals, in early May, 311 at Serdica (Sofia) in Dardania, approximately 2 1/2 years after the appointment of Licinius. (Eutrop. 10.4; *Epit.* 40.4; Lact. *De Mort. Persec.* 33.1 ff; Euseb. *Vit. Const.* 1.5; *H.E.* 8.16.3; *Anon. Val.* 3.8; Zos. II.11; Zon. XII.34). Victor is the only author to mention Galerius' reclamation of the area between Lake Balaton (Pelso) and the Danube. This area, the northern part of Pannonia Inferior, was reorganized into a separate province by Galerius in c. 294 and called Valeria after his wife, the daughter of Diocletian (Ammianus, 19.11.4; 28.1.5; Syme, *Emperors*, 226-227). Victor's knowledge of these details may be the result of autopsy or information from eyewitnesses: he was at Sirmium from c. 357 (*vid.* Introduction).

10.   Victor's figures are approximately correct. Constantius and Galerius were Caesars from March 1st, 293 until May 1st, 305, i.e. just over 12 years. Constantius was then Augustus until July 25th, 306, Galerius until early May, 311 (Lact. *De Mort. Persec.* 35.1-4), i.e. 6 years.

11.   Cf. *De Caes.* 39.26; Eutrop. 10.2; *Epit.* 40.15; Lact. *De Mort. Persec.* 9.1-2. It seems that Victor uses the terms *beneficia naturae* (= *ingenium*, natural abilities) and *eruditio* (learning) as antitheses. His ideal emperor would combine *eruditio* and its concomitant qualities, *elegantia* and *comitas* (refinement

and courtesy) with the *ingenium* of emperors like Aurelian, Probus and Diocletian. Victor attributes Rome's decline to the growth of dishonesty and the lack of education and culture (24.9). The idea was hardly novel; cf. Sall. *Jug.* 2 ff.; *Cat.* 1-5. Even Victor's mention of Cyrus may have been borrowed from Sallust (*Cat.* 2.2), although the latter used Cyrus as an example of aggrandizement. Cyrus the Great, founder of the Achaemenid Persian Empire (559-529 B. C.), defeated the Medes in 549 B.C. and the Lydians a few years later. Victor's opinion of him, like that of many in the ancient world, was influenced by Xenophon's historical romance, the *Cyropaedia*, a didactic work which disregarded historical accuracy in order to portray Cyrus as the perfect statesman, ruler and general: cf. Cic. *ad Quint. Fratr.* 1.1. Eusebius compares Constantius I with Cyrus and Alexander (*Vit. Const.* 1.7).

12.   Cf. 40.2; 41.20-21; Eutrop. 10.5; 10.6-7; *Epit.* 41.13; Lact. *De Mort. Persec.* 18.10; *Anon. Val.* 2.2; 6.30; Zos. II.29.1; 38.1; *Pan.* 7.16; 9.19.6; 10.34.4. The Anonymus Valesianus is less impressed than Eutropius with Constantine's cultural attainments. Lactantius, the first two mentioned panegyrics and even Zosimus note Constantine's imposing appearance (borne out by his statues and coins). Lactantius and the last-mentioned panegyric remark upon his affability. His ambition, evident in so much that he did, is emphasized by Victor, Eutropius, the Epitomator and Zosimus, his lavishness criticized by pagan writers in general. Even Eusebius (*H.E.* 4.54) deplores the liberal favours he bestowed upon Christians which resulted in many interested conversions. At this point Victor indicates that he lived and was old enough to remember events during Constantine's reign, i.e. he was born c. 320: cf. Bird, *S.A.V.,* 5; Nixon, *Caesares,* 21; Dufraigne, *A.V.,* xiv. Victor's criticism is less pronounced than that of other pagan authors probably because he was writing under Constantius II; the others wrote after the end of the dynasty. For Ammianus' criticisms of Constantine *vid.* 16.8.12; 17.4.13; 21.10.8; 12.25.

13. Cf. Prax. I.I. (*F.H.G.*IV.2); *Pan.* 9.2.6. This refers to Constantine's campaigns against the Franks and Alamanni along the Rhine in 309 and 310. He appears subsequently to have entered Spain and annexed it and made a compact with Licinius, to whom he betrothed his half-sister, Constantia (Lact. *De Mort. Persec.* 43.2; Zos. II.17.2) before marching against Maxentius in the spring of 312.

14. Cf. *Epit.* 40.2; 40.6; 40.20; Zos. II.12.2-3; 14.2-3; Polem. Silv. *Chron. Min.* I.522. In 308 L. Domitius Alexander, vicar of the praetorian prefect, was acclaimed Augustus in Africa and may have made overtures to Constantine (*I.L.S.* 8936). The Epitomator and Zosimus, following a common source here which is not the *Kaisergeschichte*, agree in general with Victor's description of Alexander, but state that his origin was Phrygian, which is unlikely. Victor's information may derive from local knowledge or personal opinion (Syme, *Emperors*, 229). At any rate a Pannonia origin for a man of that rank is more plausible. Alexander probably ruled until 311 when Maxentius was finally forced to send a small force under his praetorian prefect, C. Rufius Volusianus, to recapture Africa and restore the grain supply for Rome. The campaign was short for Alexander's troops were few in number and hastily levied; the pretender was captured and executed (cf. L. Laffranchi, *Numismatica* 13, 1947, 17-20; R. Andreotti, *Afrika und Rom in der Antike*, Halle, 1968, 245-276).

15. Cf. Zos. II.14.3-4; *C.I.L.* VIII.18261, line 11; *Pan.* 4.32.6; 9.16.1; 10.32.6. Victor dwells upon his native province and gives details not found in the more extensive account of Zosimus. In 40.28 he tells us that Cirta suffered serious damage during the war and had to be restored by Constantine and renamed Constantina. Maxentius took excessive reprisals against Alexander's supporters and also made heavy demands on the province to ensure Rome's grain supply and to defray the substantial expenditure incurred by his building schemes at Rome and the augmentation of his army. He thus incurred the

hatred of the Africans to such an extent that his head was sent to Africa by Constantine in 312, for the latter felt that he would thereby gain the support of the province (*Pan.* 9.16; 10.32).

16.   Cf. Lact. *De Mort. Persec.* 18.9; 43.4; *Pan.* 9.4.4; 9.14.2; 9.14.5; 9.16.2; 10.8.3; 10.9.4; Eutrop. 10.4.3; Zos. II.14.4; Julian, *Caes.* 30.329 A; Euseb. *H.E.* 8.14.3. For a full discussion of Victor's portrayal of Maxentius, who became the stereotypical tyrant, in part, at least, because of Constantinian propaganda, *vid.* Nixon, *Caesares,* 366-373. Victor is quite correct in maintaining that Maxentius was unmoved by his father's death for Maximian's sole intention was to resume power himself with Diocletian (Lact. *De Mort. Persec.* 43.6). Maxentius was not the indolent, unwarlike coward of the sources. Expecting an attack by Licinius in 312 he despatched an army to Verona, but Constantine anticipated Licinius and in spring, 312 he crossed the Alps, seized Segusio and defeated detachments of Maxentius' troops near Turin and at Brescia. At Verona Maxentius' forces actually encircled Constantine's army as it was besieging the city, but Constantine ultimately prevailed after a hard contest, captured the city, and afterwards Modena, which allowed him to march on Rome with central and northern Italy secure behind him.

17.   Cf. Eutrop. 10.3.1; Lact. *De Mort. Persec.* 28; Zos. II.11; *Pan.* 6.12.5; 7.15.2. In early spring, 308 Maximian, who had reached an agreement with Constantine the previous year and given him Fausta in marriage, returned to Rome where he seems to have had a serious disagreement with Maxentius. Finally, in April that year he summoned his old soldiers to a meeting, denounced his son for the existing troubles and tore the purple cloak from his shoulders. The soldiers rallied around Maxentius and the old emperor fled for his life to his son-in-law, Constantine. Victor, unlike Eutropius and Lactantius, chooses to ignore the rivalry between father and son and play up Maxentius' supposed apathy and inertia in

contrast with Maximian's energy and intractability.

18.   Cf. Eutrop. 10.3; *Epit.* 40.5; Lact. *De Mort. Persec.* 29.3; 30.6. In 310, left in charge of Constantine's southern army while Constantine was campaigning on the lower Rhine, Maximian proclaimed Constantine dead, won over the troops at Arelate (Arles) by bribery and had himself proclaimed Augustus. Fausta informed her husband and Constantine quickly returned to besiege Maximian at Marseilles. The citizens opened the gates to Constantine and Maximian was compelled to surrender and hanged himself, presumably at Constantine's insistence. (Barnes, *Constantine*, 32-35; Williams, *Diocletian*, 195-197). Eutropius' suggestion that Maximian engineered his rift with Maxentius in order to eliminate Constantine was probably part of Constantine's subsequent propaganda.

19.   Cf. Eutrop. 10.4; *Epit.* 40.7; Lact. *De Mort. Persec.* 44.1; 44.3; 44.9; *Anon. Val.* 4.12; *Pan.* 4.27.5; 12.14.3; 15.1; Euseb. *H.E.* 9.9.5; Praxag. 1.1. (*F.H.G.* IV. p. 2); Zos. II.16.1; Zon. XIII.I. Rome was in turmoil because of Maxentius' enforced exactions and his losses in northern and central Italy. Accordingly he was compelled to abandon the tactics which had proven so successful against Severus and Galerius and face Constantine in open battle across the Tiber near Saxa Rubra upstream from the Milvian Bridge, which he had seemingly destroyed and replaced with an easily-dismantled trestle bridge. On October 28th, 312 Maxentius' army, its main contingent being the praetorians, was severely defeated, probably by superior forces, and the temporary bridge collapsed under the weight of the fleeing army. Maxentius was swept into the Tiber and drowned, after ruling exactly six years (Barnes, *Constantine*, 41-43). For Victor's use of the words tyrant, tyranny in a pejorative sense *vid.* Bird, *S.A.V.*, 112.

20.   The normal reaction at the death of a stereotypical tyrant: cf. Lact. *De Mort. Persec.* 44.10; *Pan.* 9.19; 10.30.4; 10.31; Euseb. *H.E.* 9.9; *Vit. Const.* 1.39; Zos. II.17; Zon. XIII.1.13.

For the praetorians' massacre of the populace *vid. Pan.* 10.3.8; Euseb. *H.E.* 8.14; *Vit. Const.* 1.35.

21. For the exactions imposed upon the senators cf. *Pan.* 10.8.3; 10.31.2. They included, in part, payment in gold (*aurum oblaticium*) according to *Chron A.D. 354*, p. 148, but Maxentius' predecessors had long received such payments made at an emperor's accession, quinquennial celebrations or triumphs (Dio, 72.16.3; 77.9.2; Jones, *L.R.E.*I,430). On the other hand Victor may be alluding to the *follis* or *collatio glebalis*, a surtax on senators graded according to property owned, which Constantine imposed soon after entering Rome (Zos. II.38; Jones, *L.R.E.*I,431). Constantine may have found this tax operating when he arrived and merely confirmed it. Victor, who detested Maxentius, may have attributed this unpopular tax to the tyrant, thereby exonerating Constantine. On the misery of the farmers cf. Ruf. *H.E.* 8.16. Victor's father would presumably have experienced and discussed this.

22. Cf. Zos. II.17.2; *Pan.* 10.33.6; *Cod. Theod.* X.10.1; XIII.10.1; XV.14.3; M. Durry. *Les Cohortes Prétoriennes*, Paris, 1938, 393-396. One of Constantine's first acts upon entering Rome was to disband the praetorians and the rest of Maxentius' forces, an obvious and necessary move which would clearly please senators and people alike.

23. Cf. *Pan.* 10.35.4-5; Ammianus, 16.10.14. Ammianus cites the *Templum Urbis*, presumably the Temple of Venus and Rome restored by Maxentius (Dufraigne, *A.V.*, 195) or the Temple of Romulus (Dudley, *op. cit.*, 116-117), the *Basilica Flavii*, which was commenced by Maxentius and completed by Constantine and named the *Basilica Constantiniana* (originally the *Basilica Nova*), which Constantine radically altered, adding a Baptistry, the *Fons Constantini* (Platner and Ashby, *op. cit.*, 76-78). Furthermore Constantine built large public baths on the Quirinal dedicated by the senate in 315. The *Circus Maximus*, first built in the regal period (Livy, VIII.20.1.) between the

Palatine and the Aventine, was restored by J. Caesar (Plin. *N. H.* 36. 102; Suet. *Caes.* 39), was improved by Trajan (*C.I.L.* VI.955) and added to by Constantine. Victor fails to mention one of the best known of the emperor's edifices, the Arch of Constantine. Erected in 315 or 316 it still bestrides the street between the Palatine and the Caelian Hill at the east end of the Colosseum. The only source for it is the inscription it bears (*C.I.L.* VI.1139; Dudley, *op. cit.,* 138).

24.   A verb such a *collocatae* (*sunt*) or *positae* (*sunt*) may have been omitted here. The statues which come to mind are the gold-covered ones representing Constantine as a god (*Pan.* 9.25.4), the colossal seated statue placed in the Basilica of Constantine, some 30 feet (9 m.) in height, with its huge head 8 feet 6 inches (2.6 m.) in height, now in the Palazzo dei Conservatori at Rome. Another impressive head of Constantine, 3 feet 1 1/2 inches (95 cm.) in height, is currently displayed at the Metropolitan Museum of Art in New York City (Ramage and Ramage, *op. cit.*, 275-277).

25.   After defeating Maxentius Constantine was greeted at Rome and in Africa as a saviour and liberator (*C.I.L.*, VI.1139, 1145). To foster this he organized a college of priests for the *gens Flavia* not only in Africa but also in Italy (*I.L.S.* 705). He continued to nominate senators to priestly colleges as *pontifex maximus* and does not appear to have discouraged paganism until his break with Licinius in 316 (A. Alföldi, *The Conversion of Constantine and Pagan Rome*, Oxford, 1948, 53 ff.; 69; A.H.M. Jones, *L.R.E.*I,93; *Constantine and the Conversion of Europe*, London, 1948, 93-94; 101-102). Cirta (Constantine in Algeria), the capital of Numidia, was a readily defensible rock fortress overlooking the River Ampsaga (Rummel) and the last stronghold of L. Domitius Alexander. Badly damaged in the siege of 311 by Maxentius' prefect, Rufius Volusianus, it was rebuilt and renamed by Constantine. It contained a large Christian community and Constantine constructed two basilicas there, one for Catholics, the second

for Donatists (Jones, *L.R.E.*I,90; III,13).

26. Victor's moralizing excursus appears to be not only a veiled criticism of Constantine (cf. 41.20-21), but also of Constantius II (42. 24-25; cf. 9.12; 13.7), who was responsible for *tyrannide tantorum depulsa* (removing many powerful pretenders/tyrants; 42.21). Both emperors are censured for promoting unworthy men to high offices, a subject of considerable importance to the senatorial nobility (Alföldi, *Conflict*, 99) and to Victor (Bird, *S.A.V.*, 52-59).

41

1. Cf. Eutrop. 10.4; *Epit.* 40.8; 40.18; Lact. *De Mort. Persec.* 45.2 ff.; 46; 47.4-5; 49; Euseb. *H.E.* 9.10.14; *Vit. Const.* 1.58 ff; Zos. II.17.3 ff. In early 313 Maximinus Daia marched from Syria with a large but hastily gathered army of 70,000 to Byzantium which he captured after a brief siege. He then took Heraclea. Just beyond that city he was surprisingly defeated by Licinius' smaller army, which till then had suffered no losses, and Maximinus was forced to retreat to Cilicia, having failed to hold the Taurus passes. At Tarsus he was besieged and seemingly committed suicide, probably in July (Barnes, *Constantine*, 62-63; *New Empire*, 7). He had been Augustus from May, 311 till July, 313. For the disagreement of the sources regarding the manner of his death *vid.* Dufraigne, *A.V.*, 196.

2. Cf. Eutrop. 10.5; *Epit.* 41.1; 41.4-5; Lact. *De Mort. Persec.* 43.1; 45.1; *Anon. Val.* 5.13; Zos. II.17.1; 18.1; Constantia, daughter of Constantius Chlorus and Theodora, was Constantine's half-sister. She was betrothed to Licinius probably in 310 and married to him at Milan in 313. Peaceful coexistence between the two emperors lasted about three years. Then, in 316, Constantine proposed that his other brother-in-law, Bassianus, should be raised to the rank of Caesar and

govern a buffer zone between them. Licinius, suspicious of encroachment, suborned Bassianus' brother, Senecio, to persuade Bassianus to rebel against Constantine. The plot was discovered and Bassianus executed. Constantine then demanded Senecio be handed over to him but Licinius refused and war broke out (*Anon. Val.* 5.14-18; Euseb. *Vit. Const.* 1.50.2; Zos. II.18-20). Eutropius and Zosimus make Constantine responsible for the rupture.

3.   For Licinius' frugality *vid.* Euseb. *Vit. Const.* 1.55; Lact. *De Mort. Persec.* 46.12; for his avarice *vid.* Julian, *Or.* 1.8; *Epit.* 41.8; *Anon. Val.* 5.22. The Epitomator is especially scathing regarding his rusticity, ignorance and hostility to learning.

4.   Constantine acted with notable clemency, after his defeat of Maxentius, for he restored to his position Aradius Rufinus, Maxentius' last urban prefect, and in late 313 he re-appointed Ceionius Rufius Volusianus to that position though he, too, had held the post under Maxentius and made him consul in 314 and praetorian prefect in 321 (Alföldi, *op. cit.* in c. 40, note 25, 72-73). One must, however, remember that the aristocracy had turned against Maxentius and Constantine needed to woo them over. A similar tendency is to be seen in his modification of certain laws like the ones Victor notes, also the edict forbidding branding on the face (*Cod. Theod.* IX.40.2) of 316, and his ineffective prohibition of gladiatorial events (*Cod. Theod.* XV.12.1) in 325, his attempts to humanize the treatment of slaves (*Cod. Theod.* II.25.1), and to ensure that maternal bequests to children went to them (*Cod. Theod.* VI.60.1), that prisoners awaiting trial should not be loaded with heavy chains and kept locked up day and night (*Cod. Theod.* IX.3.1; 320, 7, 409), and should receive speedy trials (*Cod. Theod.* IX.3.6, 380; *Cod. Just.* IX.4.6, 529). Victor returns to this theme of Constantine's clemency in 41.17. Nevertheless both Eutropius (10.8) and the Epitomator (41.14) remark upon his severe enactments. Nixon (*Caesares*, 337 ff.) emphasizes the differing attitudes of Victor and subsequent

writers like Eutropius and Zosimus regarding Constantine. Victor, writing under Constantius, omits the negative aspects of Constantine's reign and exculpates the emperor.

5.   Julian (*Or.* 1.8a) observes that Constantine's soldiers revered him as a god: also *vid.* Philostorg. *H.E.* 2.17. It had been normal to do so. But his conversion to Christianity caused pagan panegyrists, accustomed to addressing the emperor as a god, to resort to a vague monotheism connecting Constantine with the Divine Mind, whereas to Christians he was the agent of God on earth (*Pan.* XII.2; Euseb. *Vit. Const.* 2.28; *Laud. Const.* 1 *ad. fin.*).

6.   Victor continues to contrast the cruelty of Licinius (he had the families of Maximinus Daia and Galerius murdered), with the clemency of Constantine: cf. Euseb. *Vit. Const.* 1.55; *H.E.*8.12; Lact. *De Mort. Persec.* 50. Eusebius accuses Licinius of inflicting on bishops punishment reserved for criminals and of treating innocent people as murderers. Constantine's cruelty, which Eutropius openly admits (10.6), is glossed over by Victor, but the Epitomator (41.7; 41.11-12) mentions Constantine's murder of Licinius, Crispus and Fausta.

7.   Cf. Eutrop. 10.6; *Epit.* 41.4-5; *Anon. Val.* 5.16-19; Zos. II.18-20; *Chron. Min.* I.232. The accounts of the Epitomator and Zosimus are practically identical and both are clearly following the same source. On October 8th, 316 Constantine attacked Licinius near Cibalae in Pannonia Secunda and won a convincing victory. Licinius retreated to Sirmium, then to Serdica and made his general, Valens, Caesar. The latter gathered a substantial army at Adrianople. Constantine, who was then at Philippopolis, refused Licinius' offers at reconciliation and again defeated Licinius near Adrianople. However, as Constantine advanced towards Byzantium Valens and Licinius cut his army off and he was forced to negotiate. Valens was removed and executed and Constantine obtained all of Licinius' European possessions except for Thrace, Moesia

and Scythia Minor. Then, on March 1st, 317 at Serdica, an agreement was reached whereby Constantine's sons, Crispus and Constantine II, and Licinius' son, Licinius II, were appointed Caesars. Thereafter Licinius ruled from Nicomedia, not Sirmium.

8.   For a contemporary's discussion of eclipses *vid.* Ammianus, 20.3.1, with reference to the solar eclipse in the East of 360, which may have caused Victor to mention the one of 316. The scientific explanation of eclipses was known to educated Romans certainly by the time of Lucretius (*D.R.N.* 5.751) and Cicero (*De Div.* 2.6), and probably much earlier, but the uneducated treated them with superstitious dread (Tac. *Ann.* I.28).

9.   Cf. Eutrop. 10.6; *Epit.* 41.5-7; *Anon. Val.* 5.20 ff; *Chron. Min.* I.232; Zos. II.22-28; Zon. XIII.1; Soc. *H.E.* 1.4. The uneasy peace became more brittle as Licinius became increasingly intolerant of his Christian subjects who favoured Constantine, and in 321 the estrangement was demonstrated by Constantine nominating his sons, Crispus and Constantine II, to the consulship. But, as Eutropius realized (10.5), Constantine had for some time aimed at universal dominion. In 323 Constantine invaded Licinius' territory in Thrace to drive the invading Sarmatians back across the Danube. Though this was allowed by the earlier agreement Licinius regarded it as a provocation and war erupted. On the 3rd and 4th of July, 324 a decisive battle occurred and ended with the surrender of Licinius' army. Meanwhile Crispus defeated Licinius' fleet in the Hellespont, allowing Constantine's army to cross the straits north of Chalcedon. On September 18th, at Chrysopolis near Chalcedon, Constantine again defeated Licinius and his newly-appointed Caesar, Martinianus, who had previously served as master of offices (*magister officiorum*). The two fled to Nicomedia where they quickly surrendered to Constantine on the condition that they be allowed to live as private citizens. They were both executed the following spring, despite

Constantine's oath to the contrary (Barnes, *Constantine*, 67-77; *New Empire*, 44-45), allegedly for intrigue, if we are to believe Constantine's propaganda. Victor, for political reasons, again chooses to gloss over this.

10.   Cf. Eutrop. 10.6; *Epit.* 41.11; *Oros.* 7.28; Zos. II.29.1; Zon. XIII.2; *Chron. Min.* 1.232. The three Caesars were Crispus, Constantine II and Constantius II, but the latter two were only 8 and 7 years old in late 324 (Barnes, *loc. cit.*) so they would not have governed provinces for some time, though Constantine wanted to accustom them early to their imperial responsibilities (Euseb. *Laud. Const.* 3.1; Lib. *Or.* 59.39).

11.   Cf. Eutrop. 10.6; *Epit.* 41.11-12; Oros. 7.28; Ammianus, 14.11.20; Zos. II.29.2; *Chron. Min.* 1.232; Sid. Apoll. *Ep.* 5.8.2. Crispus, son of Minervina, was executed at Pola in Istria in May or June, 326, possibly for sexual offences engineered by his step-mother, Fausta, for dynastic reasons. Fausta herself was forced to commit suicide that July apparently after Helena, Constantine's mother, had caused him to suspect his wife's machinations (P. Guthrie, *Phoenix* 20, 1966, 325 ff.; Barnes, *Constantine*, 220; cf. Jones, *Constantine and the Conversion of Europe*, 245).

12.   Cf. *Anon. Val.* 6.35; Oros. 7.28.30; *Chron. Min.* 1.232; Hier. *Chron. A.D. 334*; Philostorg. 207. In 335, after Cyprus had been devastated by an earthquake and Salamis destroyed, Calocerus, an imperial functionary in charge of military dromedaries, seized power. Dalmatius, the new Caesar, easily crushed him and had him crucified, the normal punishment for slaves and robbers till Constantine abolished it. According to Philostorgios Calocerus was burned alive.

13.   On November 8th, 324 Constantine had the civic boundary of his New Rome, located at the old Byzantium, formally marked out, and it soon became known as Constantinople. The city was officially dedicated on May 11th, 330 (Barnes,

Constantine, 212, 222). Cf. Eutrop. 10.8. Its foundation eventually underlined the division of the empire into two halves, the Latin-speaking west and the Greek-speaking east. Constantine's conversion to Christianity resulted in the adoption of Christianity as the official state religion subsidized by public funds, despite long and fierce pagan opposition. Believing that the unity of the Christian church was vital to the unity of the empire Constantine fruitlessly involved himself in the bitter Donatist schism in North Africa soon after defeating Maxentius. In the east he summoned and unofficially presided over the first general council of the Christian church at Nicaea in June, 325 to deal with the Arian controversy. Since the schism and disputes remained unsettled he summoned other councils at Caesarea, Tyre and Jerusalem. In the military sphere Constantine completed the establishment of a fully-fledged field army (*comitatenses*) under the command of two newly-created officers, the *magister peditum* and the *magister equitum*. Many of the units came from Gaul and Germany. He was also responsible for the further development of the *scholae palatinae* which acted as part of his personal staff and his bodyguard. For fuller discussion *vid.* Jones, *L.R.E.*I,97 ff.; H.M.D. Parker, *J.R.S.* 23, 1933, 175-189; W. Seston, *Historia* 4,'1955, 284-296; D. van Berchem, *L'armée de Dioclétien et la Réforme Constantinienne*, Paris, 1952. Victor is exceedingly brief in noting three of Constantine's most important achievements. The reasons are not difficult to detect. Victor felt himself a Roman, heir to the traditions of the city (39.45), and like the people of Rome he resented the new city (41.17) and could not bear even to mention it by name. He similarly resented Christianity, the upstart religion, and despised the army, showing no interest in its organization. Eutropius is similarly reticent regarding Constantinople and Christianity.

14.   Cf. Eutrop. 10.7; *Anon. Val.* 6.31-32; *Chron.* Min. 1.234; Euseb. *Vit. Const.* 4.5.1 ff.; Hieron. *Chron.* 315; Ammianus, 17.12.18-13.1; Philostorg. *H.E.* 216a. In 332 Constantine

defeated the Goths and forced them to acknowledge Roman suzerainty. Two years later he overcame the Sarmatians, settling some in the Danubian provinces and compelling others to serve in the Roman army (Barnes, *Constantine*, 250). Constans was raised to the rank of Caesar in 333.

15.   Cf. *De Caes.* 32.3-4 where Victor describes another portent of disaster for the state when Gallienus was made Caesar.

16.   Cf. Eutrop. 10.9; *Epit.* 41.15; 41.18; Ammianus, 21.16.8; *De Caes.* 41.22; Zos. II.39-40; Julian, *Ep.ad Ath.*, 270 CD; 281 B. Flavius Julius Dalmatius, son of Constantine's brother, Flavius Dalmatius, was appointed Caesar to rule over Thrace and Macedonia on September 18th, 335. He was killed in August or early September, 337. His father, his brother Hannibalianus, Constantine's other half-brother, Julius Constantius, Ablabius, the praetorian prefect, and other relatives and supporters were all killed in an apparently pre-arranged massacre just before the three sons of Constantine pronounced themselves Augusti on September 9th (Barnes, *Constantine*, 261-262; *New Empire*, 8, 45. Barnes notes that Constantius had most to gain but considers that Eutropius had the plausible diagnosis (*Constantine*, 398). What we have in the Latin sources is basically the official version, that the army was responsible, which accords with Victor's qualifying remark that the soldiers vigorously objected to Dalmatius' promotion.

17.   Cf. Eutrop. 10.8; *Epit.* 41.15; Oros. 7.28.31; Euseb. *Vit. Const.* 4.61; *Anon. Val.* 6.35; Hieron. *Chron.* 315; Philostorg. *H.E.* 2.16a; Zos. II.39.1; Zon. XIII.4; Socrat. 1.39; Sozom. 2.34. Sapor II attacked Mesopotamia in 335 and the next year invaded Armenia and installed a Persia puppet on the throne. Constantine countered by declaring his nephew, Hannibalianus, 'King of Kings', sent him to Caesarea in Cappadocia and had Constantius fortify Amida on the Tigris in Upper Mesopotamia. In 337 he was preparing to march in person against the Persians when he died on May 22nd at Anchyrona

near Nicomedia (Barnes, *Constantine*, 254; Matthews, *R.E.A.*, 135-136; 498-499). Constantine had ruled as sole Augustus from September 18th, 324, i.e. 12 years, 8 months. He was sixty-five years old according to Eutropius, which is fairly accurate (Barnes, *New Empire*, 39-40). Eutropius and Philostorgios also mention the comet: it was presumably in the *Kaisergeschichte*.

18. Cf. *Epit.* 41.17; *Anon. Val.* 6.35. For the mourning at Rome at the death of Constantine *vid.* Euseb. *Vit. Const.* 4.69: for his renewal of Rome, *ibid.* 3.1. Victor was very possibly at Rome in 337 and witnessed the riots in protest at the burial of Constantine at Constantinople.

19. Cf. *De Caes.* 13.4; *Epit.* 41.13; *Chron. Pasc. Ad. 328*, I.28; Zos. II.34; Philostorg. 205. According to the *Chronicon Pascale* the bridge was constructed in 328, but it may have been built in 332 when Constantine crossed the Danube to defeat the Goths. The mention was probably in the *Kaisergeschichte* (cf. *Epit., loc. cit.*). Troubles on the middle and lower Danube seemingly forced Constantine to reorganize Diocletian's system of defences (Jones, *L.R.E.*I,99) and erect additional forts. Possibly Victor learned of this from local commanders or functionaries while serving at Sirmium. Zosimus gives a fuller account of Constantine's reorganization.

20. Septimus Severus was a native of Leptis Magna, one of the three major cities of Tripolis. In gratitude for his help and benefactions the region's inhabitants furnished Rome with free oil and grain (*H.A.Sev.* 18.3; 23.2; *Alex.* 22.2). Subsequent emperors perhaps increased the amounts which Tripolis provided and what had originally been a voluntary offering became an enforced indiction. Nicaea in Bithynia was the scene of the celebrated Council of 325 where the Nicene Creed was formulated. Hipparchus (c. 190-126 B.C.) was one of the most famous astronomers of the ancient world. He was the first to propound a theory of the motion of the sun and moon

based upon observed data and to estimate the length of the tropical year accurately. Ammianus regarded him as one of the four most eminent astronomers (26.1.8). The story that M. Aurelius imposed a tax as a penalty on the Nicenes for not knowing that Hipparchus was born there is out of character and may be apocryphal. Constantine presumably removed the indictions on Tripolis and Nicaea because both were economically distressed at this period. Nicaea, in particular, had been compelled to entertain 250-300 bishops and the imperial retinue in 325 and Constantine perhaps felt bound to assist the city by remitting its normal indictions. Victor again calls M. Aurelius *Boionius*: cf. 16.1. This name is otherwise unattested for him. In Eutrop. 8.8; *Epit.* 15.1 and *H.A. Ant. Pius*, 1.1 the name is correctly ascribed to Antoninus Pius. It was therefore in the *Kaisergeschichte* (Syme, *Emperors*, 37) and erroneously transferred to M. Aurelius by Victor.

21.   For examples of Constantine's legislation in this regard *vid.* N. Lewis and M. Reinhold, *Roman Civilization* II, New York, 1966, 477-487. In one law of 331 Constantine threatens that the rapacious hands of the functionaries shall immediately stop: if they do not they shall be cut off with the sword.

22.   Cf. Eutrop. 10.7; Ammianus, 16.8.12; 21.10.8; Zos. II.38.1. It was a common criticism which Victor levels at Constans (41.23) and at Constantius in his postscript (42.24-25), which was surely appended after Constantius' death.

23.   For a similar sentiment *vid.* Sall. *Cat.* 51.12-13; "Men in positions of great power live, as it were, on an eminence, and their actions are known to all the world. The higher our station, the less is our freedom of action. We must avoid partiality and hatred, and above all anger; for what in others would be called merely an outburst of temper, in those who bear rule is called arrogance and cruelty." (trans. S.A. Handford).

24. Cf. Eutrop. 10.9; *Epit.* 41.18; 41.21; Julian, *Ad Ath.* 3.270d; *Or.* 2.121; Hieron, *Chron.* 317; Zos. II.41; 55.9; Zon. XIII.5.5-14; Socrat. 2.5. For Dalmatius' death *vid.* note 16. Victor, serving under Constantius, hedges. Julian and Zosimus openly blame Constantius for the murder. Eutropius writes that a military faction killed Dalmatius and that Constantius acquiesced rather than gave the orders. In 340 Constantine II, the eldest son of Constantine, who regarded himself as senior emperor, complained that Constans had failed to respect his authority. He invaded Italy that spring, marched along the Po valley to cut off Constans from Rome (the latter was at Naissus/Nish), but was ambushed and killed near Aquileia. Constans thereby acquired Britain, Spain and Gaul, which Constantius, occupied with the Persians, was forced to accept.

25. Cf. Eutrop. 10.; *Epit.* 41.22-23; Liban. *Or.* 14.10; Hieron, *Chron. Ann. 344-345*; Zos. II.42.1; 47.3; Zon. XIII. 5.15; 6.7-9. In 341 and 342 Constans defeated the Franks on the Rhine and in the winter of 342/343 he fought the Sarmatians on the middle Danube. Furthermore, he dealt with problems in Britain and gave the Alamanni reasons to respect him. His homosexual inclinations, however, noted by Victor and Zosimus, conflicted with Christian morality, his fiscal inability produced further tax burdens, and his favouritism in making appointments resulted in mounting unpopularity especially with the army and officer cadre. This culminated in a conspiracy led by Marcellinus, *comes rei privatae*, who, on January 18th, 350 at Autun, proclaimed Flavius Magnus Magnentius, a pagan officer of Frankish origin, emperor. Constans fled to Spain but was overtaken and killed at Helena on the Gallic side of the Pyrenees. He had ruled as Caesar and then Augustus since December 25th, 333 and was born in 320 or 323 (Barnes, *New Empire*, 8, 45). Here and subsequently there are indications that both Victor and Eutropius continued to follow the *Kaisergeschichte*, which ended in 357 (H.W. Bird, *C.Q.* n.s. 23, 1973, 375 ff.; Nixon, *Caesares*, 340: cf. T.D. Barnes, *The Sources of the Historia Augusta*, Brussels, 1978, 94, who

argues that the *Kaisergeschichte* ended in 337.

26. Cf. Eutrop. 10.9; Ammianus, 16.7.5; Zos. II.42.1-2. Victor was almost certainly at Rome at this period and these comments may stem from common knowledge. Eutropius, less of a moralist than Victor, avoids mention of Constans' homosexuality and describes his faults in general terms (*gravia vitia*).

27. Cf. Julian, *Or.* 1.40b; 2.62a; *Epit.* 42.7; Zos. II.54.1. The sources generally agree in depicting Magnentius as harsh, cruel, disloyal and audacious, but the Epitomator adds that he was actually timid but concealed this under the guise of boldness.

28. Cf. Eutropius. 10.10; *Epit.* 41.25; Oros. 7.29; Julian, *Or.* 3.76c; Zos. II.42.1 ff.; Philostorg. *H.E.* 3.22. On March 1st, 350 Vetranio, the master of the infantry who commanded the army on the middle Danube, was acclaimed Caesar at Mursa (Osijek) in Pannonia Inferior, possibly at the instigation of Constantina, Constantius' sister, as Philostorgios states, to preserve the Danubian provinces for Constantius. He temporarily recognized Vetranio, whose coins bore Constantius' image. Magnentius also sought an arrangement with Vetranio but failed. Constantius and Vetranio met at Serdica (Sofia); then travelled together for about three days to Naissus (Nish) where Vetranio had apparently gathered the bulk of his army. There, on December 25th, 350 at a general assembly of the troops Constantius made an eloquent appeal for which they seem to have been prepared (Ammianus, 21.8.1). Vetranio then laid down his imperial insignia and was granted an honourable retirement at Prusa in Bithynia. In view of Constantius' severity and intransigence towards usurpers Vetranio's actions must have received the blessing of the emperor. Both considered it expedient, however, to continue the fiction of the usurpation to avoid having the soldiers believe that they had been duped. This may account for the

varying assessments of Vetranio in the sources. To Eutropius he was "an honourable man of old-fashioned morality and pleasant disposition." According to Nixon (*Caesares*, 341) Victor was swayed by his literary and social snobbishness in denigrating Vetranio. His personal bias towards Constantius, however, may have had something to do with it.

42

1.　　Cf. Eutrop. 10.11; *Epit.* 41.25; Oros. 7.29; Ammianus, 21.8.1; Zos. II.44.3-4; Julian, *Or.* 1.25.31; 3.22.76e-77; 1.26.33a; Soz. *H.E.* 4.4.2; Philostorg. *H.E.* 3.22. Following Arntzen I read *vi* in place of *vix*. Victor and Julian warmly praise Constantius' eloquence and clemency and Eutropius calls it a novel and extraordinary event. Zosimus, corroborated in part by Ammianus' brief statement, stresses the duplicity of Constantius. Dufraigne (*A.V.*, 201) believes that Victor used themes exploited by the panegyrists of Constantius, but Nixon (*Caesares*, 342), correctly in my estimation, thinks the account may well have been in Victor's source (the *Kaisergeschichte*) and passed over by Eutropius.

2.　　For the usefulness of eloquence in war as well as in peace cf. Quint. *Inst. Or.* 2.16.8.

3.　　On the alliance of eloquence and virtue cf. Cic. *De Or.* 3.55; Quint. *Inst. Or.* 12.1.11-12. Victor's main preoccupation here is to flatter Constantius and he dwells upon those qualities which he values most highly and deems essential in a good emperor; cf. *De Caes.* 8.7. It is significant that the Battle of Mursa (Eutrop. 10.12) is totally omitted by Victor even though Constantius was victorious. Victor may not have wished to remind his readers (including Constantius) of the emperor's responsibility for such a costly Pyrrhic victory. Eutropius has no such reservations. Ammianus (21.16.4), too, paints quite a different picture of Constantius' learning and eloquence.

4.   On the difficulties of crossing the Alps, especially in winter
     and spring, *vid.* Ammianus, 15.10.4-6; Philostorg. *H.E.* 3.24.
     For the fear of blocked passes and ambush *vid.* Herod. 8.1.6.

5.   Cf. Eutrop. 10.11; *Epit.* 42.3; Oros. 7.29.11; Julian, *Or.* 2.58c;
     Ammianus, 28.1.1.; Zos. II.43.2-4. On June 3rd, 350 Flavius
     Popilius Nepotianus, son of Eutropia, Constantine the Great's
     half-sister, gathered a motley band of gladiators and ordinary
     citizens at Rome and had himself proclaimed emperor. This
     occurred after the acclamation of Vetranio but before he was
     deposed. Nepotianus' followers killed Anicetus, Magnentius'
     praetorian prefect (Zos. *loc. cit.*): the urban prefect Fabius
     Titianus was not at hand (Dufraigne, *A.V.*, 201).

6.   Victor's graphic details of the carnage, which he may have
     actually witnessed, are a common theme in historians: cf. Sall.
     Cat. 51.9; Tac. *Ann.* XIV.33; *Hist.* III.83; Flor. *Epit.* 2.9.21;
     Ammianus, 28.1.1. After twenty-eight days (Eutrop. 10.11;
     Epit. 43.2) of vicious street fighting Magnentius' master of
     offices, Marcellinus, suppressed the insurgents and Nepotianus
     was killed.   The accounts of Victor, Eutropius and the
     Epitomator again show a chronological, verbal and factual
     similarity which seems to indicate the continued use of their
     common source.

7.   Cf. Eutrop. 10.12; *Epit.* 42.4-6; Oros. 7.29; Hieron. *Chron.*
     A. D. 353; Zos. II.45.2-58.1; Zon. XIII.8.5-13. Decentius was
     appointed Caesar in July or early August, 350. Similarly
     Flavius Claudius Constantius (Gallus) was appointed Caesar at
     Sirmium on March 15th, 351. Both events occurred after the
     suppression of Nepotianus not before, as Victor and the
     Epitomator indicate.   Eutropius is also chronologically
     incorrect at this juncture, placing the Battle of Mursa before
     the appointment of Gallus. Zosimus has the correct order of
     events. The bloody Battle of Mursa, on the Drava River north
     of Sirmium, took place on September 28th, 351 and seriously
     weakened the Roman army. Magnentius offered to negotiate

but his attempt was rejected and in 352 he retreated to Gaul. The next year Constantius crossed the Cottian Alps and defeated Magnentius' army at Mons Seleuci. That July or August Magnentius and his brother committed suicide to avoid being surrendered by their troops, the former at Lyons, the latter perhaps a little later at Sens.

8.   Cf. Hier. *Chron. A.D. 356*; Soz. 4.7.5-6; Philostorg. 222; Socr. *H.E.* 2.33. In 352 a certain Patricius (only mentioned by Victor in the extant sources) was proclaimed King of the Jews. Gallus easily crushed the revolt and among the savage reprisals taken Diocaesarea, Tiberias and Diospolis were razed. This item was probably gleaned from the *Kaisergeschichte* by Victor and Jerome but ignored as insignificant by Eutropius and the Epitomator.

9.   Cf. Eutrop. 10.13; *Epit.* 42.9; Ammianus, 14.1.1 ff; Philostorg. *H.E.* 3.7; 3.28; 4.1; Zos. II.55; Socr. 2.34; *Const. Constantinop. A.D. 354.* Gallus was married to Constantius' sister, Constantia, and sent to Antioch to govern the East. He ruled for almost four years and had to suppress a conspiracy, conduct treason trials, which he mismanaged, and chastise the upper classes at Antioch for creating a grain shortage. Julian had to deal with the last-mentioned in 362(*Misopogon,* 368 D). Constantius received inflammatory reports on his conduct, instructed him to travel to Pola in late 354, and executed him. The Latin sources emphasize his cruelty but Zosimus and Philostorgios depict him as the victim of eunuchs and informers. For recent views *vid.* Matthews, *R.E.A.* 33-36, 483-484.

10.   Victor is correct: Diocletian ruled alone briefly in 285 after the assassination of Carinus and before Maximian was appointed Caesar. Cf. Eutrop. 10.13; Zos. II.55.1. All stress the return to the rule of one emperor, but Eutropius places the event after the suppression of Silvanus, Zosimus after the death of Magnentius (when Gallus was still Caesar). This detail, too,

was presumably in the *Kaisergeschichte.*

11.   Cf. Eutrop. 10.13; *Epit.* 42.10-11; Oros. 7.29; Ammianus, 15.5.1-31; 15.6.2 ff; Hieron. *Chron.* 321. Probably in August, 355 Silvanus, the master of infantry in Gaul, who was stationed at Cologne, and who had helped Constantius defeat Magnentius at Mursa by bringing his troops over to Constantius, was forced by palace intrigue at Milan to declare himself emperor. Ursicinus, master of soldiers in the east and himself an object of suspicion, was despatched to Cologne to deal with the usurpation. Constantine correctly anticipated that at least one of his dangerous subordinates would thus be eliminated. Ursicinus suborned Silvanus' auxiliary regiments, the Cornuti and Bracchiati, and had Silvanus assassinated twenty-eight days after his acclamation. For recent discussions of this episode *vid.* Matthews, *R.E.A.*, 37-38, 484-485. Ammianus served as an officer (*protector*) under Ursicinus on this mission and described it from first-hand experience. In view of the flagrantly disproportionate discussion of this affair in comparison with the dry and curt remarks about Julian's victories over the Alamanni (Dufraigne, *A.V.*, 203), it is likely that Victor knew much more about the Silvanus affair than he states. For political reasons, however, as well as for reasons of length and balance, he was induced to gloss over certain aspects, downplay Julian's achievements, and promulgate the official version.

12.   Cf. Eutrop. 10.14; *Epit.* 42.12-14; Ammianus, 15.8.1; 16.12.1 ff.; Julian, *Ep. ad Ath.* 359; Philostorg. 4.2; Socr. *H.E.* 3.1; Soz. 5.2.20. The rebellious nature of the Gauls, borne out by history, is noted by Philostorgios and the *H.A.* (*Tyr. trig.* 3.7; *Quad. tyr.* 7.1), and was probably conventional (Syme, *Ammianus*, 189). Flavius Claudius Julianus (b. 331) was the son of Constantine the Great's half-brother, Julius Constantius. After Silvanus' death Julian, who was studying at Athens, was summoned by Constantius II to Milan and appointed Caesar on November 6th, 355. Some days later he married Constantius'

sister, Helena, and on December 1st he set off for Gaul which was being ravaged by the Alamanni and Franks. The totally inexperienced twenty-four-year-old's function was essentially to be an imperial figurehead while his generals carried on the war with the Germans. Julian had other ideas. In 356 he gained military experience as a subordinate fighting in east-central Gaul. The following year he had a remarkable success. Though he probably relied heavily on his commanders he managed to claim credit for recapturing Cologne from the Franks and then that summer (357), with a small army of 13,000, he decisively defeated an Alamannic army 35,000 strong under King Chnodomarius at Strasbourg and captured the king. In 358 he overcame the Salian Franks and Chamavi on the lower Rhine, restored the frontier, and in 359 he crossed the Rhine, routed the Alamanni again, and forced them to hand over the 20,000 prisoners they had taken and pay reparations (R.C. Blockley, *Latomus* 31, 1972, 445 ff.; Matthews, *R.E.A.*, 91-92, 296-300). Julian also captured King Vadomarius in spring, 361 (Ammianus, 21.4.5; *Epit.* 42.14; cf. Ammianus, 21.5.9) which Nixon, rightly in my estimation, regards as evidence that the *De Caesaribus* was completed in the spring of 361 *(C.Ph.* 86, 1991, 120-121).

13.   Cf. Ammianus, 16.12.68-70; Zos. III.4. Zosimus notes that Julian, in his official dispatches, ascribed his successes to the emperor's good fortune. Cf. Tac. *Ann.* III.47.1.

14.   Cf. Tac. *Ann.* VI.51.5, where Tacitus commends Tiberius when he was a private citizen or while he served under Augustus; *Hist.* I.49, where Galba is similarly praised. Victor probably adds Galerius for stylistic and historical balance.

15.   I now feel that Victor, in this statement, is referring to the period after September 9th, 360 for Constantius became Augustus on September 9th, 337 (cf. Nixon, *loc. cit.* in note 12). Victor presumably did not start work on it before 358 since, in a relatively early chapter (16.12), he mentions one of

204

the consuls of that year, Cerealis (cf. Ammianus, 17.5.1) and the earthquake at Nicomedia which occurred on the 24th of August, 358 (Ammianus, 17.7.1 ff.). Furthermore, he could hardly have acquired a copy of the *Kaisergeschichte* before 358.

16.   For Constantius' almost incessant wars against the Persians between 337 and 360 (Festus, 26), with an English translation of the sources, *vid.* M.H. Dodgeon and S.N.C. Lieu, *The Roman Eastern Frontier and the Persian Wars (A.D. 226-363)*, London, 1991, 164-230. After a few years of comparative peace (353-356) fruitless negotiations took place between 357 and 359. Hostilities erupted in 359 (cf. *De Caes.* 39.37), when Reman, Busan and finally Amida were captured by Sapor, whose forces, however, incurred substantial casualties. In 360 Singara was destroyed by the Persians and Bezabde captured and garrisoned by them. Sapor was then forced to withdraw and the Romans, in turn, besieged Bezabde. The following year (361) Constantius was making further plans to besiege Bezabde and had reached Edessa with his army before learning of Sapor's retreat. He was then compelled by Julian's advance into the Danubian provinces and seizure of the pass of Succi to turn his attention to Europe. Returning to Antioch in haste he made rapid preparations and left Antioch probably in early or mid-October (Nixon, *op. cit.,* 117) but contracted fever at Tarsus and died at Mopsucrene in Cilicia on November 3rd. The powerful pretenders he removed would be Magnetius Decentius, Vetranio and Silvanus. In 358 Constantius, operating from Sirmium, had carried out extensive campaigning against the Quadi and Sarmatians. They submitted and restored the prisoners they had captured but were permitted to retain the territory they had occupied. Only the Sarmatian Limigantes were forced to pull back over the River Theiss and the Sarmatian Liberi were granted the vacant land. Constantius then chose one of their princes, Zizais, as their king (Ammianus, 17.12.9 ff.). These operations all took place in the central Danube area between Sirmium (Mitrovica)

and Brigetio (Szóny) and it is possible that Victor, probably serving on the staff of Anatolius, the praetorian prefect, was actually present, which would account for him concluding his historical account here with one of Constantius' major military and diplomatic successes. Otherwise, as is more likely, the author acquired his information from one or more eyewitnesses, for the *Kaisergeschichte's* historical account had by now ended and Victor adds the intriguing detail that Constantius "was with great honour seated as a judge among them." Moreover he deliberately manipulates the chronology of events, placing the subsequent and less successful Persian campaigns of 359/360 before the Danubian campaigns and settlements of 358 in order to end on a positive note.

17. Further flattery of Constantius by comparing him with Pompey the Great. In 66 B.C., by virtue of the *Lex Manilia,* Pompey was sent east to fight Mithridates of Pontus and his son-in-law Tigranes of Armenia. He defeated Mithridates that year and the king committed suicide in 63 B.C. Meanwhile (64 B.C.) Pompey invaded Armenia and forced Tigranes to surrender. He allowed Tigranes to retain his throne but deprived him of his foreign conquests (Plut. *Pomp.* 38; Appian, *Mith.* 114-115; Dio, 36.51-53; 37.7a; Velleius, II.373 ff; Val. Max. 5.19; Flor. 1.40.27; Ammianus, 14.8.10).

18. Cf. Eutrop. 10.15; *Epit.* 42.18-19; Ammianus, 14.5.4; 16.8.10; 16.10.11; 21.16.1 ff; Julian, *Or.* 1.8.11; 1.11.16b; 1.37.46a; 1.38.46d; 1.39.48b; 3.2.22.77a; Lib. *Or.* 59.122. For a full discussion of the character sketches of Constantius by Victor, Eutropius, Julian, the Epitomator and Ammianus *vid.* Nixon, *Caesares,* 344-364; Dufraigne, *A.V.,* 204. If, as I believe, the *Kaisergeschichte* continued to 357 it presumably ended, like the *De Caesaribus,* with a character description of Constantius II. This clearly owed much to the prevailing panegyrics and must have been as sensibly favourable as that of Victor. Neither its author nor Victor could afford to affront an emperor who was "excessively concerned with the respect owed to

him." Nevertheless the Epitomator, Ammianus, and, to a lesser extent, Eutropius could state that Constantius fared badly in external wars and the former two denigrate the emperor's oratorical skills, which Victor, for his own reason, praises. It is likely, in my opinion, that Victor completed his first draft of the *De Caesaribus* with the eulogistic statement that Constantius was "aware that the tranquillity of the state is governed by the lives of good emperors," perhaps thereby intending an implicit comparison with Trajan, (cf. 13.7-8).

19.   This postscript is a bitter indictment of Constantius' advisers and appointees; cf. Ammianus, 21.16.16.   On official corruption *vid. De Caes.* 9.12; Anon. *De Rebus Bellicis*, 4; Ammianus, 16.8.1 ff.; 21.16.17; 22.4.2-9; *Cod. Theod.* I.12.2; I.16.7; I.32.1; X.4.1. It seems unlikely that Victor could have written such a striking denunciation of Constantius' ministers before he had espoused Julian's cause (C.G. Starr, *Am. Hist. Rev.* 61, 1955/56, 582), or at least until Julian had landed at Bononia.   Victor may initially have been appointed by Constantius or one of his officials (Bird, *S.A.V.*, 9) and was consequently grateful to him, but he was shrewd enough to realize that the emperor possessed a major weakness, an excessive need for adulation, which allowed his unscrupulous ministers and favourites undue influence over him (Liban. *Or.* 62.9; Ammianus, 22.4.9). His postscript, then, may have been an attempt to set the record straight rather than to curry favour with Julian. The last phrase is telling. Victor appears to use the word *apparitores* (petty officials) (cf. the Russian *apparatchik*) as a deliberate pejorative to denote not only court flunkies, but also those ministers, governors, commanders and their subordinates who obtained their positions through sycophancy and obsequiousness and were corrupt and self-serving (cf. *De Caes.* 24.10).   Julian, who was not like Constantius, understood Victor's predicament (cf. *De Caes.* 20.11) if one compares his treatment of Lucillianus (Ammianus, 21.9.8) and Florentius (Ammianus, 20.8.21-22; 22.7.5). In addition he needed all the support he could muster

(Nixon, *op. cit.*, 125). After all, the administration and army at Sirmium were presumably supporters of Constantius until Julian arrived, and two legions from Sirmium deserted Julian as soon as they could (Ammianus, 21.11.2).

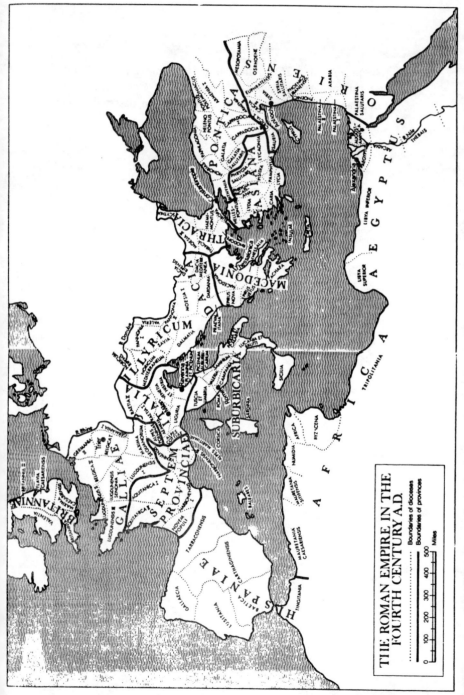

THE ROMAN EMPIRE IN THE
FOURTH CENTURY A.D.

.... Boundaries of dioceses
———— Boundaries of provinces

0   100   200   300   400   500
Miles

GAUL IN THE
FOURTH CENTURY A.D.

0   50   100   150   200
                            Miles
0   100   200   300
                          Kilometres

Reproduced, by kind permission of the Orion Publishing Group, from
Robert Browning, *The Emperor Julian*, London, Weidenfeld and
Nicolson, 1975.

ASIA MINOR & SYRIA IN THE FOURTH CENTURY A.D.

--- Approx. Frontiers

Miles
0 50 100 150 200 250 300

Reproduced, by kind permission of the Orion Publishing Group, from Robert Browning, *The Emperor Julian*, London, Weidenfeld and Nicolson, 1975.

212

SELECT BIBLIOGRAPHY

The following bibliography is restricted to books and articles pertaining to Victor and his times or to those regularly cited in the commentary. For fuller recent bibliographies reference should be made to J. Matthews, *The Roman Empire of Ammianus* (London, 1989), to T.D. Barnes, *Constantine and Eusebius* (Cambridge, Mass., 1981); *id. The New Empire of Diocletian and Constantine* (Cambridge, Mass., 1982).

Alföldi, A., *The Conversion of Constantine and Pagan Rome* (trans. Oxford, 1948).

————, *A Conflict of Ideas in the Late Roman Empire* (trans. Oxford, 1952).

Andreotti, R., "L'opera legislativa ed amministrativa dell'Imperatore Giuliano", *Nuova Rivista Storica* 14 (1930), 342.

————, *Il regno dell'Imperatore Giuliano* (Rome, 1936).

Athanassiadi-Fowden, P., *Julian and Hellenism: An Intellectual Biography* (Oxford, 1981).

Baldwin, B., "The *Caesares* of Julian", *Klio* 60 (1978), 449.

Barnes, T.D., review of J.W. Eadie, *The Breviarium of Festus, J.R.S.* 58 (1968), 262.

————, "The Lost Kaisergeschichte and the Latin Historical Tradition", *B.H.A.C.* 1968/69 (1970), 13.

————, "Some Persons in the *Historia Augusta*", *Phoenix* 26 (1972), 140.

————, "A Law of Julian", *C.P.* 69 (1974), 288.

————, "Imperial Campaigns, A.D. 285-311," *Phoenix* 30 (1976), 174.

————, "The *Epitome de Caesaribus* and Its Sources", *C.P.* 71 (1976), 258.

————, *The Sources of the Historia Augusta* (Brussels, 1978).

————, "Imperial Chronology, A.D. 337-350, *Phoenix* 34 (1980), 160.

Baynes, N.H., *The Historia Augusta: Its Date and Purpose* (Oxford, 1926).

————, *Constantine the Great and the Christian Church* (2nd ed., London, 1972).

213

Bellezza, A., "Interpretazione di un passo di Aurelio Vittore (*Caesares* 33, 34) sulla politica imperiale romana del III secolo", *Atti della Accademia Ligure di Scienze e Lettere* 17 (1960), 149.

Bidez, J., *La vie de l'empereur Julien* (2nd ed., Paris, 1965).

Bird, H.W., "Aurelius Victor and the Accession of Claudius II, *C.J.* 66 (1971), 252.

———, "A Note on the *De Caesaribus* 34.7-8", *C.J.* 67 (1972), 360.

———, "Further Observations on the Dating of Enmann's *Kaisergeschichte*", C.Q. n.s. 23 (1973), 375.

———, "A Reconstruction of the Life and Career of S. Aurelius Victor", *C.J.* 70 (1975), 49.

———, "Diocletian and the Deaths of Carus, Numerian and Carinus", *Latomus* 35 (1976), 123.

———, "The Sources of the *De Caesaribus*", *C.Q.* n.s. 31 (1981), 457.

———, "Recent Research on the Emperor Julian", *C.V.* 24 (1982), 281.

———, *Sextus Aurelius Victor: A Historiographical Study* (Liverpool, 1984).

———, "Some Reflections on the Empire and Imperial Policy in A.D. 369/370", *Florilegium* 8 (1986), 11.

———, "The Roman Emperors: Eutropius' Perspective", *Ancient History Bulletin I*, 1987, 139.

———, "A Strange Aggregate of Errors for A.D. 193", *C.B.* 65 (1989) 1.

Blockley, R.C., "Constantius Gallus and Julian as Caesars of Constantius II", *Latomus* 31 (1972), 433.

———, "The Panegyric of Claudius Mamertinus on the Emperor Julian", *A.J.P.* 93 (1972), 437.

———, *Ammianus Marcellinus: A Study of his Historiography and Political Thought* (Brussels, 1975).

———, "Constantius II and his Generals", in C. Deroux (ed.), *Studies in Latin Literature and Roman History* II (Brussels, 1980), 467.

Boer, W. Den, "Rome à travers trois auteurs du quatrième siècle", *Mnemosyne* 21 (1968), 254.

———, *Some Minor Roman Historians* (Leiden, 1972).

_____, "The Emperor Silvanus and his army", *Acta Classica* 3 (1960), 105.

Bonamente, G., *Giuliano l'Apostata e il Breviario di Eutropio* (Rome, 1986).

_____, *Eutropio e la tradizione su Giuliano l'Apostata* in *Scritti in onore di Salvatore Calderone*, II (Rome, 1987).

Bonfante, L. Warren, "Emperor, God and man in the fourth century: Julian the Apostate and Ammianus Marcellinus", *Parola del Passato* 99 (1964), 401.

Bowder, D., *The Age of Constantine and Julian* (London, 1978).

Bowersock, G.W. *Julian the Apostate* (London, 1978).

Brown, P.R.L., *The Making of Late Antiquity* (Cambridge, Mass., 1978).

Browning, R., *The Emperor Julian* (Berkely, 1976).

Calvi, A., *Eutropio. Breviarium ab Urbe Condita* (Turin, 1965).

Cameron, A.D.E., "Literary Allusions in the *Historia Augusta*", *Hermes* 92 (1964), 363.

_____, "The Roman friends of Ammianus", *J.R.S.* 54 (1964), 15.

_____, 'Two Glosses in Aurelius Victor', *C.R.* n.s. 15 (1965), 21.

_____, review of J. Straub (*q.v.*) in *J.R.S.* 55 (1965), 240.

_____, 'Three Notes on the Historia Augusta', *C.R.* n.s. 18 (1968), 17.

_____, *Claudian: Poetry and Propaganda at the Court of Honorius* (Oxford, 1970).

Cameron, Averil and Alan, 'Christianity and Tradition in the Historiography of the Late Empire', *C.Q.* n.s. 14 (1964), 316.

Chastagnol, A., *Les fastes de la préfecture de Rome au Bas-Empire* (Paris, 1962).

_____, 'Le problème de l'Histoire Auguste: État de la question', *B.H.A.C.* 1963 (1964), 43.

_____, 'L'Utilization des *Caesares* d'Aurélius Victor dans l'Histoire Auguste', *B.H.A.C.* 1966/67 (1968), 53.

_____, 'Emprunts de l'Histoire Auguste aux "Caesares" d'Aurélius Victor', *Revue de Philologie* 51 (1967), 85.

_____, 'Recherches sur l'Histoire Auguste de 1963 à 1969',

Antiquitas 4 (6), 1970, 1.

Camus, P.M., *Ammien Marcellin, témoin des courants culturels et religieux à la fin du IVe siècle* (Paris, 1967).

Capozza, M., "Nota sulle fonti di Eutropio per l'età regia," *Mem. Acc. Patav. Cl. Scienze mor. Lett. Arti* 25 (1962-63), 349.

_____, *Roma fra monarchia e decemvirato nell'interpretazione di Eutropio* (Rome, 1973).

Croke, B., and Emmett, A., (edd.), *History and Historians in Late Antiquity* (Sydney, London, New York, 1983).

Cohn, A., *Quibus ex fontibus Sexti Aurelii Victoris et Libri de Caesaribus et Epitomes undecima capita priora fluxerint* (Diss. Berlin, 1884).

Corbett, P.B., 'The 'De Caesaribus' attributed to Aurelius Victor: Points arising from an examination of the MSS and of the Teubner edition of F. Pichlmayr', *Scriptorium* 3 (1949), 254.

Dagron, G., *Naissance d'une capitale: Constantinople et ses institutions de 330 à 451* (Paris, 1974).

Daly, L.J., 'In a Borderland: Themistius' Ambivalence to Julian', *B.Z.* 73 (1980), 1.

Damerau, P., 'Kaiser Claudius II Gothicus', *Klio*, Beiheft 33 (n.f. 20), 1934.

Damsholt, T., 'Zur Benutzung von dem Breviarium des Eutrop in der Historia Augusta', *C. & M.* 25 (1964), 138.

Damsté, P.H., 'Ad S. Aurelius Victor', *Mnemosyne* 45 (1917), 367.

D'Elia, S., *Ricerche sulla tradizione manoscritta e sul testo di Aurelio Vittore e dell' "Epitome de Caesaribus"* (Naples, 1969).

Dessau, H., 'Uber Zeit und Persönlichkeit der S.H.A.', *Hermes* 24 (1889), 337.

Dill, S., *Roman Society in the Last Days of the Roman Empire* (London, 1899).

DiMaio, M., "The Antiochene Connection: Zonaras, Ammianus Marcellinus and John of Antioch on the reigns of the Emperors Constantius II and Julian", *Byzantion* 50 (1980), 158.

_____, "Infaustis ductoribus praeviis: the Antiochene Connection Part II", *Byzantion* 51 (1981), 502.

Dodgeon, M.H., and Lieu, S.N.C., *The Roman Eastern Frontier and the Persian Wars (A.D. 226-363)*, London, 1991.

216

Downey, G., 'The Emperor Julian and the Schools', *C.J.* 53 (1957), 97.

_____, *Ancient Antioch* (Princeton, 1963).

Drinkwater, J.F., "The 'pagan underground,' Constantius II's 'secret service' and the survival and the usurpation of Julian the Apostate", in C. Deroux, *Studies in Latin Literature and Roman History*, III (Brussels, 1983), 348.

Dufraigne, P., *Aurelius Victor: Livre des Césars* (Paris, 1975).

Eadie, J.W., *The Breviarium of Festus* (London, 1967).

Ebeling, P., *Quaestiones Eutropianae* (diss. Halle, 1881).

Echols, E.C., *Sextus Aurelius Victor's Brief Imperial Lives* (Exeter, N.H., 1962).

Elliot, T.G., *Ammianus and Fourth Century History* (Sarasota, Florida, 1983).

Enmann, A., "Eine verlorene Geschichte der römischen Kaiser und das Buch *De Viris Illustribus Urbis Romae*", *Philologus* suppl. bd. 4 (1884), 337.

Erickson, D.N., *Eutropius' "Compendium of Roman History": Introduction, Translation, Notes* (Syracuse University dissertation, Syracuse, N.Y., 1990).

Fuhrmann, M., "Die Romidee der Spätantike", *H.Z.* 207 (1968), 529.

Gilliam, J.F., "Ammianus and the Historia Augusta: the lost books and the period 117-284", *B.H.A.C.* 1970 (1972), 125.

Glover, T.R., *Life and Letters in the Fourth Century* (Cambridge, 1901).

Goffart, W., 'Did Julian Combat Venal *Suffragium?*', *C.P.* 65 (1970), 145.

Hamblenne, P., "Une 'conjuration' sous Valentinien?" *Byzantion* 50 (1980), 198.

Hartke, W., *De Saeculi Quarti Exeuntis Historiarum Scriptoribus Quaestiones* (Leipzig, 1922).

_____, "Geschichte und Politik im spätantike Rom", *Klio*, Beiheft 45, n.f. 32 (1940).

Hengst, D. Den, "De Romeinse Kaiserbiographie", *Lampas* 17 (1984), 367.

Hohl, E., "Die Ursprung des Historia Augusta", *Hermes* 55 (1920), 296.

_____, "Bericht über die Literatur zu den S.H.A. für die Jahre 1916-1923", *Bursians Jahresberichte* 200 (1924), 167.

_____, "Zur Historia-Augusta-Forschung', *Klio* 27 (1934), 149.

_____, "Bericht über die Literatur zu den S.H.A. für die Jahre 1924-35", *Bursians Jahresberichte* 256 (1937), 127.

_____, "Die Historia Augusta und die Caesares des Aurelius Victor", *Historia* 4 (1955), 220.

_____, "Über das Problem der Historia Augusta", *Wien. Stud.* 71 (1958), 132.

Hopkins, M.K., "Social Mobility in the Later Roman Empire: The Evidence of Ausonius", *C.Q.* n.s. 11 (1961), 239.

_____, "Eunuchs in Politics in the Later Roman Empire", *Proc. Camb. Philol. Soc.* 189 (n.s. 9), 1963, 62.

_____, "Elite Mobility in the Roman Empire", *Past and Present* 32 (1965), 12.

Jeep, L., "Aurelii Victoris de Caesaribus e l'Epitome de Caesaribus", *Riv. Fil.* 1 (1873), 505.

Jones, A.H.M., *The Later Roman Empire,* 3 vols. (Oxford, 1964).

_____, *Constantine and the Conversion of Europe* (London, 1948).

_____, Martindale, J.R., and Morris, J., *The Prosopography of the Later Roman Empire* (Cambridge, 1971), cited as *P.L.R.E.*

Jones, B.W., "Suétone et Aurelius Victor," *P.P.* 25 (1970), 346.

Kaegi, W.E., The Emperor Julian's Assessment of the Significance and Function of History", *Proc. American Philosoph. Soc.* 108 (1964), 29.

_____, "Research on Julian the Apostate 1945-1964", *Classical World* 58 (1965), 229.

_____, "Domestic Military Problems of Julian the Apostate", *Byz. Forsch.* 2 (1967), 247.

_____, "The Emperor Julian at Naissus", *L'antiquité classique* 44 (1975), 161.

_____, "Constantine's and Julian's strategies of strategic surprise against the Persians", *Athenaeum* n.s. 59 (1981), 209.

Lacombrade, C., "Notes sur les Césars de l'empereur Julien", *Pallas* 11 (1962), 47.

_____, "L'empereur Julien émule de Marc-Aurèle", *Pallas* 14

(1967), 9.

Laistner, M.L.W., "Some Reflections on Latin Historical Writings in the Fifth Century", *C.P.* 35 (1940), 241.

Liebeschuetz, J.H.W.G., *Antioch: City and Imperial administration in the Later Roman Empire* (Oxford, 1972).

Lieu, S.N.C. (ed.), *The Emperor Julian: panegyric and polemic* (Liverpool, 1986).

Leo, F., *Die griechisch-römische Biographie* (Leipzig, 1901).

Lot, F., *The End of the Ancient World and the Beginnings of the Middle Ages* (trans. New York, 1961).

MacMullen, R., *Soldier and Civilian in the Later Roman Empire* (Cambridge, Mass., 1963).

_____, *Enemies of the Roman Order* (Cambridge, Mass., 1966).

_____, *Constantine* (New York, 1969).

_____, *The Roman Government's Response to Crisis* (New Haven, 1976).

Malcovati, E., "I Breviari del IV secolo", *A.F.L.C.* 12 (1942), 23.

Marriot, I., The Authorship of the *Historia Augusta:* Two computer Studies", *J.R.S.* 69 (1979), 65.

Marrou, H.I., *A History of Education in Antiquity* (trans. New York, 1964).

Matthews, J., *Western Aristocracies and the Imperial Court* Oxford, 1975).

Mazzarino, S., *Aspetti sociali del quarto secolo* (Rome, 1951).

_____, *La fine del mondo antico* (Milan, 1959).

_____, *Il pensiero storico classico* II, 2 (Bari, 1966).

McDermott, W.C., review of E.C. Echols (*q.v.*) in *Class. World* 56 (2), (1962), 53.

Mocsy, A., *Pannonia and Upper Moesia: a History of the Middle Danube Provinces of the Roman Empire* (London, 1974).

Momigliano, A., *The Conflict between Paganism and Christianity in the Fourth Century* (Oxford, 1963).

_____, *Studies in Historiography* (London, 1966).

Mommsen, T., "Zu den Caesares des Aurelius Victor", *Sitz. der Königlich. Preus. Akad. der Wiss. zu Berlin* 2 (1884), 951.

Monks, G.R., "The Administration of the Privy Purse: An Enquiry into

Corruption and the Fall of the Roman Empire", *Speculum* 32 (1957), 748.

Moss, B.T. *Sextus Aurelius Victor: Liber de Caesaribus* (diss. N. Carolina, 1942).

Nixon, C.E.V., *An Historiographical Study of the Caesares of Sextus Aurelius Victor* (diss. Michigan, 1971).

_____, review of W. den Boer, *Some Minor Roman Historians, Phoenix* 27 (1973), 407.

_____, "Aurelius Victor and Julian", *C.Ph.* 86 (1991), 113.

Nicolle, J., "Julien apud Senones", *Riv. Stor. Ant.* 8 (1978), 144.

Noble, A.N., *Indices verborum omnium quae in Sexti Aurelii Victoris libro de Caesaribus et incerti auctoris epitome de Caesaribus reperiuntur* (diss. Ohio State University, 1938).

Norman, A.F., *Libanius' Autobiography* (London, 1965).

Nutt, D.C., "Silvanus and the Emperor Constantius II" *Antichthon* 7 (1973), 80.

Opitz, T., "Quaestionum de Sexto Aurelio Victore capita tria", *Acta Soc. Phil. Lipsiensis* 2 (1872), 199.

_____, "Sallustius und Aurelius Victor", *Jahrbücher für Phil. und Paed.* 127 (1883), 217.

Oost, S., review of W. den Boer, *Some Minor Roman Historians (q.v.)* in *C.P.* 71 (1976), 294.

Oosten, H. Van. "Keiserdatums in Eutropius", *Acta Classica* 32 (1989), 59.

Palanque, J.R., *Essai sur la préfecture du prétoire du Bas-Empire* (Paris, 1933).

Parker, H.M.D., "The Legions of Diocletian and Constantine", *J.R.S.* 23 (1933), 175.

Paschoud, F., *Roma Aeterna* (Neuchâtel, 1967).

Penella, R.J., "A Lowly Born Historian of the Roman Empire: Some Observations on Aurelius Victor and his *De Caesaribus", Thought* 55 (1980), 122.

_____, "A Sallustian Reminiscence in Aurelius Victor", *C.P.* 78 (1983), 234.

Peter, H., *Die Geschichtliche Litteratur über die römische Kaiserzeit bis Theodosius I und ihre Quelle* (Leipzig, 1897).

Pflaum, H-G., "La séparation des pouvoirs civil et militaire avant et

220

sous Dioclétien (et *De Caes.* 33, 34)", *BSAF* 1958 (1960), 78.

Piganiol, A., *L'Empereur Constantin* (Paris, 1932).

————, *L'Empire Chrétien* (Paris, 1947).

Ridley, R.T., "Notes on Julian's Persian Expedition", *Historia* 22 (1973), 317.

Romanelli, P., *Storia delle Province Romane dell'Africa* (Rome, 1959).

Rosen, K., "Beobachtungen zur Erhebung Julians", *Acta Classica* 12 (1969), 121.

Sanford, E.M., "Contrasting Views of the Roman Empire", *A.J.P.* 58 (1937), 437.

Schanz, M. and Hosius, C., *Geschichte der römischen Literatur* (Munich, 1914).

Schemmel, F., "Die Schule von Karthago", *Phil. Woch.* 47 (1927), 1342.

————, "Die Schulzeit des Kaisers Julian", *Philologus* 82 (1927), 455.

Schlumberger, J., *Die "Epitome de Caesaribus": Untersuchungen zur heidnischen Geschichtsschreibung des 4. Jahrhunderts n. Chr.* (Munich, 1974).

Schmidt, P.L., "S. Aurelius Victor,. *Historiae Abbreviatae"*, *Pauly's Realencyclopädie* Supplementband XV (Munich, 1978), 1660-71.

Scivoletto, N., "La 'civilitas' del IV secolo e il significato del 'Breviarium' di Eutropio", *G.I.F.* 22 (1970), 14.

Segoloni, M.P., Corsini. A.R., *Eutropii Lexicon* (Perugia, 1982).

Selem, A., "A proposito del comando militare di Giuliano in Gallia secondo Ammiano", *Rivista di Cultura Classica e Medioevale* 13 (1971), 193.

————, "L'Atteggiamento storiografico di Ammiano nei confronti di Giuliano dalla proclamazione di Parigi alla morte di Giuliano Constanzo", *Athenaeum* 49 (1971), 81.

————, "Ammiano e la morte di Giuliano (25.3.3-11)", *Rediconti dell' Instituto Lombardo, Acc. di Scienze e Lettere* 107 (1973), 1119.

Sokolov, V.S., "Sekst Avrelij Viktor, Istoriograph IV v.n.e.", *Vestnik Drevnej Istorii* 86 (1963), 215; 87 (1964), 229.

Starr, C.G., Aurelius Victor, Historian of Empire", *A.H.R.* 61

(1955/56), 574.

Stern, H., *Date et Destinaire de l'Histoire Auguste* (Paris, 1953).

Straub, J., *Heidnische Geschichtsapologetik in der christlichen Spätantike* (Bonn, 1963).

_____, *Vom Herrscherideal in der Spätantike* (Stuttgart, 1939 [1964]).

Syme, R., *Tacitus* (Oxford, 1958).

_____, *Sallust* (Berkeley, 1964).

_____, *Ammnianus and the Historia Augusta* (Oxford, 1968).

_____, *Emperors and Biography* (Oxford, 1971).

_____, *The Historia Augusta: A Call of Clarity, Antiquitas* 4 (8), Bonn, (1971).

Tarrant, R.J., review of P. Dufraigne (*q.v.*) in *Gnomon* 50 (1978), 355.

Thompson, E.A., *The Historical Work of Ammianus Marcellinus* (Cambridge, 1947).

_____, *A Roman Reformer and Inventor* (Oxford, 1952).

_____, "Ammianus Marcellinus and the Romans", *G. & R.* 11 (1941/42), 130.

_____, "Three Notes on Julian in 361 A.D.", *Hermathena* 62 (1943), 83.

_____, "The Emperor Julian's Knowledge of Latin", *C.R.* 58 (1944), 49.

Tomlin, R.S.O., The Army of the Late Empire", in J.S. Wacher (ed.) *The Roman World* I (London & New York, 1987), 107.

Valensi, L., "Quelques réflexions sur le pouvoir impérial d'après Ammien Marcellin", *Bull. del'Assoc. Guillaume Budé 4.4 (Supplément: Lettres d'Humanité, t. XVI), (Paris, 1957)*, 62.

Warmington, B.H., "Objectives and Strategy in the Persian Wars of Constantius II", *Akten des XI Internationalen Limeskongresses* 1976 (Budapest, 1977), 509.

_____, "Ammianus and the Lies of Metrodorus", *C.Q.* n.s. 31 (1981), 464.

Williams, S., *Diocletian and the Roman Recovery* (London, 1985).

Wölfflin, E., "Aurelius Victor", *Rh.M.* 29 (1874), 282.

_____, "Epitome", *Arch. für Lat. Lex. und Gramm.* 12 (1902), 333.

_____, "Zur Latinität der Epitome Caesarum", *Arch. für Lat. Lex. und Gramm.* 12 (1902), 445.

CLASSICAL SOURCES

Ammianus Marcellinus, *Historia* (Loeb Transl., Heinemann, 1939).

Anonymus Valesianus (Loeb Transl., Heinemann, 1939).

Dio Cassius, *Historia* (Loeb Transl., Heinemann, 1927).

Eusebius, *Vita Constantini* (Transl. in *Nicene & Post-Nicene Fathers*, Oxford, 1890).

Eusebius, *Historia Ecclesia* and *De Martyribus Palestinae* (Trans. H. Lawlor and J.E.L. Oulton, London, 1927).

Eutropius, *Breviarium ab Urbe Condita* (C. Santini, Teubner, Leipzig, 1979).

Herodian, *Histories* (Loeb, Transl., Heinemann, 1969).

Jerome, *Chronicle*, Eusebius Werke 7 (ed. R. Helm, Berlin, 1956).

Lactantius, *De Mortibus Persecutorum* (ed. S. Brandt, Vienna, 1897). (Trans. W. Fletcher, *The Works of Lactantius*, Vol. II, 1871).

Malalas, *Chronographia* (ed. L. Dindorf, Bonn, 1831).

Orosius, *Adversum Paganos* (Teubner, Leipzig, 1889).

Panegyrici Latini (ed. R.A.B. Mynors, Oxford, 1964).

Scriptores Historiae Augustae (Trans. D. Magie, Loeb, London, 1932).

Sextus Aurelius Victor, *Liber de Caesaribus and Epitome* (R. Gruendel, Teubner, Leipzig, 1966).

Zonaras, *Epitome* (ed. Lindorf, Leipzig, 1868-75).

Zosimus, *Historia Nova* (Teubner, Leipzig, 1887).

223

INDEX

Names and Places in the translation

Abgarus, 23
Abrittus, 31
Achaea, 32
Achilleus, 43, 44
Adiabene, 23
Aegean, 6
Aelius, Lucius, 16, 17
Aemilianus, Aemilius, 31
Africa/Africans, 28, 29, 39, 43, 44, 45, 48, 49
agentes in rebus, 45
Agrippa, 2
Alamanni, 25, 32, 37
Albinus, Clodius, 22
Alexander (the Great), 30
Alexander (usurper), 47, 48
Alexander Severus, 26, 27
Alexandria, 43, 44
Allectus, 45
Alps, 44, 52
Altinum, 19
Amandus, 42
Anatolius, 15
Anchyrona, 50
Antinous, 17
Antioch, 16
Antoninus (title), 24, 25, 26
Antoninus Pius, 17
Antony, Mark, 1
Aper, 40, 42
Aquileia, 29
Aquitaine, 34
Arabia/Arabs, 6, 23, 29

Archelaus, 2
Arce/Caesarea, 26
Aristobulus, 42
Armenia, 44
Armentarius, 43, 46 (*vid.* Galerius)
Asclepiodotus, 45
Asia/Asians, 19, 32
Athenaeum, 16
Athenian, 16
Attalus, 33
Attitianus, 33, 34
Augustus (Octavian), 1, 2, 3, 10
Aurelian, 35, 37, 38, 39, 44, 45
Aureolus, 34

Bacchants, 3
Bactrians, 1
Bagaudae, 42
Baiae, 17
Balbinus, Caecilius, 28, 29
Bassianus (*vid.* Caracalla)
Bithynia, 19
Black Sea, 15
Boionius (M. Aurelius), 18, 51
Bonosus, 39
Britain/Britons, 5, 22, 23, 24, 27, 43, 46
Brutus, 4

Caelian Hill, 37
Caligula, 2, 3, 4, 5, 41
Calocerus, 50
Campania, 18
Capitol, 10, 11, 13
Cappadocia, 2
Capri, 2
Caracalla (Bassianus), 24, 25, 26, 27
Carausius, 43, 45
Carinus, 40, 41, 42
Carnuntum, 19
Carpi, 45
Carthage, 29, 28, 45, 48
Carus, 40, 42
Cerealis, 19
Ceres, 16
Chaerea, 4
Chalcedon, 50
Chatti, 13
Chosroes, 15
Circus Maximus, 49
Cirta/Constantina, 49
Claudius, 4, 5, 6, 11
Claudius II, 35, 36
Coenofrurium, 38
Cologne (Colonia Agrippinensis), 33, 39
Commodus, 19, 20, 22, 24
Constans, 50, 51
Constantine (the Great), 36, 37, 46, 47, 48, 49
Constantine II, 50, 51
Constantius I, 36, 37, 43, 44, 45, 46, 47
Constantius II, 1, 50, 52, 53, 54

Cottian Alps, 7
Cottius, 7
Cremona, 10
Cretan, 14
Crispus 50
Ctesiphon, 40
Curii, 20
Cyprus, 50
Cyrus, 47
Cyzicus, 22

Dacia/Dacians, 13, 15
Dalmatius, 50, 51
Danube, 5, 15, 31, 47, 51
Dardanians, 15
Decebalus, 15
Decentius, 52
Decii, 36
Decius, 30, 31
Diadumenus, 26
Diocletian, 41, 42, 43, 44, 45
Domitian, 11, 13, 15, 41
Domitius, L., 7
Domitius (praet.pref.), 28
Druids, 5
Drusus, 2

Edessa, 26
Egypt, 6, 22, 25, 43, 44
Eleusinian Mysteries, 16
Ephesus, 19
Epirus, 4
Etruria/Etruscan, 30, 32
Etruscus, 30
Euphrates, 15

Fabricii, 20

Fate, 13, 40
Faustinus, 37
Felicissimus, 37
Flaminian Way, 11
Flavius (Constantine I), 49, 52
Florianus, 39, 40
Fortune, 5
Franks, 32
frumentarii, 45

Gaetuli, 2
Gaius (*vid.* Caligula)
Galba, 8, 9
Galerius, 43, 44, 46, 47, 53
Gallienus, 32, 33, 34, 35, 36, 37, 40
Gallus, 31
Gallus Caesar, 52, 53
Garamantes, 1
Gaul/Gauls, 5, 9, 15, 19, 22, 27, 32, 33, 37, 39, 40, 42, 43, 44, 47, 52, 53
Gemonian Steps, 10
Germanicus, 2, 13
Germany/Germans, 1, 3, 10, 27, 28, 32, 33, 37, 43, 53
Geta, 24, 25
Gordian I, 28, 29
Gordian II (III), 29
Goths, 30, 31, 32, 36, 50
Greece/Greeks, 4, 7, 13, 16, 38

Hadrian, 16, 17
Hannibal, 39
Helianus, 42
Heliogabalus (Elagabalus), 26, 27
Helvius, 21
Herculius (= Maximian), 43, 44, 45, 46, 48
Hipparchus, 51
Hostilianus, 31

Illyricum, 1, 15, 30, 32, 41, 43, 44, 46, 47, 52
Indians, 1
Ingebus (Ingenuus), 32
Italica, 15
Italy/Italians, 10, 12, 14, 16, 29, 32, 41, 44, 46, 48, 49, 52
Janus, 1, 29
Jotapianus, 30
Jovius (=Diocletian), 43, 44, 47
Judaea/Jews, 9, 12, 53
Julia (Augustus' daughter), 43
Julia (Domna), 25
Julia (Mammaea), 27
Julian (emperor), 1, 53
Julianus (usurper), 41, 43
Julianus, Didius, 21
Julianus, Salvius, 21
Jupiter, 3

Lacus Curtius, 9
Laelianus, 33
Lanuvium, 17
Leptis, 23
Liber, 3
Libera, 16
Licinianus, 50
Licinius Licinianus, 47, 49, 50
Licinius Valerianus, 32

Livy, 1
Lorium, 18
Lucania, 37
Lyons (Lugdunum), 22

Macedonia, 30, 31, 32
Macrinus, 26
Magnentius, 51, 52, 53
Main River, 25
Mainz (Mogontiacum), 33
Marcomanni, 19, 45
Marcomarus, 19
Marcus Aurelius, 18, 19, 24, 29, 51
Margus, 42
Marius, Gaius, 33, 41
Marius (usurper), 33
Maroboduus, 2
Martinianus, 50
Maxentius, 46, 47, 48
Maximian (also *vid.* Herculius), 42, 43, 44
Maximinus, C. Julius (Thrax), 27, 28, 29
Maximinus Daia, 46, 49
Menapia, 43
Mesopotamia, 5, 32, 40, 44
Messalina, 5
Milan (Mediolanum), 34, 36, 45
Milvian Bridge, 21, 48
Minerva, 14
Moesia/Moesians, 10, 39, 42, 52
Moors, 5
Mucapor, 39
Mursa, 32

Musulamii, 5

Narbonne (Narbo), 42
Narses, 44
Nepotianus, 52
Nero, 7, 8, 9, 29
Nerva, 14, 16
Nicaea, 51
Nocomedia (Izmit), 19, 45, 50
Nola, 1
Numa Pompilius, 1, 16
Numerian, 40

Ocean, 3, 23
Octavian (*vid.* Augustus)
Octavius, 1
Ostia, 5, 6
Otho, 9, 10

Palestine, 12
Pannonia/Pannonians, 10, 19, 32, 39, 47
Papinian, 25
Parthia/Parthians, 8, 12, 23, 32, 40
Patricius, 53
Pelso Lake, 47
Persia/Persians, 18, 23, 26, 29, 32, 37, 40, 43, 44, 47, 50, 54
Pertinax, 20, 21, 22
Pervium, 14
Pescennius Niger, 22
Philippopolis, 29
Philip, M. Aurelius (emperor), 29, 30
Phoenix, 6

Pipa, 33
Plotina, 16
Polemon, 7
Pompey, 54
Pontus, 7, 14
Postumus, 33
Priscus, L., 30, 31
Probus, 39, 40, 44
Punic, 47
Pupienus, Clodius, 28, 29

Quadi, 19
Quinquegentiani, 43
Quinquennial Games, 29

Raetia, 1, 32, 34
Ravenna, 47
Reate, 10
Regalianus, 32
Rhine, 5
Romulus, 27, 38

Sabinus, 10
Salonina, 33
Saloninus, 32
Sapor (Shapur), 32
Sarmatians, 15, 50, 54
Saturninus, 39
Saxa Rubra, 48
Scaeva, 20
Scythians, 1
Septimius Severus, 21, 22, 27, 51
Sequani, 14
Severus (emperor), 46
Sibylline Books, 36
Sicilia, 27

Silvanus, 53
Sirmium (Mitrovica), 30, 39
Spain/Spanish, 8, 15, 32
Suburanus, 16
Suebi, 2
Sulpicii, 9
Sura, 15
Suranae, 15
Syria/Syrians, 10, 12, 16, 21, 26, 30

Tacfarinas, 2
Tacitus (emperor), 38, 39, 40
Tarquinius Priscus, 7, 14
Tarquinius Superbus, 4
Tarsus, 39, 49
Temple of Peace, 11
Tetricus, 34, 37
Thrace, 29, 30, 32, 47, 50
Thraconitis, 29
Thysdrus, 28
Tiber, 10, 29, 32, 48
Ticinum, 35
Tigranes, 54
Titus, 11, 12
Tivoli (Tibur), 16
Trajan, 7, 15, 16
Trebellica, 28
Tripolis, 23, 51
Tyana, 39

Ulpian (Domitius Ulpianus), 27

Valens, Julius, 30, 31
Valeria (province), 47
Valerian, 32

Valerius, *vid.* Diocletian
Venetia/Veneti, 19, 41
Venus, 4
Verona, 9, 30, 48
Verus, Lucius (emperor), 18, 19
Vespasian, 9, 10, 11
Vesta, 8
Vetranio, 52
Victoria, 34
Victorinus, 33, 34
Vienna, 19
Vimius, 4
Vitellius, 9, 10
Vologeses, 12, 18
Volusianus, 31
Volusianus, Rufius, 48

Xerxes, 26
York (Eboracum), 24

TRANSLATED TEXTS FOR HISTORIANS
Published Titles

Gregory of Tours: Life of the Fathers
Translated with an introduction by EDWARD JAMES
Volume 1: 176pp., 2nd edition 1991, ISBN 0 85323 327 6

The Emperor Julian: Panegyric and Polemic
Claudius Mamertinus, John Chrysostom, Ephrem the Syrian
edited by SAMUEL N. C. LIEU
Volume 2: 153pp., 2nd edition 1989, ISBN 0 85323 376 4

Pacatus: Panegyric to the Emperor Theodosius
Translated with an introduction by C. E. V. NIXON
Volume 3: 122pp., 1987, ISBN 0 85323 076 5

Gregory of Tours: Glory of the Martyrs
Translated with an introduction by RAYMOND VAN DAM
Volume 4: 150pp., 1988, ISBN 0 85323 236 9

Gregory of Tours: Glory of the Confessors
Translated with an introduction by RAYMOND VAN DAM
Volume 5: 127pp., 1988, ISBN 0 85323 226 1

The Book of Pontiffs (*Liber Pontificalis to AD 715*)
Translated with an introduction by RAYMOND DAVIS
Volume 6: 175pp., 1989, ISBN 0 85323 216 4

Chronicon Paschale 284-628 AD
Translated with notes and introduction by
MICHAEL WHITBY AND MARY WHITBY
Volume 7: 280pp., 1989, ISBN 0 85323 096 X

Iamblichus: On the Pythagorean Life
Translated with notes and introduction by GILLIAN CLARK
Volume 8: 144pp., 1989, ISBN 0 85323 326 8

Conquerors and Chroniclers of Early-Medieval Spain
Translated with notes and introduction by KENNETH BAXTER WOLF
Volume 9: 176pp., 1991, ISBN 0 85323 047 1

Victor of Vita: History of the Vandal Persecution
Translated with notes and introduction by JOHN MOORHEAD
Volume 10: 112pp., 1992, ISBN 0 85323 127 3

The Goths in the Fourth Century
by PETER HEATHER AND JOHN MATTHEWS
Volume 11: 224pp., 1991, ISBN 0 85323 426 4

Cassiodorus: *Variae*
Translated with notes and introduction by S.J.B. BARNISH
Volume 12: 260pp., 1992, ISBN 0 85323 436 1

The Lives of the Eighth-Century Popes (*Liber Pontificalis*)
Translated with an introduction and commentary by RAYMOND DAVIS
Volume 13: 288pp., 1992, ISBN 0 85323 018 8

Eutropius: Breviarium
Translated with an introduction and commentary by H. W. BIRD
Volume 14: 248pp., 1993, ISBN 0 85323 208 3

The Seventh Century in the West-Syrian Chronicles
introduced, translated and annotated by ANDREW PALMER
including two seventh-century Syriac apocalyptic texts
introduced, translated and annotated by SEBASTIAN BROCK
with added annotation and an historical introduction by ROBERT HOYLAND
Volume 15: 368pp., 1993., ISBN 0 85323 238 5

Vegetius: Epitome of Military Science
Translated with notes and introduction by N. P. MILNER
Volume 16: 182pp., 1993, ISBN 0 85323 228 8

Aurelius Victor: De Caesaribus
Translated with an introduction and commentary by H. W. BIRD
Volume 17: 264pp., 1994, ISBN 0 85323 218 0

Bede: On the Tabernacle
Translated with notes and introduction by ARTHUR G. HOLDER
Volume 18: 224pp., 1994, ISBN 0 85323 378 0

Caesarius of Arles: Life, Testament, Letters
Translated with notes and introduction by WILLIAM E. KLINGSHIRN
Volume 19: 176pp., 1994, ISBN 0 85323 368 3

For full details of Translated Texts for Historians, including prices and ordering information, please write to the following:

All countries, except the USA and Canada: **Liverpool University Press, PO Box 147, Liverpool, L69 3BX, UK** *(tel* **051-794 2235,** *fax* **051-708 6502).**

USA and Canada: **University of Pennsylvania Press, Blockley Hall, 418 Service Drive, Philadelphia, PA 19104-6097, USA** *(tel* **(215) 898-6264,** *fax* **(215) 898-0404).**